When Two or More are Gathered... in PRACER

When *Two or More* *are Gathered...* in
PRAYER

How Praying *Together* Can Change Our World
Includes Study Guide

James "Micky" Blackwell

United Writers Press, Inc.
226 Chestnut Lake Way
Lilburn, GA 30047
www.unitedwriterspress.com

ISBN: 978-1-934216-58-3

To Christians everywhere

who are committed

to advancing the Kingdom of God

through praying together

Contents

Appendices   **241**

Foreword

Those of us who are lucky have mentors. I am especially fortunate because Micky Blackwell is mine. Most would think that a retired executive vice president of Lockheed Martin Corporation would have taught me how to be an engineer or executive. Instead, Micky is my *spiritual* mentor. He taught me how to pray together with other people.

Three years ago, my husband David and I were visiting Sunday School classes when we found the Kindred Spirits class at First United Methodist Church of Marietta, Georgia. The class seemed incredibly typical at first—chairs in a neat semi-circle, polite young couples wearing smiles, and Bibles stacked in the back. But what was remarkably atypical was the teacher. We knew almost instantly that this man, Micky Blackwell, was someone who really knew the Bible and had a passion for teaching it. Over the weeks that followed, it became very clear that Micky was a mentor for *all* of these couples—couples struggling with raising children, office politics, divorce, and sick parents. He used his experience and passion for faith and prayer to provide us with Bible-based answers to the questions we had about everyday life.

I had just begun to get to know Micky personally when he asked me to review and comment on a book he was writing on "corporate prayer," the title of which is *When Two or More are Gathered...in Prayer*. I was honored but scared to death. As a former executive producer at CNN, I was used to proofreading "important" pieces, but a book on corporate prayer seemed way out of my league. Admittedly, I had never even heard the term, and felt incredibly unprepared to comment on the book. But what I *really* wasn't prepared for is how it would open my mind and heart to a whole new dimension of faith. Immediately after starting the book, I became obsessed with knowing more about God's will and getting on what Micky calls "praying ground." *Was I on praying ground? Were the other people in my Sunday School class, church and weekday Bible study on praying ground? And if not, would God answer our prayers anyway?*

My interest in the book sparked the first question in our Sunday School class's Hot Topics Box—a box of anonymous questions for Micky to research and then teach to the class. My question, "Does God hear and answer our prayers when we haven't asked forgiveness for our sins?" was of enormous interest. Micky taught from his book and thoroughly answered the question to everyone's satisfaction. He showed us the reasons why believers are not on "praying ground" in the first place, and how to get on "praying ground" through confession and forgiveness. Through personal, heartfelt examples, Micky explained how to find out what's wrong in your life, and how to get in line with God's will. He outlined seven specific ways the Holy Spirit reveals God's will to His people. As Micky pointed out, "once we know His will, God has committed to answer our prayers." The book doesn't just identify problems but explains how to solve them through prayer, specifically by two or more praying together.

I have been a Christian all my life. I pray regularly at night and silently in church; but, like most other Christians I know, I'm not comfortable praying in front of people. In fact, I have always had a strict policy against it. What I discovered in Micky's book is that praying in front of others doesn't really come naturally to anyone. On the contrary, it's actually a supernatural exercise that takes time to become comfortable doing, especially in front of others.

I am confident that the inspiration of this book will empower you to start a prayer group of your own. What could be more valuable for a Sunday School class, church or community! It gives you a step by step guide to finding God's will, and the courage to pray "faith-sized prayers." You will overcome the fear of praying out loud and move closer to God—closer to real answers for your prayers.

Micky Blackwell has a deep knowledge of the Bible, loves young adults, and has the gift of teaching, all of which will be obvious when you settle down with *When Two or More are Gathered...in Prayer*. I feel blessed to have Micky as a spiritual mentor, and I am also delighted that countless more Christians will have the opportunity to learn from him.

So sit back, immerse yourself, and prepare to embark on a supernatural, faith-based journey that will deepen and enrich your prayer life.

— Lisa Tyler, President
Kindred Spirits Young Adult Sunday School Class
First United Methodist Church, Marietta, GA

Acknowledgments

I want to acknowledge the contributions of so many people who enabled the writing of this book about how two or more Christians gathered in corporate prayer can change our world.

This book could not have been written without my wife, Billie, who has supported me with love and been my prayer partner for over nearly half a century.

I am eternally grateful to my mother and father, Jean and James Blackwell, Sr., who were Christ-like role models and prayed for me every day they were here on earth.

Donald Adcock, an outstanding Christian businessman, introduced me to the Holy Spirit controlled life and started me on the journey of understanding the awesome power available when Christians gather to pray together. He will always have a special place in my heart.

I am thankful for the many people God has brought through my life to teach me about the power of "two or more" praying together. I am specifically indebted to Lance Lambert and Stephen Kaung for their in-depth teaching on prayer by the church.

I owe a debt of gratitude to all the Christian book writers whose thoughts and words have helped shape the message of this book. I am especially grateful for the books by R. A. Torrey, Rosalind Rinker, and Watchman Nee which have been incredible resources in helping me learn about prayer.

The lives of so many prayer intercessors such as Rees Howells, George Mueller, David Brainerd, and John Hyde have been a major source of inspiration.

I am also greatly indebted to those who over the years have shared their insights and concepts with me about prayer.

I will always be grateful for my Christian friends that have prayed with me as we learned how to pray together in small prayer groups.

The notes for this book were accumulated as I taught on the subject of "corporate prayer" over a period of 35 years. I would like to acknowledge all the inquiring minds whose questions prompted my quest for answers.

Many thanks to Dr. Nelson Price, Dr. Charles Sineath, Dr. James Speed, Bernie Brown, the late Charlie "Tremendous" Jones, Rev. Brian Foster, Rev. Mark Barbour, Gary Bottoms, Mack Henderson, Phil Hodges, Lisa Tyler, Dolan Falconer, David Varner, and many other friends for their encouragement and many helpful suggestions.

Finally, I want to gratefully acknowledge the help of Vally Sharpe and Janice Lowe in the editing and publication of this book.

Preface

My Spiritual Journey

I began a spiritual journey many years ago to understand God's directions for how Christians can use the multiplying power of "two or more" gathered together in prayer to accomplish great and mighty things in our world. I searched for what God had to say in His Word about why Christians need to pray together in public, how Christians can pray together with power and receive answers to prayer, and how to put public prayer into practice by two or more Christians gathered together. This book describes that journey.

By training, I am an aerospace engineer. I was fortunate enough to lead the Lockheed team that developed the world's most sophisticated military fighter aircraft for the United States Air Force—the F-22 Raptor stealth fighter. Later, as an executive vice president of the Lockheed Martin Corporation, I led their worldwide aircraft business. You might ask, "Why is an engineer writing a book on prayer?" To explain, I need to start at the beginning.

I gave my heart to Jesus when I was twelve years old, in a small rural Baptist church in North Alabama. Through high school and college, I continued to be active in church. My wife and I were married in my senior year of college. Her background in church was similar to mine, so it was natural that we would continue to actively participate in church as a married couple.

Soon after I got my first job as an engineer with NASA in Hampton, VA, and had joined a local Baptist church, I was asked to teach a Sunday School class of young adults. This started my love affair with teaching the Bible. I was ordained a deacon while still in my mid-twenties. Our seven years in Hampton were happy years.

In 1969, we moved to Marietta, GA, and I went to work for the Lockheed Corporation. Again, we joined a local Baptist church, but our church experience was not as joyful as before. It was about this time that God sent some men and women to our church for a lay-led revival. For the first time, I heard that Jesus wanted to control my life and fill me with His Holy Spirit. I recognized that, while God had truly blessed me, I had not relinquished control of my life. At that revival, I allowed God, for the first time, to control all of my life.

Whenever I had the opportunity over the next several years to experience and take part in praying together with an international group of laymen, I realized that there was much more to praying together than a minister offering a few minutes of prayer on behalf of the congregation. As our group prayed together, praise and thanksgiving were offered to God, burdens were shared, God's will was sought for our burdens, and answers were claimed by faith. There was no doubt that Jesus was in the midst of us as He had promised (Matthew 18:20). Every believer in the group had the opportunity to pray without feeling uncomfortable. It was exciting to see God use His people.

Following the lay-led revival, several men and women in our church formed a small prayer group that met every week for several years to pray together for whatever the Holy Spirit put in our hearts. Our first attempt at praying together was not pretty, and we quickly realized that we didn't know much about how to pray together as a group.

Why hadn't our church taught us how to pray together as a group of believers? I have gone to church my entire life, and I can't ever recall hearing a sermon or studying in Sunday School the subject of "why and how people should pray together in public." Recognizing our lack of knowledge, I, in the same spirit as the disciple in Luke 11:1, said to Jesus, "Lord, teach us how to pray when two or more are gathered in your name so that our prayers are always answered!"

The Lord answered my prayer. He took my wife and me under His wing and sent wonderful people to teach us about spiritual things. Through small weekly prayer group experiences, praying together with an international group of laymen, reading as many books on prayer as I could find, reading about the lives of great prayer warriors and intercessors, and studying scripture dealing with prayer in God's Word, I began to understand God's directions for how two or more people can pray together with power so that their prayers are answered.

I am not a theologian, nor do I pose as an authority on the subject of prayer. However, I believe that God, who wants us to talk to Him so He can answer our prayers, made the directions for how His people are to pray together plain enough for the simplest of us to comprehend if we would just try. As an engineer, I loved the challenge of identifying God's directions and finding ways to make them easy for every Christian to understand and put into practice.

I must confess that, even after spending many years studying about how to pray together, I still have much to learn. Also, I, like most of you, still struggle every day to allow Jesus to control my life and to have the prayer life I know God wants me to have.

I close with the hope that, as a result of your understanding the importance and power that comes from gathering to pray together with other Christians and your learning to follow God's directions on how to gather in public to pray together, God will use you and your fellow Christians to accomplish great and mighty things for His Kingdom.

— James "Micky" Blackwell

Chapter 1

Introduction

Let me introduce you to seven friends, who are all Christians and members of the same young adult Sunday School class at their church. Some of the friends have been Christians since childhood. Others have recently become a Christian. We will encounter these friends in several places throughout this book.

In our first encounter with the seven friends, they have gathered on a Sunday morning at the Christian Education Center's coffee pot. After getting coffee, they head to their class while catching up on recent events. Jack is the class president. Let's listen in on the class:

Jack: "Would everyone take a seat. Sue, would you tell us about the upcoming church activities of interest to the class?"

Sue: "I would like to remind everyone of the special revival focused on living a Spirit-filled life that is coming up next month. Also, the church is beginning to organize small prayer groups that meet in homes if you are interested. Finally, we will all meet at Hemingway's for Trivia Pursuit after church on Wednesday night. We came in first place last month."

Jack: "Bill what is the latest on church visitation?"

Bill: "Visitation of prospective new members is tomorrow night. Let me know after class if you can come."

Jack: "Are there any prayer requests?"

Amanda: "Please pray for the safety of my father who is in the
           Army and has just been deployed to a war zone."

Mary: "My next door neighbor, Pamela, has cancer, is sepa-
           rated from her husband, and has two small boys. Please
           pray for her and her family."

Joe: "I would like us to pray for our President. I believe he
           is in real need of prayer."

Hank: "This week, I finally graduated from college. Would
           you pray that I find a job?"

Jack: "Are there any other prayer requests? If not, let's go to
           the Lord in prayer. Would someone lead us in prayer?"

There is a period of silence. Since no one speaks, Jack prays:

Jack: "Father, we ask that you keep Amanda's father safe. We pray
           that your healing hand would touch Pamela that she might
           be healed. Let your Holy Spirit guide our President in these
           uncertain days. He needs the wisdom only you can give. Fi-
           nally Lord, we pray that you would show Hank your will for
           his life. Thank you for our class and bless our teacher as he
           teaches the lesson. Father, we ask these things in Jesus' name.
           Amen."

Jack's prayer asks for God to use His power and resources to intervene in
our world and honor the class member's prayer requests. I am sure the prayer
requests and Jack's subsequent leading of the class in prayer sound familiar and
are similar to the prayer time that takes place each week in many Sunday School
classes or in other religious groups that meet on a regular basis.

છ

Asking for God's Supernatural Power and Resources

From the very beginning of creation, God gave His people the responsibility
(Genesis 1:26-28) to use their free will to take control of the world in which

they live—to be masters of all life upon the earth, in the skies, and in the seas. Like the seven friends above, when we have needs or burdens that are beyond our human ability to control or resolve, God expects us to depend on Him by asking Him in prayer to provide the supernatural spiritual power and heavenly resources to deal with the burdens. The Bible is full of stories about praying men and women asking God to intervene in our world and about people receiving answers to their prayers when their requests are consistent with God's will.

God makes up the difference in what we can do in our power and the power required to meet a need on earth. If a family is in need of food and shelter, the church generally has the means and power to help them. If someone is sick, we often have the power through technology to relieve this sickness. If friends are not yet Christians, we have the power to share Jesus with them. However, if the monetary requirement to resolve a need is greater than the ability of the church, we need access to God's power and resources to meet the requirement. If a person's sickness is beyond today's technology to cure, we need God's power to heal them. If our friends reject Jesus as Savior, we need God's power to bring them to salvation.

The Multiplying Power of Two or More Praying Together

In the prayer time with the seven friends above, why did the Sunday School class members who had prayer requests ask others to share their burdens in prayer with God? Why didn't they just pray to God about their burden privately at home by themselves? I believe it is because somewhere in our spiritual DNA we know that the power of prayer is multiplied when *"two or more"* believers gather together and approach the throne of God with a shared burden.

When we ask other Christians to pray with us, we seek to unite them with us in one voice to ask God to intervene in our world with His power so that Amanda's father is kept safe from harm, Pamela is physically healed and her marriage restored, our President receives wisdom to govern well, and Hank can find a job.

Jesus taught in Matthew 18:19-20 that *the most effective way to access God's awesome power when it is needed in the world* **is through two or more uniting together in prayer to the Father.** Listen to the words of Jesus:

> "Again I say to you, that if **two of you** agree on earth about
> anything that they may ask, it shall be done for them by My
> Father who is in heaven. For where **two or three** have gathered
> together in My name, there I am in their midst."
> — Matthew 18:19-20 (NAS, emphasis added)

We have a greater authority to appropriate God's power and resources to address the burdens on our hearts when two or more pray together than we do through individual efforts. When two or more gather together in prayer, agree on the will of God concerning a need, and act as one, Jesus has promised that the Father will use His unlimited power and resources to answer their prayer. The above scripture also indicates that God will do things when two or more pray together that He may not do when we pray alone. When we pray together, the prayer power is multiplied. By praying together, we enlarge the channel through which God will act. Individual streams of prayer become a river of prayer. What a terrific promise!

Pastor Jack Hayford has described the principle behind the increased power that comes from two or more praying together:

> "There is a biblical principle that the multiplying of partnership in prayer multiplies the dimension of impact. It's taken from the Lord, who said that five will chase a hundred, and a hundred will put ten thousand to flight (Leviticus 26:8). It's not a matter of saying God is obligated because of number, but there is a penetrating power when there's agreement in prayer."[1]

God works in our world through the church, and works in our churches through His people's uniting together in prayer. The power God manifests on earth is directly related to the number of people participating in the public prayer ministry of the church and the amount of time they devote to prayer. I call this the *"prayer capacity"* of the church. The bigger the prayer capacity, the more heaven is opened to shower down God's will on earth.

Corporate Prayer

In this book, prayer by two or more people gathered together to pray as one united body for the purpose of making intercessory prayer to the

Father regarding a shared burden is referred to as *"corporate prayer."* The word *"corporate"* is used to describe this type of prayer because it means *"two or more people united together and acting as one."* Corporate prayer also includes two or more people offering praise and thanksgiving or confessing corporate sin to the Father. Prayer by a single Christian in private to the Father is referred to as *"individual prayer."*

Individual prayer and corporate prayer are two sides of the same coin. Both are necessary in a believer's life to appropriate all that God has for us. Corporate prayer by two or more Christians is impossible without being preceded by individual private prayer. It is in individual prayer that we prepare our hearts before coming to pray with others in corporate prayer.

A corporate body that gathers together in prayer to ask for God's power and resources can vary in size from two to large numbers of people participating in the prayer. Here are a variety of examples of how we can engage in corporate prayer.

- A husband and wife pray together
- Two or more friends pray together
- A family prays together at mealtime
- A small group prays together
- A cell group prays together
- An affinity group (members who have something in common) prays together
- An accountability group prays together
- A Sunday School class prays together
- A local church prays together
- Multiple churches pray together for a specific burden
- A city or nation prays for a specific burden

Bringing God's Will from Heaven to Earth

Corporate prayer is God's way for His people to bring all that the Father wants us to have from heaven to earth. Noted pastor and author Andrew Murray has remarked, "We must begin to believe that God, in the mystery of prayer, has entrusted us with a force that can move the heavenly world, and can bring its power down to earth."[2]

Through corporate prayer when two or more are gathered together, we can change our world by bringing God's will and resources from heaven to earth, as illustrated in Figure 1-1.

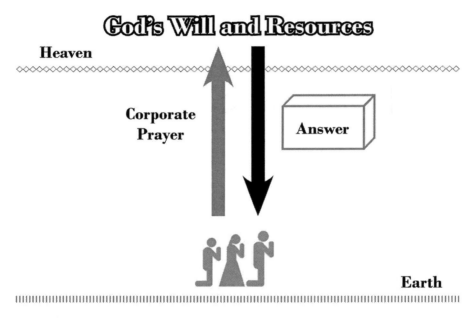

Figure 1-1. Corporate prayer brings God's will and resources from heaven and earth.

We see in the following scripture that Jesus gave His believers the keys to unlock the door of heaven and have free access to heaven's infinite power and resources to meet their needs on earth:

> And I will give unto thee the keys of the kingdom of heaven:
> — Matthew 16:19a (KJV)

God will only move His power and resources to earth to meet a need if we ask Him to do it in prayer. Everything on earth is determined by our choice to use or not to use the keys through prayer. With the keys, we can take control of our lives here on earth. How well we use the keys will determine how much of God's power and resources come from heaven to earth.

If we use the multiplying power of corporate prayer to unlock heaven and appropriate God's will, power, and resources, Jesus promised His people that they could do even greater things than He did:

> Verily, verily, I say unto you, He that believeth on me, the works that I do shall he do also; **and greater works than these shall he do**; because I go unto my Father. — John 14:12 (KJV, emphasis added)

It's astonishing to think that Jesus actually said believers today can not only minister to people spiritually and physically like He did, but can, with God's power, have a greater impact on the world than Jesus did! It follows that for believers to be able to do these extraordinary things, we as a corporate body must spend much time together in prayer.

Why Do We Spend So Little Time Praying Together?

For the seven friends we met earlier, their brief time of corporate prayer in Sunday School is the only time all week that they gather to pray with other Christians about their burdens. The friends had not yet become involved in a prayer group. Also, when they did gather to pray with others, they were comfortable sharing their prayer requests but were uncomfortable praying about them in front of others.

If Jesus ordained prayer by two or more gathered together as the ***most effective*** way for us to appropriate God's awesome power to do His work on earth, why is it then that we seldom pray together with other Christians, spend so little time in corporate prayer when we do pray with others, and find it uncomfortable to pray even in front of our friends? I believe this is due to:

- Our not understanding the importance of the public prayer ministry of the church in carrying out God's work here on earth
- Our failure to understand that when two or more are gathered together in prayer, the power of prayer is multiplied

- Our churches' failure to help people set aside a regular time to pray together in public
- Our being afraid to pray aloud in public
- Our past experiences with corporate prayer have been boring

Most Christians understand and engage in individual private prayer to some extent for themselves and for others. The Bible has much to say about how to pray as an individual believer to the Father. In addition, many wonderful books and materials are available to help us understand how to pray as individuals.

Most Christians, however, do not understand the awesome power available through corporate prayer and do not engage in praying with other Christians in public corporate prayer. In contrast to the abundant information available on how to pray as an individual believer, there are very few books and materials available, other than the Bible, to help us understand how two or more Christians should engage in prayer together.

God's Directions for When Two or More Are Gathered in Prayer

In our first encounter with the seven friends at the beginning of the chapter, Jack asked God the Father to grant the prayer requests made by the class members. Any prayer made to God by those that love Him is a good prayer. However, based on Jack's prayer, do you think Amanda, Mary, Joe, and Hank went home confident that their prayer requests had been answered by God? Did Jack's corporate prayer for the friend's burdens meet God's requirements, as given in the Bible, for their prayers to be answered? What do the friends need to do to be confident that God will answer their prayers?

To answer the above questions, we would have to see if the seven friends praying as a corporate body followed God's "directions" in the Bible for them to receive answers to their prayer requests. To answer our corporate prayers, God requires His people to individually have clean hearts (by confessing their sins and surrendering their lives to the control of the Holy Spirit), to be united together in one Spirit as they pray, to earnestly seek the will of God together regarding each prayer request, and as a corporate body claim God's will by faith for each burden.

To draw on God's awesome power and resources, we must follow God's directions for praying together. Unfortunately, most Christians do not understand the directions that God has established for how two or more are to pray together to receive answers to their prayers. Here are some possible reasons:

- Our lack of knowledge about what the Bible says about corporate prayer (what we don't know, we can't use)
- Our lack of understanding God's directions for how two or more people pray together to receive answers to their prayers
- Our failing to obey God's directions for corporate prayer after we have understood them
- Our not knowing how to put corporate prayer into practice

Purpose of This Book

The purpose of this book is to pass on to other Christians the knowledge and wisdom I have learned on my spiritual journey to understand and apply God's directions for how two or more people pray together with awesome power and receive answers to their prayers. Specifically, I would like to help others discover the answers to the following questions:

- Why is it important for the church to have a public prayer ministry where its people regularly gather to pray together?
- What does the Bible say about corporate prayer?
- What are God's directions as given in the Bible for how we should pray together with other people so that our prayers receive answers?
- How do we put into practice God's directions for praying together so that all believers can comfortably (without fear) participate in the public prayer ministry of the church?

Overview of Book

In Part I, our journey to understand the awesome power of corporate prayer will begin with learning what God's Word has to say about two or more gathering to pray together. Part II contains eight steps that summarize God's directions as given in the Bible for how people are to pray together with great power to receive answers to their prayers. In Part III, we will look at the practical aspects of applying God's directions for praying together to small prayer groups, the local church, and the nation.

At the end of each chapter are questions to stimulate personal reflection on the contents of the chapter. At the end of the book, a study guide for each chapter is included to provide an opportunity to gain a deeper understanding of corporate prayer and to help you put God's directions into practice.

Points to Remember

In the Introduction, the important points discussed were:

1. Jesus taught that the most effective way to access God's power, when it is needed in our world, is through two or more united together praying to the Father.

2. By praying together, we enlarge the channel through which God will act, and we multiply the power of our prayers.

3. Corporate prayer is defined as when two or more gather to pray in public as one united body for the purpose of making intercessory prayer to the Father regarding a shared burden, offering praise and thanksgiving, or confessing corporate sin.

4. The corporate body that gathers together in prayer to ask for God's power and resources can vary in size from two people to a large number of people participating in the prayer.

5. Jesus established that prayer by two or more is to be used to obtain answers to prayer regarding our burdens and to bring all He wants us to have from heaven to earth!

6. The "prayer capacity" of the church is the number of people involved in the prayer ministry of the church and the amount of time they devote to prayer.

7. When there is a major burden on our heart, we should engage the largest prayer capacity possible to intercede on behalf of the burden with the Father.

8. Jesus promised that after He was gone His people would have the power to do extraordinary things.

Questions for Personal Reflection

Before going to the next chapter, take time to reflect on your answers to the following questions:

1. Do you accept the biblical principle that there is more spiritual power when two or more believers gather to pray together?

2. Does the prospect of learning how to pray with other people in order to draw on the awesome power of God to do extraordinary things excite you?

Part I

What the Bible Says About Corporate Prayer

Chapter 2

Why Should We Pray Together Corporately?

In Part I, our journey to understand corporate prayer will begin with learning what the Bible has to say about corporate prayer. Specifically, we will study why we should pray together; learn what Jesus taught about prayer; look at the differences in prayer by the early church and today's church; and examine the corporate prayers found in the Bible.

As we saw in the last chapter, Jesus has given us the promise that when two or more Christians pray together as one corporate body there is a multiplying in the power of prayer. The natural question that follows is "Why has God given the church this increased prayer power?" In this chapter, we consider the many important reasons that the Bible gives for why we should gather together in public and use the power of corporate prayer. *

We should pray corporately with other Christians because:

- God desires to talk and to have fellowship with His children!
- Corporate prayer gives God glory!
- Corporate prayer will bring God's will from heaven to earth for ourselves, for believers, for the unsaved, for our ministers, for our church, and for our nation!
- God is looking for a people that will spend much time in prayer!
- The Bible commands us to pray!

---

*You will recognize that many of the reasons for why we should pray corporately also apply to why we should pray in individual prayer.

Let's look at these reasons for why we should gather to pray with other Christians in more detail.

God Desires to Talk and Have Fellowship with His Children!

Why should we pray corporately? We should pray because God desires to talk to His children and to have fellowship with them.

Our relationship to God in prayer is similar to the relationship we had as children with our earthly fathers. As a child I could go boldly to my father and ask him for anything—a new toy, a snack, more allowance and, later, the car keys. If my request met with my father's approval, it was granted. This was usually followed by a hug and kiss. Also, I often enjoyed the fellowship of just being in my father's presence when no one spoke—watching a ballgame together, holding hands while walking, or fishing quietly together on a river bank.

Because we are His children, God wants us to come boldly to His throne room in prayer so that we can spend time together with Him, feel His love, express our love for Him, listen to Him, and tell Him our needs.

Our talking to God in prayer is a two-way conversation between ourselves and the Heavenly Father. In prayer, we express our repentance, feelings, thoughts, and requests to God. Through prayer, we are speaking and listening to God, and God is listening and speaking to us. Corporate prayer is a conversation between God and His children gathered together.

Fellowship with God in prayer is enjoying an intimate relationship with the Father in the throne room of heaven without necessarily God or us speaking. We enjoy keeping company with the Father and He enjoys keeping company with His children. As we corporately commune with the Father, we make ourselves available to God.

Prayer Gives God Glory!

Why should we pray corporately? We should pray because the *ultimate purpose of corporate prayer is "To Give God Glory!"* It is not the act of corporately praying that gives God glory. It is our *receiving answers* to prayer that gives God glory. Look at what Jesus had to say about this:

And whatsoever ye shall ask in my name, that will I do, **that the Father
may be glorified** in the Son. — John 14:13 (KJV, emphasis added)

God is given glory when our corporate prayers:

- Praise Him and thank Him for answers to prayer
- Appropriate the blessings God has already promised us
- Ask and receive
- Bring God's will to earth
- Help us gain victory over Satan

Prayer Brings All God Has For Us from Heaven to Earth!

Why should we pray corporately? We should pray corporately because
corporate prayer brings God's will from heaven to earth for ourselves, for believers, for the unsaved, for our ministers, for our church, and for our nation.

Corporate prayer for believers results in their receiving power for service
through the continual filling of the Holy Spirit. The Father wants us to have
more and more of the Holy Spirit. All we have to do is ask:

If you then, evil-minded as you are, know how to give good gifts—gifts
that are to advantage—to your children, how much more will your
heavenly Father give the Holy Spirit to those who ask and continue to
ask Him! — Luke 11:13 (AMP)

Corporate prayer for believers results in God supplying our every need.
In Paul's letter to the Philippians, he says:

But my God shall supply all your need according to His riches in glory
by Christ Jesus. — Philippians 4:19 (KJV)

Corporate prayer for believers results in their being protected and delivered from future temptation as we see from the Lord's Prayer:

And lead us not into temptation, but deliver us from evil…
— Matthew 6:13a (KJV)

Corporate prayer for believers results in God giving them a bountiful supply of wisdom:

> If you want to know what God wants you to do, ask him, and he will
> gladly tell you, for he is always ready to give a bountiful supply of
> wisdom to all who ask him; he will not resent it. — James 1:5 (LVB)

Corporate prayer for believers results in God granting His people the desires of their hearts:

> Delight yourself in the Lord; And He will give you the desires
> of your heart. — Psalms 37:4 (NAS)

Corporate prayer for believers brings physical healing as we read in the book of James:

> Is any sick among you? Let him call for the elders of the church; and let
> them pray over him, anointing him with oil in the name of the Lord:
> — James 5:14 (KJV)

Corporate prayer for unsaved souls results in their being saved. God longs for all to be saved as we see in I Timothy:

> Here are my directions: Pray much for others; plead for God's mercy
> upon them; give thanks for all he is going to do for them. This is good
> and pleases God our Savior, for **he longs for all to be saved** and to
> understand this truth: — I Timothy 2:1, 3-4 (LVB,emphasis added)

Corporate prayer can impact the salvation of our family members, friends, neighbors, and co-workers. Corporate prayer can release the power of the Holy Spirit upon unbelievers' spirits and souls with such might that they will want to accept the Lord Jesus into their heart and be saved rather than remain unbelievers.

Corporate prayer for our ministers and church leaders brings them power. Many Christians are not happy with their ministers. Christians should pray together for their ministers until God changes them into what He desires them to be. We should pray for them until God fills them with power and gives them wisdom.

The great evangelist and author R. A. Torrey wrote, "Oh, any church can have a minister who is a man of power, a minister who is baptized and filled with the Holy Ghost, if they are willing to pay the price, and the price is prayer, much prayer, and much real prayer, prayer in the Holy Ghost."[1] We should never cease to pray for our ministers and church leaders.

Corporate prayer changes our churches. Prayer brings revival. All great revivals have begun with much intercessory prayer by God's people gathered together. Prayer will cause the church to identify and confess its corporate sin. Prayer brings the power of the Holy Spirit to the ministries of the church. Prayer resolves problems in the church. Prayer transforms the church into what it was intended to be—the corporate body of Christ.

God has infinite resources and does not limit how many resources the church can have. All limitation is based on the church's willingness to spend time united as one in corporate prayer. If we pray a little, we get few of heaven's resources. If we pray a lot, we get a lot of heaven's resources. John Wesley said, "God will do nothing but in answer to prayer." God is ready to act, but will only do so when we pray and ask.

Corporate prayer will heal our nation and bring God's blessings to our country if only His people will humble themselves and pray:

> If my people, which are called by my name, shall humble themselves,
> and pray, and seek my face, and turn from their wicked ways; then will I
> hear from heaven, and will forgive their sin, and will heal their land.
> — II Chronicles 7:14 (KJV)

Paul exhorts us to pray for those who lead our nation so that we can live quiet and peaceable lives:

> I exhort therefore, that, first of all, supplications, prayers, intercessions,
> and giving of thanks, be made for all men; For kings, and for all that
> are in authority; that we may lead a quiet and peaceable life in all
> godliness and honesty. — I Timothy 2:1-2 (KJV)

19

God Is Looking For a People That Will Pray!

Why should we pray corporately? We should pray because God is looking for men and women who will spend much time in prayer together. Who will become God's prayer warriors? In Ezekiel, God says:

> And I sought for a man among them that should make up the hedge, and stand in the gap before me for the land, that I should not destroy it: but I found none. — Ezekiel 22:30 (KJV)

God is asking, "Where are the people that will be my church and are willing to stand in the gap by gathering together to pray. I will do wondrous things if they will just pray to me." The great preacher Charles H. Spurgeon in his sermon "The Story of God's Mighty Acts" expressed the need for a people to pray in this way:

> "Oh! men and brethren, what would this heart feel if I could but believe that there were some among you who would go home and pray for a revival of religion—men whose faith is large enough, and their love fiery enough to lead them from this moment to exercise unceasing intercessions that God would appear among us and do wondrous things here, as in the times of former generations."[2]

Our Father desires His church to spend much time in praise and intercessory prayer and be called a house of prayer. Jesus, quoting from Isaiah, said:

> "...It is written, my house shall be called **the house of prayer...**"
> — Matthew 21:13b (KJV, emphasis added)

A church that prays together can be assured that God's presence is there with them. Prayer is the one feature that sets apart the house of God from all other organizations who gather together.

God is not only looking for a people that will pray, but He is also looking for churches that will teach His people to pray. E. M. Bounds a Methodist minister, who wrote many books on prayer, observes:

"As God's house is a house where the business of praying is carried on, so is it a place where the business of making praying people out of prayerless people is done. The house of God is a divine workshop, and there the work of prayer goes on."[3]

The Bible Commands Us To Pray!

Why should we pray corporately? We should pray because the Bible commands us to pray! As Christians we have no choice. Look at the following words from Jesus:

> One day Jesus told his disciples a story to illustrate their need for
> constant prayer and to show them that they must keep praying
> until the answer comes. — Luke 18:1 (LVB)

Paul echoes this theme in I Thessalonians 5:17 when he writes that we are to *"pray without ceasing."*

Points to Remember

In this chapter, answers were given to the question, "Why should we pray corporately?" They are:

1. Because God desires to talk and to have fellowship with His children!
2. Because corporate prayer gives God glory!
3. Because corporate prayer will bring God's will from heaven to earth for ourselves, for believers, for the unsaved, for our ministers, for our church, and for our nation!
4. Because God is looking for a people that will spend much time in prayer!
5. Because the Bible commands us to pray!

Questions for Personal Reflection

Before going to the next chapter, take time to reflect on your answers to the following questions:

1. In what areas of your life could corporate prayer make a difference?
2. Do you feel a burden to pray together with other believers?
3. Are you willing to spend time with other believers in corporate prayer?

Chapter 3

What Did Jesus Teach About Prayer?

What is the Holy Spirit saying to you and your church about the need for corporate prayer? Do you feel inadequate to pray individually and corporately? Do you feel a need to learn to pray in the manner God has set forth? If your answer is "yes" to these questions, let's see what Jesus taught the disciples about how to pray.

"Lord, Teach Us to Pray"

After about a year and a half into His ministry, Jesus chose twelve disciples. He did this after praying to the Father all night about whom He should choose. Until that time the future apostles had just hung around Jesus as He moved from place to place, taking in all that Jesus said and did. With the selection of the twelve, Jesus used the remaining year and a half of His ministry on earth to focus on teaching and training the disciples. It would be up to them to carry the gospel to the world.

Shortly after selecting the twelve, Jesus gave the disciples power and authority over all demons and the power to heal diseases. He then sent them out on a mission to the nearby villages to minister to the people. Later, they came back and reported to Jesus all the wondrous things that had been done. A few days later, Jesus took Peter, John, and James up to a mountain to pray. Here they experienced the transfiguration. This was heady stuff for the disciples.

After coming down from the mountain, a man pleaded with Jesus to heal his mentally deranged son. He had already brought his son to the disciples, and they could not cure him. Jesus was disappointed that His disciples could not cure the boy. Jesus healed the boy at once. The disciples were vexed as to why they had not been able to cure the boy. Jesus told them they had insufficient faith and that they had to earnestly seek that faith by prayer and fasting.

It was now time for mission number two. Jesus appointed seventy disciples and sent them out to minister. The mission was a great success. In Luke, it says:

> And the seventy returned again with joy, saying, Lord, even the devils
> are subject unto us through thy name. — Luke 10:17 (KJV)

The disciples had now experienced God's power working through them in a mighty way. They had also experienced failure. The cure for their failure, Jesus told them, was to increase the size of their faith through prayer and fasting.

One day as Jesus had finished praying, one of His disciples said to Him:

> "**Lord, teach us to pray**, as John also taught his disciples."
> — Luke 11:1b (KJV, emphasis added)

Did the disciples not know how to pray? William Barclay suggests this disciple may have been looking for a *model* prayer since most rabbis of that day had simple model prayers.[1] Was this disciple looking for a formula? Had not John the Baptist already instructed many of them?

I believe the disciple noticed something special about the prayers of Jesus—that His prayers were always answered by the Father without fail. Now, this was truly remarkable! More than likely the disciple had not had the same success in his own prayers. Could he have been saying, "Lord, teach us to pray like you so that our prayers will also be answered every time?"

Aren't most of us in the same boat as this disciple? We too want God to do great and wondrous things in our church, so our cry from the church today should be, "Lord, teach us how to *pray together corporately* so that our prayers are answered!"

Jesus responded to the disciple's request to be taught how to pray by teaching the disciples what is referred to today as the "Lord's Prayer" that is recorded in Matthew 6:9-13. Jesus also taught the disciples how to pray by example.

As we study what Jesus taught about prayer, we will see that He taught prayer, whether individual or corporate, contains four basic elements: *

- Praise
- Thanksgiving
- Pardon
- Petition

The first element of prayer is *praise*. Praise includes the adoration and worship of God where we describe His character, wonder, mercy, ability and love, and recognize His greatness, achievements, and majesty.

The second element of prayer is *thanksgiving*—thanksgiving for actions that God has taken in the past or is currently taking, whether for blessings or for supporting us in our trials and temptations; thanksgiving for all that He has so generously given us.

Thanksgiving and praise are closely related and are often mentioned together in the Bible (e.g. Psalm 106:1).

The third element of prayer is *pardon*. Pardon refers to confessing our sins individually or corporately to God, asking Him to forgive us of our sins, and committing to correct our actions.

The fourth element of prayer is *petition*. Petition includes personal requests to God and intercession for other people's burdens to God.

Jesus Taught the Lord's Prayer to His Disciples

In answer to the disciple's request for Jesus to teach the disciples how to pray, He said:

---

*Other authors use the word ACTS to describe the elements of prayer. "A" stands for adoration, "C" for confession, "T" for thanksgiving, and "S" for supplication. I have used praise, thanksgiving, pardon, and petition to describe the elements of prayer since I think they are more descriptive.

> After this manner therefore pray ye: Our Father which art in heaven,
> Hallowed be thy name. Thy kingdom come. Thy will be done in earth, as
> it is in heaven. Give us this day our daily bread. And forgive us our debts,
> as we forgive our debtors. And lead us not into temptation, but deliver
> us from evil: For thine is the kingdom, and the power, and the
> glory, for ever. Amen. — Matthew 6:9-13 (KJV)

The Lord's Prayer contains three of the basic elements of prayer — praise, pardon, and petition.

Jesus said we should open our prayer by addressing the Father —*"Our Father which art in heaven..."*

The second part of the Lord's Prayer is praise to the Father —*"Hallowed be thy name."*

The third part is our petition to bring God's will to earth —*"Thy kingdom come. Thy will be done in earth, as it is in heaven."*

The fourth part is a petition for today's provisions —*"Give us this day our daily bread."*

The fifth part is for pardon asking God to forgive us as we likewise have forgiven others —*"And forgive us our debts, as we forgive our debtors."*

The sixth part is to petition God to protect us from future temptation and evil —*"And lead us not into temptation, but deliver us from evil..."*

The seventh part closes with praise: *"For thine is the kingdom, and the power, and the glory, for ever. Amen."*

As will be seen in Chapter 5, corporate prayer can contain any or all of the basic elements of prayer.

Each of the elements of prayer in the Lord's Prayer carries with it a burden that is initiated by God. For instance, the Holy Spirit places on our hearts the burden of wanting to come to the Father and offer praise, thanksgiving, and worship because we love Him. Also, the Holy Spirit will burden our hearts with the need to seek pardon for our sins so that we can be in right relationship with the Father. Finally, the Holy Spirit will burden our hearts with specific petitions to bring before the Father. In the Lord's Prayer, Jesus says there are three definite petitions that every believer should have on his or her heart and discuss with God daily.

The *first petition* is for pardon from our sins: *"Forgive us our debts"* Matthew 6:12a (KJV). It involves confessing our sins daily (more about this in Chapter 6). Each day because of our fallen nature, we disobey God in many areas of our lives. This is sin. There can be no unconfessed sin in our lives if we want God to answer our prayers. If there is sin in our hearts, the first thing to go is faith. For effective corporate prayer, we must have clean hands and clean hearts.

The *second petition* is for our provision: *"Give us this day our daily bread"* Matthew 6:11 (KJV). God knows our needs. However, we must ask daily for his provision. As a husband and wife, it is your privilege to ask God daily in corporate prayer to give your family what it needs to sustain life.

Remember the story of Moses and the children of Israel in the wilderness. God fed them with manna. The manna came from heaven every day. People could only gather what their families needed for that day. Yesterday's manna was not good for today—it had to be gathered anew every day. Similarly our prayers must appropriate God's provisions on a daily basis.

The *third petition* is for our protection: *"And lead us not into temptation"* Matthew 6:13a (KJV). As individual believers and as a church, we need future protection from Satan. God has allowed Satan freedom to roam around our earth.

God permits temptations to be given to us just as He permitted Satan to test Job by taking away his earthly blessings and health (Job 1:6-12). As individual believers and as a church, we experience more temptation than God desires us to have simply because we do not ask for protection. Assume that one day Satan wants to tempt you. If you pray daily for God's protection, God decides if the temptation will help you mature as a Christian and either permits it or protects you. However, if on that day we have failed to pray for protection, Satan has a free hand to tempt us. The question is, "Why subject ourselves to more than God desires us to have?"

The famous missionary C. T. Studd said, "If you don't desire to meet the devil during the day, meet Jesus before dawn."[2]

It is important to remember, however, that God will not allow us to have more temptation than we can stand as we see in the following scripture:

27

> There hath no temptation taken you but such as is common to man:
> but God is faithful, who will not suffer you to be tempted above that ye
> are able; but will with the temptation also make a way to escape, that
> ye may be able to bear it. — I Corinthians 10:13 (KJV)

It is spiritual negligence on the part of parents to send their children into the world each day without asking God to protect them. It is so important for a husband and wife to pray together corporately each day for the protection of their family.

Jesus Taught the Disciples by Example

Jesus spent many hours in prayer talking with His Father while He was here on earth. Sometimes Jesus was too busy to eat or sleep; however, He always had time to pray. Many times, He prayed all night. It was through prayer that Jesus asked for and obtained God's will and power for His life. As a result of His prayer ministry, lives were changed, people were healed, and miracles were performed. Jesus taught the disciples how to pray through His personal example.

In the Bible verses below, we can see where Jesus used the elements of praise, thanksgiving, and petition in His own prayers. Jesus gave *praise* to the Father out of a joyful heart:

> Then he was filled with the joy of the Holy Spirit and said, "I praise you,
> O Father, Lord of heaven and earth, for hiding these things from
> the intellectuals and worldly wise and for revealing them to those who
> are as trusting as little children. Yes, thank you, Father, for that is the
> way you wanted it." — Luke 10:21 (LVB)

Jesus gave *thanks* to the Father for the provisions that God had given as we see in the following scripture:

> Jesus therefore took the loaves; and having given thanks, He distributed
> to those who were seated; likewise also of the fish as much
> as they wanted. — John 6:11 (NAS)

Jesus *petitioned* the Father with intercession for others. Jesus interceded for Peter that he would be protected from Satan (Luke 22:31-32). Jesus petitioned the Father for all of us that would believe on Him in the future to be united as one:

> Neither pray I for these alone, but for them also which shall believe on me through their word; That they all may be one; as thou, Father, art in me, and I in thee, that they also may be one in us: that the world may believe that thou hast sent me. — John 17:20-21 (KJV)

Jesus also petitioned the Father for himself:

> And he went a little further, and fell on his face, and prayed, saying, O my Father, if it be possible, let this cup pass from me: nevertheless not as I will, but as thou wilt. — Matthew 26:39 (KJV)

Points to Remember

In this chapter, we looked at what Jesus taught the disciples about how to pray. The important points were:

1. The disciples asked Jesus to teach them how to pray. Jesus responded by teaching the disciples the "Lord's Prayer."
2. The four basic elements of prayer are praise, thanksgiving, pardon, and petition.
3. In the Lord's Prayer, Jesus gives us three specific petitions to pray for daily: petition for pardon of our sins, petition for life's necessities, and petition for protection from Satan.
4. God through the Holy Spirit burdens our hearts to praise Him, to thank Him, to ask Him to pardon our sins, and to petition Him for our needs and other's needs.
5. Jesus spent much time in prayer. Many times, He spent the whole night in prayer. It was through prayer that Jesus sought and obtained God's will and power for His life.

Questions for Personal Reflection

Before going to the next chapter, take time to reflect on your answers to the following questions:

1. What important things did you learn about how you should pray from looking at what Jesus taught on prayer and Jesus' personal prayer life?
2. Are you comfortable using praise, thanksgiving, pardon and petition in your prayers? If not, why not?

Chapter 4

Prayer in the Early Church and Today's Church

Are there differences in the way the early church and today's church have used what Jesus taught us about prayer? Yes. The early church, like Jesus, spent much time in prayer and, as promised, did extraordinary things. Many of today's churches spend little time in corporate prayer, have little power, win few souls to Christ, grow slowly if at all, have little joy, and are disappointed when prayers go unanswered.

Let's compare prayer in the early church and prayer in today's church to see what these differences teach us.

Prayer in the Early Church

The early church continued to follow the example Jesus set for them on how to pray. After Pentecost, the book of Acts tells us that the church did indeed spend much time in corporate prayer, and extraordinary things happened just as Jesus promised! The early church was empowered with the Holy Spirit and viewed corporate prayer as a ministry to get things done. Through the apostles, many signs and wonders were done. Many people were saved daily and added to the fellowship of believers. The early church was dynamic and thrilling. All felt a sense of awe. The believers:

- Worshiped regularly in the temple
- Met constantly in small groups in homes for communion and fellowship with each other

- Were of one heart and mind
- Shared their meals with great joy, happiness, and thankfulness
- Listened to powerful sermons from the apostles
- Joined with other believers in the regular attendance at the apostles' teaching sessions
- Shared their possessions with those in need
- Shared their faith with unbelievers
- Regularly joined with other believers in prayer

Even when trouble came to the early church, they found the answer by praying together in corporate prayer. Peter and John were arrested for claiming Jesus had risen from the dead. They were threatened by the High Priests and let go. As soon as they were freed, all the believers came together and prayed corporately that they might have boldness, continue to heal the sick, and do miracles and wonders in the name of Jesus. Following this corporate prayer, the house where they were gathered shook, and all the believers were filled again with the Holy Spirit. God answered their prayer for boldness, because the Bible says Peter immediately began to preach boldly the Word of God with power.

Trouble in the church arose again when the Greek-speaking widows felt they were being discriminated against in the daily distribution of food. The apostles called a meeting of all believers. They set aside seven men full of faith and the Holy Spirit's power to help with the administration of the food program; so they could spend their time in prayer, preaching, and teaching. The apostles understood that they needed to spend much time in prayer.

Trouble in the form of persecution soon hit the early church. Peter was arrested this time by King Herod, whose intention was to deliver Peter to the Jews for execution. However, the church united in earnest intercessory corporate prayer to God the Father asking for the safety of Peter during the time he was in prison:

> Peter therefore was kept in prison: but prayer was made without ceasing of the church unto God for him. — Acts 12:5 (KJV)

32

The result was God answered the church's prayer by sending an angel to release Peter from prison.

Think about the early church. The believers prayed together as a corporate body. The leaders of the church prayed. The early church lived in victory, and extraordinary things happened just as Jesus promised!

Prayer in Today's Church

In the first centuries after Christ's ascension, the church flourished and spread throughout the world. This was followed by periods of darkness. In the last several centuries, several great revivals in the church have occurred, such as:

- Three great awakenings in America: 1730s to 1740s, 1800s to 1830s, and 1880s to 1900s
- Ulster revival of 1859-1860
- Welsh revival of 1904-1905
- Shantung revival in China of 1930-1933
- Asbury revival of 1970
- Wheaton College revival of 1995

In each of these revivals, the power of the Holy Spirit was present, there was joy, and souls were saved just as in the early church. All the revivals came about as a result of the church confessing its sin, surrendering to the control of the Holy Spirit and spending much time together in intercessory prayer. Unfortunately, the revivals were not sustained. In many cases, the revival died when the prayer meetings died.

Today, there are churches and communities seeing many souls saved and spiritual growth in their people. However, we ask, "Is today's church taken as a whole like the early church?" The answer is no.

If the early church had power, joy, unity, spiritual growth, souls being saved, and needs being met, then we have to ask ourselves the following questions.

- Why does today's church have so little power?
- Why is today's church declining/disappearing in so many countries?
- Why does today's church win so few people to Christ?
- Why are so many ministers boring and powerless?
- Why does the church have so little growth?
- Why is there so little spiritual growth in our lives?
- Why is today's church so ignorant of spiritual things?
- Why does the church have so little joy and victory?
- Why do our prayers in church seem more like just religious ritual?
- Why do we spend so little time praying together corporately in church?
- Why do we fear praying in public with other believers?
- Why do our corporate prayers go unanswered?
- Why do our hearts crave revival of our churches and none comes?

God's answer to these questions is found in the book of James:

> ...ye have not, because ye ask not. Ye ask, and receive not, because ye ask amiss... — James 4:2b-3a (KJV)

In this verse, we see two reasons that the churches of today are different from the early church. The first is that the church neglects to pray (if you don't ask, you don't get). The second is that, when the church does ask, it asks with wrong motives or doesn't follow God's directions for answered prayer.

Ye Ask Not

When the church neglects to ask in prayer for God's will to come to earth, we are not following God's directions. Our Father desires that His church spend much time in prayer, and the church, as we saw earlier, is to be known foremost as a house of prayer. Prayer by the church is how God's work on earth gets done.

When we go to our local church, we spend much of our time socializing, hearing a sermon, singing hymns, and studying the Bible. While there are short prayers, the church neglects to spend the time in intercessory corporate prayer needed to change our world. Jonathan Graf, editor of *Pray!* magazine, notes that, "at best, five percent of churches have a significant mobilized prayer ministry."[1]

F. B. Meyer, the great Baptist pastor and evangelist, made this comment on the lack of prayer by the church: "The greatest tragedy of life is not unanswered prayer, but unoffered prayer."

Unfortunately, we don't think of the local church as a place to spend time in corporate prayer. I remember that as a child my family went to church on Wednesday nights to "prayer meeting." Today in many churches, a weekly meeting dedicated for believers to pray together in public has been lost to other activities.

The intercessory corporate prayer ministry of the church should be on equal footing with preaching the gospel, teaching the Bible, witnessing to the lost, and helping those in need.

Without the intercessory ministry of prayer, the church is not carrying on the work of our Lord here on earth in the same way Jesus would do it if He were here. As we have already seen, Jesus spent much time in prayer. So as the body of Christ, we should also expect to spend much time in the ministry of prayer. Make no mistake, this ministry takes time and is work.

Our churches today neglect to pray because they depend more on organizational machinery to accomplish God's work than on intercessory corporate prayer. Unfortunately, without prayer the organizations have no power. When our organizations don't produce the results we want, we look for new people, programs, processes, plans, or other institutional methods to fix the organizations rather than looking to God in corporate prayer. Paul E. Billheimer writes: "Any church without a well-organized and systematic prayer program is simply operating a religious treadmill."[2]

The church needs the power of the Holy Spirit that comes through corporate prayer. E. M. Bounds observes:

> "What the Church needs today is not more or better machinery, not new organizations or more and novel methods. She needs men whom the Holy Spirit can use—men of prayer, men mighty in prayer.

The Holy Spirit does not flow through methods, but through men. He does not come on machinery, but on men. He does not anoint plans, but men—men of prayer."[3]

Corporate prayer in the church, where Christians are asked to pray together in public, often strikes fear in the hearts of God's people. Many believers fail to spend time praying together in public because they fear the opinion of man more than God. We are afraid of praying aloud in front of other people because:

- We are afraid we will embarrass ourselves in front of others
- We feel unworthy to pray together with those of greater spiritual maturity
- We don't know what to say
- We are afraid we will say something wrong and others will notice it
- We are uncomfortable since we have never prayed in front of other people
- We feel that we do not speak well and will not sound as good as others
- We are intimidated by others' abilities to pray

Because of this fear many Christians simply fail to gather together to pray in public—"ye ask not." God does not want us to be afraid of praying with other Christians. He wants us to love and enjoy each other as we see in the following scripture:

> For the Holy Spirit, God's gift, does not want you to be afraid of people,
> but to be wise and strong, and to love them and enjoy being with them.
> — II Timothy 1:7 (LVB)

In chapter 16, we will return to the subject of the fear of praying in public with other Christians. We will describe how every believer in the church can be comfortable and enjoy participating in corporate prayer no matter what their backgrounds, speaking abilities, or where they are in terms of Christian maturity.

Today's church can be like the early church and have power and answered prayer if its people will spend much time together in corporate prayer. Exciting things will begin to happen in a church when its people pray in earnest. The Bible says:

> The earnest prayer of a righteous man has great power and wonderful results. — James 5:16b (LVB)

What a marvelous statement! If we would just take time to passionately pray together with purpose like the early church, we will receive great power and have wonderful results. Jesus says that God will act when the church kneels to pray.

Ye Ask Amiss

We ask amiss when we pray without letting God be in control and when we do not spend time earnestly seeking His will concerning a burden. How often have we gone to a church committee meeting where the chairman of the committee opens with prayer? In the prayer, the chairman asks God to show us His will. Then, the chairman quickly proceeds to tell everyone the plan *he* has developed. Finally at the end of the meeting, the chairman, in a closing prayer asks God to bless the plan.

Did this chairman and committee spend time together in corporate prayer seeking God's will before they made a plan? The answer is no. We ask God to get in on what *we* want to do, and we do not get in on what *God* wants to do. We ask amiss, and God will not answer our prayers.

We ask amiss when we pray and do not follow God's directions for answered prayer. (We will discuss God's directions for answered prayer in Part II.) Here are some other ways we ask amiss.

- We pray and do not keep his commandments
- We pray and have known sin in our hearts that is unconfessed
- We pray and have not surrendered control of our lives to the Holy Spirit
- We pray and do not do those things that are pleasing in His sight

We ask amiss, too, when we ask God for something to satisfy our own selfish desires. For instance, most of us reading this book are guilty of praying selfishly for material things. We have prayed for our sports team to win a game, or we have prayed for success in our careers. Did we ask for these things to give God glory, or did we ask out of wrong motives because of our selfish desires?

Jesus is clear that we are not to pray for our own selfish desires in His story about the "hypocrite":

> "And now about prayer. When you pray, don't be like the hypocrites
> who pretend piety by praying publicly on street corners and in
> the synagogues where everyone can see them. Truly, that is all
> the reward they will ever get."
> — Matthew 6:5 (LVB)

In the case of the hypocrite, his selfish desire was to be seen of men and praised for his piety.

Points to Remember

In this chapter, we saw the differences in prayer by the early church and prayer by today's church. The important points were:

1. The early church, like Jesus, spent much time in prayer and, as promised, did extraordinary things.
2. When today's church emulates the early church by following God's directions, they also can do great and wonderful things.
3. Many of today's churches spend little time in corporate prayer, have little power, win few souls to Christ, grow slowly if at all, have little joy, and their prayers go unanswered.
4. There are two reasons that many of today's churches are not like the early church: they fail to take time to pray, and they don't follow God's directions when they do pray.

Questions for Personal Reflection

Before going to the next chapter, take time to reflect on the answers to the following questions:

1. Are you willing to follow God's directions for praying corporately?
2. What can you do to elevate the importance of corporate prayer in your church?

Chapter 5

Corporate Prayers in the Bible

In this chapter, we will look at the corporate prayers found in the Bible to guide us as we learn how to pray corporately.

As defined in Chapter 1, corporate prayer is when the church gathers together to pray in public as a united body for the purpose of making intercessory prayer to the Father regarding a shared burden, offering praise and thanksgiving, or confessing corporate sin.

It was also pointed out that the word *"corporate"* means two or more people united together and acting as one body. In our case, the church is two or more people acting like one body—Jesus. The apostle Paul, using an analogy of the human body, refers to the church as the *"body of Christ"* with Christ as the head. The church as it prays acts with one mind, one heart, one will, and one Spirit (more on this in Chapter 7).

There is greater spiritual power when we pray together corporately. It is more difficult for our pride and egos to be exalted when we pray with other people. Corporate prayer humbles us when we pray publicly in front of others. Also as we pray corporately, the will of God concerning a personal burden can more easily be discerned through others that have greater objectivity.

As we pray corporately for each other, our love and concern for each other grows. Herbert Lockyer writes: "Unison in prayer greatly helps to banish the spirit of self-independence and narrowness of personal outlook, and benefits our spiritual life in general."[1]

The key to corporate intercessory prayer, as noted before, is found in Matthew 18:19. It is instructive to look at this verse in the Amplified Bible:

> "Again I tell you, if two of you on earth agree (harmonize together, together make a symphony) about—anything and everything—whatever they shall ask, it will come to pass and be done for them by My Father in heaven."— Matthew 18:19 (AMP)

"Agree" in this verse means symphony. That is, everyone is in concert (harmony) regarding the prayer. The key is when "two or more" agree on earth. Agreeing on earth is not agreeing to pray with a friend about a burden. Agreement is when the Holy Spirit puts the same burden on "two or more" hearts and they agree on the will of God regarding the matter as revealed by the Holy Spirit.

The Bible is a book that chronicles the life of praying men and women. It also describes what God accomplished through their prayers. By studying the corporate prayers of praying men and women in the Bible, we can look for and distill God's directions as to how we in today's world can pray together corporately with power and receive answers to our prayers.

Looking at the corporate prayers found in the Bible, there are three general types. Corporate prayer can occur:

1. When people from multiple geographies (a nation or multiple local churches) unite in prayer for a common burden.
2. When the local church is gathered together to pray.
3. When two or more believers pray in a small group.

As we look at the different types of corporate prayers in the Bible, we can identify the prayer elements (praise, thanksgiving, pardon, and petition) contained in each corporate prayer, and can observe how God answered the corporate prayers through the power of the Holy Spirit.

Corporate Prayer by a Nation or Multiple Churches

The Bible has many examples where God's people were called together by a king or prophet to a national time of corporate prayer for a specific need which was generally a crisis of some kind. All the people recognized they had a crisis and responded to God in prayer as one. Examples of corporate prayer by a nation in the Bible are: King Josiah and the people of Judah, the prophet Ezra and the people of Jerusalem, and King Jehoshaphat and the people of Judah.

While we do not have a specific example of a prayer offered by multiple churches in the Bible, we have evidence in the Apostle Paul's letters where corporate prayer was requested of multiple churches for a specific burden.

Let's look at what we can learn about corporate prayer from these Bible stories.

King Josiah and People of Judah

In II Kings, during the repair of the temple, a scroll was found which contained God's laws. When King Josiah of Judah read the scroll, he was terrified because they had not followed God's laws and God had promised to destroy the city because of their sin. He sent the priests to see Huldah the prophetess to ask for help. Huldah, through a supernatural word of prophecy from the Holy Spirit, sent a message to the king that Judah would not be destroyed during his reign because they had confessed their sin.

King Josiah then convened all the elders and leaders of Judah and Jerusalem to hear God's laws read to them. All that were assembled promised the Lord to obey his laws:

> Then the king sent for the elders and other leaders of Judah and Jerusalem to go to the Temple with him. So all the priests and prophets and the people, small and great, of Jerusalem and Judah gathered there at the Temple so that the king could read to them the entire book of God's laws which had been discovered in the Temple. He stood beside the pillar in front of the people, and he and they made a solemn promise to the Lord to obey him at all times and to do everything the book commanded. — II Kings 23:1-3 (LVB)

The elements of prayer highlighted in this story are ***pardon***, where the nation confessed its corporate sin, and ***petition***, where they asked God what they should do.

Prophet Ezra and People of Jerusalem

In the book of Ezra, Ezra wept and prayed to God before the temple regarding the sins of the people returning to Jerusalem from exile. The people gathered around Ezra. Recognizing their sins, they began to cry and corporately confess their sin to God as one:

> As I lay on the ground in front of the Temple, weeping and praying and making this confession, a large crowd of men, women, and children gathered around and cried with me. — Ezra 10:1 (LVB)

The element of prayer at work here is ***pardon***.

King Jehoshaphat and the People of Judah

This corporate prayer is found in II Chronicles 20:3-26. The nations of Ammon, Moab, and Mount Seir had combined their armies and were marching against the Kingdom of Judah. King Jehoshaphat was afraid. He called the people of Judah to a time of fasting and intercession with God. The people united as one in their prayer. King Jehoshaphat stood among the people of Judah and began to praise God:

> "O Lord God of our fathers — the only God in all the heavens, the Ruler of all the kingdoms of the earth — you are so powerful, so mighty. Who can stand against you?" — II Chronicles 20:6 (LVB)

Jehoshaphat asked the Lord to save them. Then the Holy Spirit spoke to one of the men present:

> As the people from every part of Judah stood before the Lord with their little ones, wives, and children, the Spirit of the Lord came upon one of the men standing there-Jahaziel..."Listen to me, all you people of Judah and Jerusalem, and you, O King Jehoshaphat!" he exclaimed. "The Lord says, 'Don't be afraid! Don't be paralyzed by this mighty army! For the battle is not yours, but God's! Tomorrow, go down and attack them! You will find them coming up the slopes of Ziz at the end of the valley that

opens into the wilderness of Jeruel. But you will not need to fight! Take
your places; stand quietly and see the incredible rescue operation God
will perform for you, O people of Judah and Jerusalem! Don't be afraid
or discouraged! Go out there tomorrow, for the Lord is with you!'"
— II Chronicles 20:13-17 (LVB)

King Jehoshaphat and all the people fell to the ground and worshiped
the Lord with thanks and songs of praise. Early the next morning, they went
out to battle continuing to sing praises to the Lord. At the moment of their
singing, the Lord caused Judah's enemies to turn and destroy each other. When
the army of Judah arrived at the battlefield all their enemies were dead. After
Judah had carried off the spoils of war, they gathered to praise the Lord again:

On the fourth day they gathered in the Valley of Blessing, as it is called
today, and how they praised the Lord! — II Chronicles 20:26 (LVB)

This corporate prayer contains the prayer elements of *praise, thanksgiving,
pardon, and petition*. They began their corporate prayer with praising God.
They were penitent. Then, in petition they asked God to protect them from the
invading armies. Finally after God answered their prayer, they again praised and
thanked God for the answered prayer.

As a result of the people's prayer, we see the Holy Spirit gave a supernatural
"word of prophecy" to one of the men praying to reveal God's will in this crisis.
His name was Jahaziel. Jahaziel shared with the people what God had said.
God did indeed answer their prayer since the invading armies fought among
themselves and destroyed each other. Judah was saved by corporate prayer.

Paul Requesting Corporate Prayer from Multiple Churches

Whenever the Apostle Paul wrote a letter to one of the churches that he
had helped to establish, he asked them to pray for him. Paul knew there was
unlimited power available from God when men everywhere united in corporate
prayer for him and his ministry. More people praying in concert for a common
burden meant more "prayer capacity" to open wider the treasury of heaven. E.
M. Bounds writes:

"He (Paul) knew that in the spiritual realm, as elsewhere, in union there is strength; that the concentration and aggregation of faith, desire, and prayer increased the volume of spiritual force until it became overwhelming and irresistible in its power. Units of prayer combined, like drops of water, make an ocean that defies resistance."[2]

To the Romans, Paul asked:

Will you be my prayer partners? For the Lord Jesus Christ's sake, and because of your love for me--given to you by the Holy Spirit--pray much with me for my work. — Romans 15:30 (LVB)

To the Ephesians, he wrote:

Pray for me, too, and ask God to give me the right words as I boldly tell others about the Lord, and as I explain to them that his salvation is for the Gentiles too. — Ephesians 6:19 (LVB)

To the Colossians, Paul said:

Don't forget to pray for us too, that God will give us many chances to preach the Good News of Christ for which I am here in jail. Pray that I will be bold enough to tell it freely and fully, and make it plain, as, of course, I should. — Colossians 4:3-4 (LVB)

To the Thessalonians, he asked:

Finally, dear brothers, as I come to the end of this letter I ask you to pray for us. Pray first that the Lord's message will spread rapidly and triumph wherever it goes, winning converts everywhere as it did when it came to you. Pray too that we will be saved out of the clutches of evil men, for not everyone loves the Lord. — II Thessalonians 3:1-2 (KJV)

To the Corinthians, he wrote:

But you must help us too, by praying for us. For much thanks and praise will go to God from you who see his wonderful answers to your prayers for our safety! — II Corinthians 1:11 (LVB)

To the Philippians, Paul said:

> I am going to keep on being glad, for I know that as you pray
> for me, and as the Holy Spirit helps me, this is all going to
> turn out for my good. — Philippians 1:19 (LVB)

Over and over, Paul asked the churches to unite in pray for him. When multiple churches, regardless of denomination or location, covet to come together in corporate prayer for a common burden, God answers their prayers.

Corporate Prayer by the Local Church

In the local church during times of public worship, ministers and prayer leaders pray corporately on behalf of the entire church. As a leader prays, the others in the meeting silently agree with the praise, thanksgiving, pardon, and petitions voiced by the prayer leader. Peter praying for the early Jerusalem church is an example of this type of corporate prayer by the church.

In addition, the entire local church can be called to corporate prayer where all the members of the local church pray for a specific burden. This is usually intercessory prayer for a church-wide burden. The early church praying in one accord for the promise of the Holy Spirit, the early church praying for boldness and power, and the early church praying for Peter's release from prison are examples of this type of corporate prayer by the local church. Let's look at these three examples in more detail.

Early Church Prays for the Promise of the Holy Spirit

Jesus told the disciples to stay in Jerusalem and wait for the promise of the Holy Spirit. The early church met together in an upstairs room and began to pray continuously to the Father in one accord (as one corporate body):

> These all continued with one accord in prayer and supplication, with
> the women, and Mary the mother of Jesus, and with his brethren.
> — Acts 1:14 (KJV)

47

In the disciples' prayers to the Father, they claimed the promise of Jesus to baptize them with the Holy Spirit. They prayed continuously for seven weeks. Then one day when the disciples were all in one place and united in one accord, the Father answered their prayer, sent the promise of the Holy Spirit, and filled their souls. As a result, the disciples spoke in different languages and told about the wonderful miracles of God.

The element of prayer in evidence here is *petition*. The disciples petitioned God for the promise of the Holy Spirit.

Peter and the Early Church Pray for Boldness and Power

This corporate prayer is found in Acts 4:24-31. Peter and John had healed a lame man as they were going to the Temple to pray. A crowd gathered and Peter spoke to the people about Jesus' resurrection from the dead. Peter and John were dragged in front of the High Priests, who threatened them and told them not to speak (about Jesus) anymore.

Peter and John were released, and they returned to the meeting place of the early church. Once there, they and the other believers united in prayer and lifted up their voices to God in one accord:

> Then all the believers united in this prayer: "O Lord, Creator of heaven
> and earth and of the sea and everything in them..." "And now, O Lord,
> hear their threats, and grant to your servants great boldness in their
> preaching, and send your healing power, and may miracles and wonders
> be done by the name of your holy servant Jesus." After this prayer, the
> building where they were meeting shook and they were all filled with
> the Holy Spirit and boldly preached God's message.
> — Acts 4:24, 29-31 (LVB)

This corporate prayer includes the prayer elements of *praise* and *petition*. In adoration they praised God. In petition, they asked for specific things— boldness in their preaching and power to heal and perform miracles and wonders in the name of Jesus. God immediately answered their prayer by filling them with the Holy Spirit and giving them boldness to preach. Also, the apostles, empowered by the Holy Spirit, performed many miracles in the name of Jesus.

The Early Church Prays for Peter's Release from Prison

King Herod arrested Peter with the intention of turning him over to the Jews to be executed. He put him in prison. The early church began to pray earnestly all the time he was in prison. No doubt they were praying for Peter's safety. This corporate prayer is found in Acts 12:5:

> Peter therefore was kept in prison: but prayer was made without ceasing of the church unto God for him. — Acts 12:5 (KJV)

As a result, an angel of the Lord came to Peter and released him from prison. God answered the early church's corporate prayer. The English Puritan preacher Thomas Watson observed: "The angel fetched Peter out of prison, but it was prayer that fetched the angel."[3]

The element of prayer demonstrated here is ***petition***. In intercession, the local church asked for Peter's release from prison and safety. God answered their prayer by sending an angel to release Peter from jail.

Corporate Prayer in Small Groups

Corporate prayer by small groups is the foundation on which the intercessory prayer ministry of the church is built. It is in smaller groups that the church can involve all the people of the church in prayer, and sufficient time can be spent in corporate prayer to determine God's will and act on it.

Intercessory prayer in small groups was commissioned by Jesus. Even with just two or three believers praying, the body of Christ is gathered corporately, and Jesus tells us in Matthew 18:19-20 that He will be in their presence when they pray.

The Bible gives several examples of small group corporate prayers for specific burdens or tasks. We will look at Daniel and his friends, Jesus' instructions on how to pray, Jesus and his closest friends at the transfiguration, the dedication of Paul and Barnabas for missionary work, Paul and Silas praying after being thrown in prison, and the instructions in the book of James for how to pray for the sick.

Daniel and Friends

King Nebuchadnezzar had a dream and none of the court's wise men could tell the king what the dream was about. As a result, Daniel and his companions Hananiah, Mishael, and Azariah were going to be killed with the rest of them. Daniel went in to see the king and asked for some time. Then, Daniel and his three friends prayed together to ask God to tell them about the dream and what it meant. This corporate prayer is found in Daniel 2:16-23:

> They asked the God of heaven to show them his mercy by telling them the secret, so they would not die with the others. And that night in a vision God told Daniel what the king had dreamed. Then Daniel praised the God of heaven, saying, "Blessed be the name of God forever and ever, for he alone has all wisdom and all power. World events are under his control. He removes kings and sets others on their thrones. He gives wise men their wisdom, and scholars their intelligence. He reveals profound mysteries beyond man's understanding. He knows all hidden things, for he is light, and darkness is no obstacle to him. I thank and praise you, O God of my fathers, for you have given me wisdom and glowing health, and now, even this vision of the king's dream, and the understanding of what it means." — Daniel 2:18-23 (LVB)

God answered their corporate prayer by appearing in a vision to Daniel. Following the receipt of God's answer, Daniel ended his prayer with praise and thanksgiving to Almighty God. This corporate prayer highlights the elements of *praise*, *thanksgiving*, and *petition*. In addition, we see the Holy Spirit gave Daniel a supernatural "word of knowledge" that allowed him to know the dream and to interpret the dream to the king. Corporate prayer saved Daniel and his friends.

The Lord's Prayer

While the Lord's Prayer is not an actual example of prayer, it is a corporate prayer to be used as a model prayer by small or large groups. Jesus gave this prayer to the disciples in response to their asking Him to teach them how to pray.

The Lord's Prayer begins with "Our" which is plural and denotes two or more people praying together. As we have already seen in Chapter 3, the Lord's Prayer instructs us to pray about several specific *petitions*. It also includes *confession* and *praise*.

Jesus and the Transfiguration

Jesus took Peter, James, and John (who were his inner circle) up into the hills to pray. He did not take all His disciples or even all the apostles. Jesus was closest to these three men and needed unity of spirit as He entered into prayer to the Father. He needed the combined prayer power of a group to pray through to the Father. With these three, Jesus could concentrate on praying. Even though Peter, James, and John went to sleep while they were praying, it was comforting to Jesus to know His friends were nearby as He continued to pray.

The transfiguration did not happen automatically. It happened because Jesus was able to "pray through" to the Father:[4]

> Eight days later he took Peter, James, and John with him into the hills to pray. And as he was praying, his face began to shine, and his clothes became dazzling white and blazed with light. Then two men appeared and began talking with him — Moses and Elijah! They were splendid in appearance, glorious to see; and they were speaking of his death at Jerusalem, to be carried out in accordance with God's plan.
> — Luke 9:28-31 (LVB)

In this corporate prayer, the element of prayer used by Jesus is *petition*. Jesus needed to know the Father's will regarding His death at Jerusalem. Jesus' prayer was answered in the form of Moses and Elijah coming to minister to Him.

Paul and Barnabas

One day, five men who were prophets and teachers of the local church at Antioch gathered together in a small corporate group to worship and fast. During this time of communication with God, the Holy Spirit told them to dedicate Barnabas and Paul for a special job as missionaries:

> Among the prophets and teachers of the church at Antioch were
> Barnabas and Symeon (also called "The Black Man"), Lucius (from
> Cyrene), Manaen (the foster-brother of King Herod), and Paul.
> One day as these men were worshiping and fasting the Holy Spirit
> said, "Dedicate Barnabas and Paul for a special job I have for them."
> So after more fasting and prayer, the men laid their hands on
> them--and sent them on their way. — Acts 13:1-3 (LVB)

After more fasting and prayer by the small group, the men laid hands on Barnabas and Paul and sent them on their way.

The men in the small group were open to pray about whatever burden the Holy Spirit put on their hearts. To make sure they had heard the will of God correctly, they continued in prayer. Obviously the men's hearts were in neutral concerning the burden, because they were willing to be part of the answer. The elements of prayer at work in this story are *praise* and *petition*. As the small group met, they worshiped the Lord. Also, they asked in petition for an anointing of the Holy Spirit for Barnabas and Paul as they dedicated them to missionary work.

Paul and Silas

Paul and Silas, following the leading of the Holy Spirit, journeyed to Philippi. There, they were followed day after day by a demon-possessed slave girl who told fortunes to make money for her masters. In the name of Jesus Christ, Paul commanded the demon to leave her, and it departed. Her masters were very upset at the loss of income derived from the slave girl's telling of fortunes. As a result, they had Paul and Silas beaten and thrown in jail.

Wounded but unbowed, Paul and Silas began to pray together and sing praises to God. As a result, God sent an earthquake to loosen their shackles and open the prison doors:

> And at midnight Paul and Silas prayed, and sang praises unto God: and
> the prisoners heard them. And suddenly there was a great earthquake, so
> that the foundations of the prison were shaken: and immediately all the
> doors were opened, and every one's bands were loosed.
> — Acts 16:25-26 (KJV)

This corporate prayer group was made up of two people—Paul and Silas. While it does not explicitly say so, it is highly probable that in their prayers they petitioned God for deliverance from prison and for the salvation of the prisoners and jailer. As a result of Paul and Silas' corporate prayers and praise, the Philippian jailer and his entire household were saved. The elements of prayer at work in this corporate prayer are ***praise*** and most likely ***petition***.

Prayer For the Sick

In James 5:14-16, we do not have an actual example of a small group praying together, but we have instructions from James as to how to conduct a small corporate prayer group that has been called together to pray for someone that is sick. Here is what James has to say:

> Is any sick among you? Let him call for the elders of the church;
> and let them pray over him, anointing him with oil in the name
> of the Lord: And the prayer of faith shall save the sick, and the
> Lord shall raise him up; and if he has committed sins, they shall
> be forgiven him. Confess your faults one to another, and
> pray one for another, that ye may be healed.
> — James 5:14-16a (KJV)

In this scripture, a person is physically sick. The sick person is told to call for the elders of the church to pray over him. The elders of the church were men filled with the Holy Spirit. The sick person is also told to confess his sins to God and to any person he has wronged so that he will have clean hands and a clean heart as he approaches the throne of God. The elders come together to pray with a single burden on their heart which is to seek healing for the sick person. The elders are told to pray for the sick person in faith and anoint him with oil in the name of the Lord.

The corporate prayer group in this scripture is the elders of the church. The elements of prayer at work here are ***confession*** and ***petition***.

Points to Remember

In this chapter, we looked at examples of corporate prayer found in the Bible. The important points were:

1. Corporate prayer works for nations/multiple-churches, local churches, and small prayer groups.
2. Corporate prayer works when the people are united in one accord and praying harmoniously as one body of Christ.
3. Sometimes God used supernatural spiritual gifts during corporate prayer to tell us His will.
4. Praise nearly always precedes and follows a corporate time of intercessory prayer.
5. Corporate prayer can contain any or all of the four basic prayer elements: praise, thanksgiving, pardon, and petition.

Questions for Personal Reflection

Before going to the next chapter, take time to reflect on your answers to the following questions:

1. Do you agree that the Bible has numerous examples of corporate prayer?
2. Review the examples of corporate prayer given in this chapter. How did God answer these corporate prayers?

Part II

God's Directions for How to Pray Together with Other People

Chapter 6

Step 1: Getting on Praying Ground

In Part I, we considered why we should pray together corporately, what Jesus taught about prayer, and how corporate prayer was used by the early church and is used in today's church. We also studied examples of corporate prayer found in both the Old and New Testaments.

It has been said that if all else fails, read the directions. We have already seen that we fail in prayer because we do not ask and we ask amiss. In Part II, we will build on what we learned in Part I and discuss God's directions for how "two or more" believers may pray together with power so that their prayers are answered.

The discussion of God's directions in Part II will be divided into eight steps that will serve as the guidebook on your journey to understand and use corporate prayer. Part II will conclude with a look at the many answers to prayer that God gives us as we journey through those steps.

The directions given in Part II apply to small prayer groups, the local church, and the nation. For ease of presentation, the discussion focuses primarily on the small prayer group and secondarily on the local church and nation.

Step 1 of the directions for corporate prayer covered in this chapter deals first with each individual believer *getting on praying ground* before gathering with other people to pray corporately. When "two or more" believers come together for prayer, each individual believer must meet God's conditions for Him to answer their prayer. If we meet God's conditions for answered prayer, then we can come into God's presence, and He will hear our prayer. Meeting God's conditions for answered prayer will be referred to as "getting on praying ground."

Step 1 also addresses the need for local churches and nations to meet God's conditions for answered prayer by getting on praying ground.

෴

The seven friends we met in Chapter 1 arrive at the entrance to the church sanctuary at about the same time and pause to chat before going inside. They are attending the first night of the special revival focused on living a Spirit-filled life. There are two revival speakers: Miss Bertha Smith a retired missionary to China and Dr. Jack Taylor a pastor and author of the book *The Key to Triumphant Living*. Let's listen to the friends comments as they talk about the special revival:

Jack:	"Bill I thought you couldn't make it tonight."
Bill:	"I changed my schedule so I could come. I was intrigued by all the talk about the filling of the Holy Spirit."
Mary:	"I must tell you that I am put off by the term "Spirit-filled." It sounds like if you are Spirit-filled you are holier-than-thou."
Amanda:	"The Holy Spirit didn't come into the world until after Pentecost. Right?
Hank:	"This past week, I have been studying the phrase "filled with the Spirit." I discovered that this phrase, as well as the Holy Spirit himself, is found all over the Bible in both the Old and New Testaments. Filled with the Spirit means surrendering your life totally to the Lordship of Jesus Christ and letting the Holy Spirit control your life. I am really looking forward to hearing what Jack Taylor has to say."
Sue:	"I have a friend that has read Bertha Smith's book *Go Home and Tell*. She says Bertha is strong on obedience to God's commands and really tough on sin! I'm not sure I'm looking forward to what she has to say."
Joe:	"Don't worry. None of us are perfect. We all sin. Also, don't we all ask forgiveness for our sins every Sunday

	when we recite together the part of the Lord's prayer
	that says *"and forgive us our sins, just as we have forgiven*
	those who have sinned against us."
Jack:	"I think we are going to hear over the next several days
	that we must individually repent of each individual sin
	that we commit daily, so we have clean hands and
	clean hearts as we approach a Holy God in prayer and
	worship. After repenting of our sins, God wants us to
	individually surrender our lives to Him and be filled
	with His Holy Spirit. Meeting these conditions puts
	each of us on praying ground."

The seven friends are about to begin a new and exciting spiritual journey that starts with each of them learning why they may not be on praying ground, and what they must do to get there.

ન્ટ

Why Believers Are Not on Praying Ground

When I went to work for Lockheed, my wife and I joined a very large church, the First Baptist Church of Marietta, Georgia. We faithfully attended Sunday morning, Sunday night, and Wednesday night services. After a few years, I was asked to be a deacon of the church and became Director of the youth Sunday School, which had many problems. Frustration with the church's bureaucracy mounted as we tried to find teachers, establish a teen center, and implement new programs. I wondered in my frustration if what I was experiencing was "all there was" to religion—I felt spiritually dry. Our church began to form "search groups" whose purpose was to deepen our spiritual lives. My wife and I eagerly joined a group looking for the answer to our spiritual dryness. I blamed our pastor and told myself his sermons were not inspirational. When I did pray, I felt as though my prayers never rose above the ceiling.

What was my problem? Me! I had substituted "religious activity" for obedience. That I was spiritually dry should not have been a surprise—while very "active" in church, I did not read my Bible or pray regularly. I did not understand the need to confess my sins daily and let the Holy Spirit control my life. All of the things I was *not* doing kept me from having God's Spirit refresh my soul and being on praying ground.

In the following two scripture passages, three reasons can be deduced as to why believers are not on praying ground:

> And whatsoever we ask, we receive of him, because we keep his commandments, and do those things that are pleasing in his sight.
> — I John 3:22 (KJV)

> Listen now! The Lord isn't too weak to save you. And he isn't getting deaf! He can hear you when you call! But the trouble is that **your sins have cut you off from God**. Because of sin he has turned his face away from you and will not listen anymore.
> — Isaiah 59:1-2 (LVB, emphasis added)

The reasons that believers are not on praying ground are (1) we do not keep God's commandments; (2) our sins have cut us off from God; and (3) we are not doing those things that are pleasing in His sight. Let us look at each of these reasons.

We Do Not Keep God's Commandments

The first reason we are not on praying ground is that we do not keep God's commandments. He wants us to be obedient to his commands. The mark of our spiritual maturity is how obedient we are to God's laws and commands.

In I Thessalonians 5:17 (KJV), God commands us to *"Pray without ceasing."* We are not keeping that commandment if we neglect to pray. We are commanded to study the Word of God in II Timothy 2:15b (LVB): *"Know what his Word says and means."* We are not keeping His commandment if we neglect to study God's Word. Paul in Hebrews 10:25 (LVB) says *"Let us not neglect our church meetings, as some people do, but encourage and warn each other…"* We are not obeying God's Word if we do not meet together on a regular basis for instruction and encouragement. Jesus said in John 15:17 (KJV) "These things I command you, that ye love one another." We are not keeping His commandment if we do not love one another. If we do not keep His commandments to pray, to study His Word, to regularly assemble together, and to love one another or any other commandment of which we are aware, we are not on praying ground.

F. B. Meyer tells the following story. He encountered C. T. Studd, the great missionary to Africa, early one morning reading his Bible by candlelight. Studd had risen early and been reading for three hours. Meyer asked him, "What have you been doing this morning?" Studd replied, "You know the Lord says, 'If ye love Me, keep my commandments' and I was just looking through all the commandments that I could find that the Lord gave, and putting a tick against them if I have kept them, because I do love Him."[1]

The Holy Spirit over time will reveal to us the commandments that we must keep in order to be able to claim God's promises. We should desire with all our hearts to keep all of God's commandments. The Bible is clear. If we know His commandments and don't keep them, we should not expect to be on praying ground when the small prayer group comes together to pray.

Our Sins Have Cut Us Off

The second reason we are not on praying ground is that our sins have "cut us off." In Isaiah 59:1-2, quoted earlier in this chapter, it says that God is not too deaf to hear our prayers, and He is strong enough to answer our prayers no matter how difficult the request. But our sins have cut off communication with the Father. This is echoed in Psalm 66:18 and John 9:31:

> If I regard iniquity in my heart, the Lord will not hear me.
> — Psalms 66:18 (KJV)

> Now we know that **God heareth not sinners**: but if any man be a
> worshipper of God, and doeth his will, him he heareth.
> — John 9:31 (KJV, emphasis added)

The impact of sin on our prayers is illustrated in Figure 6-1. As Christians we are not on praying ground if there is sin in our heart. If we do not meet the conditions of answered prayer, God is not obligated to make good on

His promises to a disobedient child. If there is sin in our heart, the prayer goes unheard—God's hearing is passive. While God listens to every prayer we speak, if there is sin in our heart God does not "hear" our prayer in the sense that He is obligated to act on it. If we have a clean heart, God hears and answers our prayers.

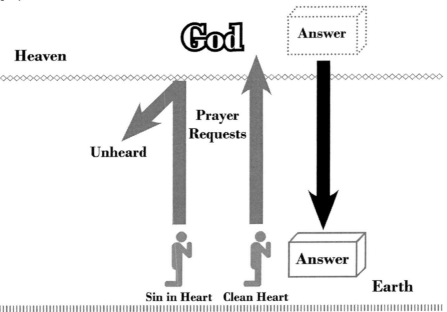

Figure 6-1. God hears our prayers if we have a clean heart,
but if we have sin in our heart the prayer goes unheard.

As a further example of the impact of sin in our heart, let's consider ourselves to be like an electric light bulb in a lamp with an on/off switch. When we become a Christian, the lamp cord is plugged into the power source—God. We are permanently connected. With the switch on, the power (Holy Spirit) can flow through the lamp cord and light the bulb (us). The light bulb will continue to give light until the switch is turned off.

When we commit a single sin, the switch is turned off. The power is still available to the bulb, but can't get by the switch. To turn the switch back on, have power, and return to praying ground, we must confess (acknowledge) the sin to God and ask God for His forgiveness.

The Psalmist says that God will listen to our prayers only when we confess our sins:

> For I cried to him for help, with praises ready on my tongue. He would not have listened if I had not confessed my sins. But he listened! He heard my prayer! He paid attention to it! Blessed be God who didn't turn away when I was praying, and didn't refuse me his kindness and love.
> — Psalms 66:17-20 (LVB)

To come before a Holy God, we must have clean hands and clean hearts. Listen again to the Psalmist:

> Who shall ascend into the hill of the Lord? or who shall stand in his holy place? **He that hath clean hands, and a pure heart**; who hath not lifted up his soul unto vanity, nor sworn deceitfully. He shall receive the blessing from the Lord, and righteousness from the God of his salvation.
> — Psalms 24:3-5 (KJV, emphasis added)

God will not answer any other prayer other than for forgiveness of sin if a single unconfessed sin is still in the believer's heart. Again the Psalmist enlightens us:

> But God says to evil men: Recite my laws no longer, and **stop claiming my promises**. — Psalms 50:16 (LVB, emphasis added)

These are hard words. If we have sin in our heart from disobeying God, we can not claim His promises!

Jesus wants to forgive us and cleanse us if we will come to Him with a repentant heart and confess our sins:

> If we confess our sins, he is faithful and just to forgive us our sins, and to cleanse us from all unrighteousness. — I John 1:9 (KJV)

Paul tells us in Hebrews that once your sins are forgiven, the Lord never again remembers them:

> And their sins and iniquities will I remember no more.
> — Hebrews 10:17 (KJV)

This is terrific! When we confess our sins, God chooses to no longer remember our sins!

As a postscript to this section, it should be noted that in order to accomplish His divine will God may decide in His sovereignty and grace to answer our prayers anyway, even though there is sin in our hearts. Such was the case with King Jehoahaz (II Kings 13: 1-6) who was an evil king that prayed to the Lord for deliverance of Israel from the Syrians. The Lord answered his prayer in spite of King Jehoahaz being evil, because God saw how oppressed His people were and had compassion on them.

We Are Not Doing Those Things Pleasing In His Sight

The third reason we are not on praying ground is we are not doing those things that are pleasing in His sight. We please *ourselves*. The glory is for ourselves in what we do and not for God. Further, we don't do the will of God every time we discover it.

As we see in Romans 12:1, it is God's will that we surrender our whole being for Him to control:

> I beseech you therefore, brethren, by the mercies of God, that ye present
> your bodies a living sacrifice, holy, acceptable unto God, which is
> your reasonable service. — Romans 12:1 (KJV)

When we let "self" stay in control, we are not following God's will. If God is not in absolute control of our lives, we are not on praying ground. The Holy Spirit is grieved by us unless He controls our lives:

> And grieve not the Holy Spirit of God... — Ephesians 4:30a (KJV)

We are commanded to be filled with the Holy Spirit:

> And be not drunk with wine, wherein is excess; but **be filled with the
> Spirit**... — Ephesians 5:18 (KJV, emphasis added)

Being filled with the Holy Spirit is not optional. It is God's will that we be continually filled with the Holy Spirit by surrendering every aspect of our lives to Him. If we are not filled with the Holy Spirit, we are disobeying God and cannot expect to be on praying ground.

How Do We Get On Praying Ground Individually?

Answered prayer is directly related to individual holiness. We are told in I Peter 1:16 *"Be ye holy; for I am holy."* This is a command. "Holy" means separated. God's people are to be holy by being separated from sin, consecrated to God, and set apart for His use. This is only possible when, in our hearts, we have no unconfessed sins of which we are aware, we obey His commandments, and we do those things pleasing in His sight. We get on praying ground by consecrating our lives for His use by becoming spiritually clean. This is done by identifying and confessing to God the individual sins in our life as revealed to us by the Holy Spirit, asking God to forgive us our sin, and surrendering our minds, emotions, and wills to God's control so that His life can be expressed through us. This process is illustrated in Figure 6-2.

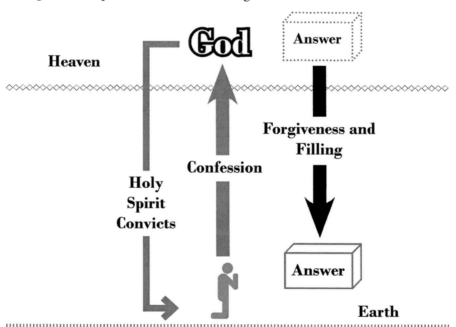

Figure 6-2. We attain praying ground when we have confessed our
sins to God and surrendered ourselves to the control of the Holy Spirit

The importance of individual holiness to attain praying ground is illustrated in a story told by J. Oswald Sanders:

> "Around 1950, there was a powerful movement of the Spirit in
> the Hebrides. The awakening did not just happen. For some months,
> a number of men met three nights a week for prayer; they often spent
> hours. The weeks passed and nothing happened until one morning at
> about two o'clock; a young man read Psalm 24:3-5, *'Who may stand in
> His holy place? He who has clean hands and a pure heart, who has not sworn
> deceitfully. He shall receive a blessing from the Lord.'*
> [He] closed the Bible and looking at his companions on their
> knees before God, he cried: "Brethren, it is just so much humbling to
> be waiting thus night after night, month after month, if we ourselves
> are not right with God. I must ask myself—'Is my heart pure? Are my
> hands clean?'" And at that moment....something happened. God swept
> into that prayer group and at that wonderful moment seven Elders dis-
> covered what they evidently had not discovered before, that revival must
> be related to Holiness...They found themselves lifted to the realm of the
> supernatural. These men knew that Revival had come."[2]

Identifying and Confessing Your Sins

Believers should desire clean hearts so that they can communicate and
have fellowship with a Holy God. David, after grievously sinning against God,
prayed the following prayer:

> Have mercy upon me, O God, according to thy loving kindness:
> according unto the multitude of thy tender mercies blot out my
> transgressions. **Wash me thoroughly from mine iniquity, and cleanse
> me from my sin**. For I acknowledge my transgressions: and my sin is
> ever before me. Against thee, thee only, have I sinned, and done this evil
> in thy sight: that thou mightest be justified when thou speakest, and be
> clear when thou Judgest. Behold, I was shapen in iniquity; and in sin
> did my mother conceive me. Behold, thou desirest truth in the inward
> parts: and in the hidden part thou shalt make me to know wisdom.
> Purge me with hyssop, and I shall be clean: wash me, and I shall be
> whiter than snow. Make me to hear joy and gladness; that the bones
> which thou hast broken may rejoice. Hide thy face from my sins, and
> blot out all mine iniquities. **Create in me a clean heart, O God; and
> renew a right spirit within me**. Cast me not away from thy presence;

and take not thy Holy Spirit from me. **Restore unto me the joy of thy salvation**; and uphold me with thy free spirit. Then will I teach transgressors thy ways; and sinners shall be converted unto thee. Deliver me from bloodguiltiness, O God, thou God of my salvation: and my tongue shall sing aloud of thy righteousness. O Lord, open thou my lips; and my mouth shall shew forth thy praise. For thou desirest not sacrifice; else would I give it: thou delightest not in burnt offering. **The sacrifices of God are a broken spirit: a broken and a contrite heart**, O God, thou wilt not despise. — Psalms 51:1-17 (KJV, emphasis added)

David recognized he had sinned and deeply regretted what he had done. He wanted to restore his relationship to God, which had been disrupted by his sins of adultery and murder. In David's prayer, he asked God to pardon him by washing away his sins and giving him a clean heart.

Most Christians know they should confess their known sins to God. Unfortunately, many Christians think they can use a shortcut by praying: "Lord, forgive us of all our sins. Amen." We are not taught to think about identifying and confessing the individual sins of which we are conscious such as when we spoke harshly, when we told a lie, when we were full of pride, when we were selfish, or when we gossiped. To have unimpeded access to God, every sin in our hearts must be removed as an obstacle. God expects us to recognize each single thing we do that is sin and confess it separately. We need to open our hearts to the inspection of God and say with David:

Search me, O God, and know my heart: try me, and know my thoughts: And see if there be any wicked way in me, and lead me in the way everlasting. — Psalm 139:23-24 (KJV)

To help readers search their hearts to identify individual sins in their lives, a list of frequent sins has been compiled for you to consider. This list is included as Appendix I and is called a "Sin Sheet." To illustrate the use of this list, let me share with you the impact it had on my life.

Some years ago, Miss Bertha Smith who was a Baptist missionary to China introduced me to a tract that listed many of the sins on the "Sin Sheet."[3] As I considered this list of sins, the Holy Spirit reminded me that I had left college without paying my dues to an honorary engineering fraternity. I could have no peace in my heart until I had (1) confessed the sin of stealing and asked God to forgive me, (2) written a letter asking the fraternity's forgiveness for my not paying before I left school, and (3) made restitution by enclosing a check for the delinquent amount.

Our sins include not only sins of commission but also include sins of omission. To understand what I mean by a sin of omission, consider my response to an event that occurred when we lived in Washington D.C.

My wife asked me to go to the drug store to get a prescription filled. There was an elderly lady and her daughter ahead of me. They were discussing her prescriptions with the pharmacist. I was in a hurry and they seemed to be taking a long time. The elderly lady had three prescriptions, but she only had enough money for one. They were discussing with the pharmacist which of the three prescriptions was the most important. I passively listened and silently wished they would hurry. Finally, the lady got a single prescription and left. When I returned to my car after getting my prescription filled, the Holy Spirit said to me, "You had plenty of money. Why didn't you pay for this poor lady's medicine? You missed an opportunity to have great joy and a wonderful blessing by thinking only of yourself." I truly believe God had me there to help this lady, and I failed. If I had it to do over again, I would have stepped forward and paid for the elderly lady's medicine. Since I had missed the opportunity to help a person in need, I asked God to forgive me of my sin of being insensitive to this lady's need and not acting to help her.

If your heart is open to God, the Holy Spirit will scrub your heart clean and show you the ***known sins*** of which you need to confess and repent. As a caution, what to one believer is a sin may not be recognized as a sin by another person at the present time. We are all on different paths to maturity and will come to grips with specific ***unrecognized sins*** in our lives at different times.

Our ultimate goal is to remove all sin from our lives and be made over in the image of Jesus. In Matthew 5:48 Jesus tells us we are to strive to be perfect even as the Father in heaven is perfect. The Holy Spirit will get around to dealing with us in every area of our lives in His process of perfecting us to look like Jesus. Paul addresses his situation in Philippians 3:12:

> I don't mean to say I am perfect. I haven't learned all I should even yet,
> but I keep working toward that day when I will finally be all that Christ
> saved me for and wants me to be. — Philippians 3:12 (LVB)

This process is depicted in Figure 6-3. At any given time, each person must decide, in the light they have, what are the known sins in their life and how are they going to deal with them. If they confess and repent of the known sins, they are washed clean and take a step toward perfection.

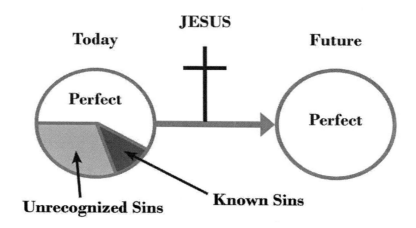

Figure 6-3. The Holy Spirit continuously shows
us our sin in the process of perfecting us to look like Jesus.

Let me illustrate how the Holy Spirit helped me become aware of an unrecognized sin in my life. During college summer breaks, I worked for a construction company as a laborer. No piece of lumber could be nailed without being roundly cursed. I picked up the habit of using bad language. However, I was careful not to take God's name in vain because I knew from the Ten Commandments that this was a sin. I could turn the cursing on and off depending on whom I was with. Looking back, I guess I didn't think using bad language was a sin as long as you didn't take God's name in vain.

My first job out of college was with NASA where I worked in a wind tunnel laboratory on night shift with a group of men. Needless to say, as something went wrong, I would utter a blue stream. Then one night as I uttered an oath, Griff, one of the old grizzled mechanics, looked up at me and said, "I thought you were a Christian."

Through the moving of the Holy Spirit speaking to my heart through Griff, I had just come face to face with the sin of cursing. It was like I had been slapped across the face. Using bad language had been a sin all along, as we see in Ephesians 5:4a (LVB) *"Dirty stories, foul talk and coarse jokes--these are not for you."* I had just not recognized it as a sin. It had now come time in my Christian growth for me to deal with and repent of the sin of bad language.

After we have agreed with the Holy Spirit regarding our sins, we need to repent and ask God to forgive us for each individual sin. As we saw earlier in I John 1:9, God has promised to forgive us for each individual sin for which we repent and ask His forgiveness. When we ask God for forgiveness, our sins are forgiven, we are washed whiter than snow, and God entirely forgets about the sin. This is not just a mental exercise. It also involves the heart. True repentance results in a changed direction in our lives. It is a broken and contrite heart that God wants. When we have repented of our known sins, we are not in a "sinless" state, but are in a state of "forgiveness" provided by God's grace.

Some of our sins are against other people. These can only be completely forgiven when we have made apology or restitution to those we have hurt. If our sin against other people is public, then the apology must be as public as the sin. Hear Jesus' words in Matthew 5:23-24:

> If therefore you are presenting your offering at the altar, and there remember that your brother has something against you, leave your offering there before the altar, and go your way; first be reconciled to your brother, and then come and present your offering.
> — Matthew 5:23-24 (NAS)

We can't get by with just telling God we are sorry when we have hurt someone. We must also go to the people we have hurt and make apology. Only then can healing begin in our relationship.

God has promised to cleanse us from our sin. We need to take Him at His Word and have the confidence that He has done what He said he would do:

> But if we walk in the light, as he is in the light, we have fellowship one with another, and the blood of Jesus Christ **his Son cleanseth us from all sin**. — I John 1:7 (KJV, emphasis added)

Surrender Control of Your Life to God

We must now choose to put the Lord Jesus on the throne of our lives, replacing our selves. Our "thrones" are the seats of our intellects, emotions and wills. We must choose God's will in every part of our life. We must surrender control of everything we possess to God one by one—our health, our families, our money, our material possessions, our careers, our natural talents, our intellects, our emotions, our wills.

A list of things you might consider surrendering to God, called a "Surrender Sheet," has been compiled and included at the back of the book as Appendix II. In prayer, surrender everything you possess to God's control. Again, this is not just a mental exercise—it must also involve the heart. After surrendering control of everything you possess, you need to ask God to control your life. Give as much of yourself to God as you understand.

Let me demonstrate how surrender works. I had worked as an aerospace engineer for ten years. I was doing extremely well in my career. One day the Holy Spirit said that He wanted me to surrender control of my career. In our first discussion, I was not willing to give Him control. I liked what I was doing, and I was afraid the Holy Spirit might want me to do something else. The Holy Spirit continued to strive with me on this point. It was not until I said, "Okay, God, you win, you can have control of my career. What do you want me to do?" At that point, I had peace with God. God did not want me to change careers after all. All He wanted was for me to be willing for Him to decide. I have no doubt that the success I have had in business was a direct result of my letting God have control of my career.

Ask God to Fill You with the Holy Spirit

As we saw earlier in this chapter, God's Word (Ephesians 5:18) commands us to be filled with the Holy Spirit. In prayer, after you have confessed your sins and surrendered your life to God, ask God to fill your heart with the Holy Spirit and empower your life. By faith, believe you have received the filling of the Holy Spirit. As an individual believer, you now have clean hands and a clean heart. You are now filled and being controlled by the Holy Spirit and available for the Holy Spirit to use. You are holy and acceptable to God as a living sacrifice. You are now on praying ground!

Caution!

Once we are filled with the Holy Spirit, the Spirit will prompt us to avoid any kind of sin and to continue to let God control our lives. Because we love God, we will want to stay on praying ground so that we can freely talk to Him. However, a single sin on our part will remove us from praying ground and cut our communication with the Father. Because we are human, we will commit another sin against God or take back control of our life from God sometime in the next several hours. You do not need to start over with the Sin and Surrender Sheets. You just have to deal with the specific sin that you have committed.

When you commit a specific sin, the Holy Spirit will tell you that what you have done is sin. At the moment you are convicted that you have sinned, you should confess the sin to God asking for His forgiveness, make restitution to others if needed, and surrender control of your life back to God. Then ask God to again fill you with the Holy Spirit. This is the way to stay on praying ground.

My wife and I had just finished a wonderful time of worship at our church, and I was feeling very close to God. I met all the conditions of being on praying ground. After church, we decided to get a country breakfast for lunch. One of my major weaknesses is food. I love a southern country breakfast with eggs, grits, country ham, and biscuits with gravy. For obvious health reasons, I can't have this kind of breakfast very often.

On the following Monday, I had an early business meeting at our local diner which also has a great breakfast. When the time came to take the order, I knew I should order cereal, but I ordered another country breakfast instead. It was so good! After the breakfast meeting, I returned home. The first words out of my wife's mouth were, "What did you have for breakfast?" The dilemma: tell a little lie and not get yelled at or tell the truth and....I chose the easy way and lied.

The Holy Spirit said to me, "You have told a lie, and this is sin." I recognized that I had indeed sinned and was no longer on praying ground. I immediately asked God to forgive me for this sin. I also knew that I would have to confess to my wife that I had lied and ask her forgiveness. I went to her and told her I had lied about what I had for breakfast and asked her to forgive me. And yes, I did get yelled at. Sin, even though it is forgiven, still has consequences. Then in prayer, I again surrendered my life to the Father and asked Him to again fill me with His Holy Spirit. Hooray, I was back on praying ground!

The process of *conviction, confession, restitution, surrender* and *filling* repeats itself over and over throughout our lives, as we commit sins daily and seek to stay on praying ground. Getting on praying ground should become a daily ritual as each believer prepares themselves to pray.

This daily ritual is similar to that observed by the early Israelite priests in the Old Testament (Exodus 30). Each day, before Aaron and his sons could go into the tabernacle and minister to God (talk to a Holy God in prayer), they had to be cleansed by washing their hands and feet in a large brass vessel called the laver (washing represents the cleansing of sins). They were also consecrated for ministry to God by being anointed with holy anointing oil (representing the Holy Spirit). In the tabernacle, incense was burned every morning and evening on the altar of incense (representing prayers of praise and intercession).

How Do Groups, Churches, and Nations Get on Praying Ground?

In addition to God's requirement for individuals to get on praying ground, groups, churches, and nations who depart from God and sin must also repent and get on praying ground to receive answers to prayer. God's directions for a corporate body to get on praying ground are the same as for individuals, as we see in II Chronicles 7:14:

> If my people, which are called by my name, shall humble themselves, and pray, and seek my face, and turn from their wicked ways; then will I hear from heaven, and will forgive their sin, and will heal their land.
> — II Chronicles 7:14 (KJV)

This passage tells us that God will hear His people if we, as a corporate body, will humble ourselves, repent of our corporate sins, and seek His face together in prayer. Purity of the corporate body must come before the corporate body begins to pray. (These are the same directions as we saw for an individual in the previous section.)

To distinguish between individual sin and corporate sin, corporate sin is any sin committed by a corporate body of "two or more" believers acting together in concert consciously or unconsciously. Corporate sins of commission and omission occur in families, groups, churches, and nations.

In Revelation, Chapters 2 and 3, Jesus addresses the seven churches of Asia and commands the churches to repent of their corporate sin. Each church as a corporate body had the option of being obedient or disobedient to Jesus' commands. The sins of the seven churches included the church's losing its first love for Jesus, tolerating sexual sin in the church, permitting false doctrine to be taught in the church, hypocrisy, lack of the church doing good deeds in the world, and the church being lukewarm to passionately following Jesus.

Jesus wants His church to recognize and repent of their corporate sins so they can be returned to a state of purity and be on praying ground. When corporate groups are on praying ground, they maximize their "prayer capacity" to bring God's will from heaven to earth.

Corporate sin by a corporate body is as serious as sin by an individual. If the corporate sin is not identified and confessed, continued association with the sin will keep the corporate body from being on praying ground. As a result, God will withdraw His presence, blessings, and power from the corporate body.

Henry T. Blackaby and Claude V. King in their book *Fresh Encounter* describe a church that recognized its corporate sin and how the church dealt with this recognition:

> "In April 1994, a small rural church in Tennessee had a special emphasis on prayer. After a two-hour study, time was given for members of the body to share what God had been saying to them. The bivocational pastor stood and confessed, 'I have not been a man of prayer, and I have not led you to be a people of prayer. I need to ask you to forgive me.'
>
> The conference leader first asked the pastor to pray publicly, confessing his sin to the Lord and seeking God's forgiveness. Then the members of the congregation expressed their forgiveness to their pastor. Then the leader asked the group, 'As I have been teaching tonight, how many of you sensed conviction by the Holy Spirit that you have not been a

people of prayer or a house of prayer?' Everyone raised their hands. Then he asked, 'Is prayerlessness a sin?' They all agreed that it was. That was corporate confession of sin.

The leader then asked if the church wanted to repent of its prayerlessness and experience God's forgiveness. They were all ready to get right with the Lord. The Holy Spirit had prepared them by revealing their sin, changing their mind about the nature of prayerlessness, and giving them a deep grief for sinning against the Lord. As a body, they were ready to repent with a whole heart. They stood before the Lord to acknowledge their sin, and their pastor led in a corporate prayer of confession. He prayed for God's forgiveness, and he asked the Lord to enable them to become a people of prayer."[4]

In the Old Testament, we have example after example of corporate sin by cities and nations. The corporate sins of the nation Israel as described in the Bible are unfortunately quite numerous. The most blatant corporate sin by Israel was the sin of idolatry, which they committed over and over even though God warned them repeatedly. As a result of this corporate sin, God withdrew from them. When the Israelites repented of their sin, God restored to them His blessings, protection, and power.

Recognizing that His people, because they were human, would eventually commit corporate sins wittingly or unwittingly, God made provision for their forgiveness. In Leviticus, Chapter 4, God tells Moses what to do if the entire nation of Israel commits a corporate sin:

> If the entire nation of Israel sins without realizing it, and does something that Jehovah has said not to do, all the people are guilty. When they realize it, they shall offer a young bull for a sin offering, bringing it to the Tabernacle... He shall follow the same procedure as for a sin offering; in this way the priest shall make atonement for the nation, and everyone will be forgiven. The priest shall then cart the young bull outside the camp and burn it there, just as though it were a sin offering for an individual, only this time it is a sin offering for the entire nation.
> — Leviticus 4:13-14, 20-21 (LVB)

As we see in this scripture, the process for God's forgiving a corporate sin by a nation is the same as the process for His forgiving a sin by an individual. Because the sin of the people was done in a corporate manner, the repentance by the people must also be made in a corporate manner.

75

Churches and nations should measure themselves on a regular basis relative to God's commands to see if they have committed a corporate sin. Just as we daily confess our sins individually, a corporate body should regularly confess their corporate sins to God together as a whole. This can be accomplished in several ways.

The corporate body can periodically set aside a time of prayer for self examination and ask the Holy Spirit to show them their corporate sins. Following recognition and agreement by the corporate body of their specific sins, the corporate body then asks God to forgive them of each sin. The process of a corporate body asking forgiveness is identical to that for an individual believer.

As part of a church's worship service, many denominations provide a prayer of confession to be read together to remind believers of their need to confess their corporate sin. For example, the prayer of confession for corporate sin from *The United Methodist Hymnal* prayed together prior to observing communion is:

> "Merciful God, we confess that we have not loved you with our whole heart. We have failed to be an obedient church. We have not done your will, we have broken your law, we have rebelled against your love, we have not loved our neighbors, and we have not heard the cry of the needy. Forgive us, we pray. Free us for joyful obedience through Jesus Christ our Lord. Amen."[5]

The corporate body as a whole can also recognize that it has sinned when a spiritual or secular leader leads them to see the need of repentance. If a leader recognizes the corporate body has committed a corporate sin, it is the responsibility of the leader to issue a call for repentance.

The Apostle Paul recognized that the church in Corinth was committing a corporate sin by tolerating a church member who was openly involved in sexual sin. Paul instructs the church in I Corinthians 5:1-13 on how to deal with this issue so that the church can be returned to a state of purity. Other examples of leaders who recognized the need of their people to repent were the prophet Ezra who prayed on behalf of the people of Jerusalem that they might recognize and confess their sins (Ezra 10:1), Moses interceding with God on behalf of the Israelite people after they had built a golden calf (Exodus 32:1-

35), Nehemiah praying to God and confessing the corporate sin of the Jewish people (Nehemiah 1:4-11), and Daniel confessing the sin of Israel and pleading to God to allow the Israelites to return to Jerusalem (Daniel 9:1-24).

An example of a spiritual leader leading a church to examine itself relative to the Word of God is found in a story told by Charles M. Sheldon in his book *In His Steps.*[6] Let me paraphrase this story:

> One day a young man who was out-of-work, shabbily dressed, sick, and homeless came to a minister's house looking for help in finding a job. The minister was too busy preparing his Sunday sermon to give him help. Others in the community were also approached by the young man. No one gave him a word of comfort or sympathy.
>
> The minister's Sunday sermon topic was "Following Christ." In the sermon, he planned to outline the steps needed to follow Christ's example with the following verse as his text: *For even hereunto were ye called: because Christ also suffered for us, leaving us an example, that ye should follow his steps: — I Peter 2: 21 (KJV)*
>
> On Sunday, after the minister had finished his sermon, the young man arose from his seat and began to walk towards the minister and speak. He spoke about his current situation, and then he said, "But I was wondering as I sat there under the gallery, if what you call following Jesus is the same thing as what He taught. What did He mean when He said: 'Follow me!'?" [7] He went on to say "What do you Christians mean by following the steps of Jesus?"[8] He asked "what do you mean when you sing 'I'll go with Him, with Him, all the way?' Do you mean that you are suffering and denying yourselves and trying to save lost, suffering humanity just as I understand Jesus did?"[9] The young man indicated that he had heard people singing the song "All for Jesus" at the Wednesday night prayer meeting as he sat on the church steps. He wondered out loud to the congregation "It seems to me there's an awful lot of trouble in the world that somehow wouldn't exist if all the people who sing such songs went and lived them out. I suppose I don't understand. But what would Jesus do?"[10]
>
> Having spoken what he had to say, the young man collapsed near the communion table. He was carried to the minister's home and died later that week. The minister was deeply moved by what the young man had to say.
>
> The next Sunday, the minister shared with the congregation what had happened to the stranger during the week. The minister talked about his own questioning of what exactly it meant to follow Jesus. He then

issued a challenge to the congregation: "I want volunteers from the First Church who will pledge themselves, earnestly and honestly for an entire year not to do anything without first asking the question, 'What would Jesus do?'"[11]

Over fifty percent of the church stayed after the service, took the pledge, and committed to do everything in their daily lives after asking the question, "What would Jesus do?" regardless of what the result might be. Everyone present felt the distinct presence of the Holy Spirit.

As a result of taking the pledge, every facet of the church member's everyday lives was measured against the question "What would Jesus do?" The newspaper editor would only print what he thought Jesus would print. Businessmen decided to only conduct business like Jesus would do.

The point of telling this story is that when a leader recognizes that a church is falling short of Jesus' commands, they have the responsibility to issue a call for repentance and change. In this case, this church clearly fell short of loving their neighbor, and the minister issued a call for change by asking them to measure themselves against Jesus. Throughout the history of the church, great preachers have been used by God to call churches and communities to repentance of corporate sin. When the churches and communities responded with repentance, revival occurred.

On the larger scale of nations, there have been several notable times in the United States when our nation has corporately sinned against man and God. For example, most Christians today would agree that the United States as a nation committed major wrongs against Native American Indians and African-Americans. As a nation, we needed to repent of these corporate sins. In February 2008, the U. S. Senate as leaders of our nation apologized for atrocities committed against Native Americans. In July 2008, the U. S. House of Representatives formally apologized to African Americans for slavery and segregation. Several U. S. states including Virginia, North Carolina, Florida, and Alabama have also issued apologies for slavery. The above apologies represent recognition of corporate wrong by secular leaders and ask the offended parties for forgiveness.

Using God's Word as a standard, what kind of corporate sins might occur in churches today? Many are the same as in Appendix I (e.g. gossip, selfishness, pride, critical spirit, complacency, moral failure, factions, poor stewardship).

For instance, how is your church doing relative to the following commands found in the Word of God?

- Jesus says His church is to be a house of prayer. Is your church a house of prayer? If not, your church is committing corporate sin and needs to repent.
- Jesus commands us to love our neighbor in the Great Commandment. Is your church loving and inviting to all people regardless of sex, race, national origin, age, or social status? If your church does not love all kinds of people, your church is committing corporate sin and needs to repent.
- Jesus says we are to help the poor. Is your church helping the poor in your community? If not, your church is committing corporate sin and needs to repent.
- Jesus says in the Great Commission that we are to witness to the lost, instruct the converts, and incorporate them into the fellowship of the church. Is your church making a concerted effort to share the gospel, teach its members about spiritual things, and welcome all members into its fellowship? If not, your church is committing corporate sin and needs to repent.

Corporate sin may also be recognized when an event or crisis in the life of churches or nations prompts them to measure themselves relative to God's Word to see if they are on praying ground. This can occur when a church collectively desires with all their heart for God to intervene in an event or crisis to bring His supernatural power to bear. As a result, the church is willing to examine itself to make sure that there is no corporate sin remaining unconfessed that would rob the corporate body of being able to access God's power and resources.

Crises or events that could prompt churches and nations to want to look at themselves to see if they are on praying ground might include: the church's desire for the healing of a member's child with a critical illness, the church's concern for the safety of a military person serving our country in a highly dangerous location, the church's longing for harmony among diverse groups, the nation's desire for relief from a natural disaster, the nation seeking an end to a national economic crisis, and the nation's earnest desire for peace.

Points to Remember

In this chapter, the need to get on praying ground by individual believers, churches, and nations before praying together corporately was discussed. The important points were:

1. To get on praying ground, we must desire clean hands and clean hearts.
2. We must get on praying ground individually before we gather to pray corporately.
3. To get on praying ground, we must repent of our individual sins, keep His commandments, and do those things pleasing in His sight.
4. To get on praying ground, we must ask forgiveness and make restitution to others if our sins are against other people.
5. To get on praying ground, we must surrender the control of our lives to God and ask Him to fill us and empower us with the Holy Spirit.
6. We must repeat the process of conviction, confession, restitution, surrender and filling as often as we sin or self takes back control of our life, so that we can stay on praying ground.
7. God's directions for a group, church, or nation to get on praying ground are the same as for individuals to get on praying ground.
8. Corporate sin is any sin committed by a corporate body of "two or more" believers acting together in concert consciously or unconsciously.
9. Churches and nations should examine themselves on a regular basis relative to God's Word to see if they have committed corporate sins and need to confess them to the Father.

Questions for Personal Reflection

Before going to the next chapter, take time to reflect on your answers to the following questions:

1. Do you have clean hands and a clean heart?
2. Is the Holy Spirit in control of every aspect of your life?
3. If Jesus spoke to your church today like He did the seven churches in Revelation, are there corporate sins for which He would ask your church to repent?

Chapter 7

Step 2: Gathering to Pray
in the Unity of the Spirit

Having completed Step 1 by getting on praying ground as individual believers, we are ready to join a group of other believers gathered together for the purpose of praying corporately. To enter into effective corporate prayer, the believers praying together must be united in one Spirit.

❧

The seven friends meet for supper at church on the Wednesday night after the special revival. During the revival, all seven friends confessed their sins and surrendered their lives to the control of the Holy Spirit. Let's listen as they talk:

Hank: "This is as close to God as I have ever been. I feel a real refreshing of my soul."

Amanda: "I feel a real unity with you guys. You are great friends. If I have a burden, I know I can come to you and ask you to pray with me."

Mary: "Sue you mentioned in Sunday School that the church is organizing small prayer groups that meet in homes. I think we should consider meeting weekly as a small prayer group."

Joe: "A great idea. We can pray for ourselves, for others, and for the world."

Sue:	"I was really impressed when our revival speakers said how important it is that when we gather together to pray as a corporate body we all need to be on praying ground. They called this *Unity of Spirit*."
Hank:	"I agree. We are all parts of the body of Christ and must work in harmony to gain access to the multiplying power of corporate prayer."
Jack:	"We can meet at my house next Sunday night to start. I will contact the church and get whatever information they have on how to start a small prayer group."
Sue:	"I think they are asking everyone that wants to be in a small prayer group to first study a new book called *When Two or More are Gathered...in Prayer*."

The seven friends who individually are now on praying ground have united together to embark on an exciting journey to learn how to pray together. They have started meeting weekly and are studying the suggested book.

∾

Unity of Spirit

By unity of the Spirit, it is meant that all participants in the corporate prayer group are individually on praying ground with clean hearts and open to the guidance of the Holy Spirit. It cannot be emphasized enough that all those praying together must individually meet the conditions for being on praying ground. Those conditions are to confess all known sin, be filled with the Holy Spirit, and be under the Lordship of Jesus Christ. Only under these conditions will the Father listen to what the individual believers have to say and will the Holy Spirit speak and guide the individual believers during corporate prayer.

This may sound like an exclusive group that is gathered to pray. Not so. If believers individually meet the conditions for having God answer their prayers, they can be productive parts of a corporate prayer group.

If believers that are out-of-fellowship with God and unbelievers are present when the corporate prayer group begins to pray, there is not complete unity of Spirit, and the effectiveness of the prayer group to do the work of the church in corporate prayer is diminished.

We may all be of different maturities spiritually. We may all have different opinions about our beliefs. It is being united in the Spirit that is important. Jesus prayed that we would be of one Spirit:

> Neither pray I for these alone, but for them also which shall believe on me through their word; That they all may be one; as thou, Father, art in me, and I in thee, that they also may be one in us: that the world may believe that thou hast sent me. — John 17:20-21 (KJV)

The Apostle Paul tells us that we are to take every care to preserve the unity of the Spirit:

> Endeavoring to keep the unity of the Spirit in the bond of peace.
> — Ephesians 4:3 (KJV)

When there is unity of the Spirit, the anointing of the Holy Spirit flows and refreshes all of those gathered to pray.

What Happens if Believers Gather and All Are Not on Praying Ground?

As we saw in Chapter 5, when faced with critical times in His life, Jesus brought only a small inner circle with Him to pray. He was closest to Peter, James, and John. Perhaps he felt they could help Him more than the others pray through to get the answers He needed. Jesus did not bring His entourage because there were probably many that followed Him for selfish reasons and many still did not believe that He was the Son of God. In corporate prayer, these followers would have hindered Jesus' effort in praying through to the Father to get an answer to His prayer. It is far better to have two people praying that are united in the Spirit than to have many people praying together that are not united.

85

There were times in Jesus' life that He faced so much unbelief from the people, that He could not do mighty works. For example, when Jesus went home to Nazareth, Mark records:

> And Jesus said to them, "A prophet is not without honor except in his home town and among his own relatives and in his own household." And He could do no miracle there except that He laid His hands upon a few sick people and healed them. And He wondered at their unbelief.
> — Mark 6:4-6a (NAS)

Similarly, when many believers in our churches are not on praying ground, it causes our ministers to struggle to preach. The Spirit of God is not filling the place. Because there is no unity, the anointing of the Holy Spirit to preach with power does not happen.

The fact is that if there are believers in a corporate prayer group that are not on praying ground, they are a drag on the prayer ministry. God will not hear their intercession, nor will He speak to the prayer group through them.

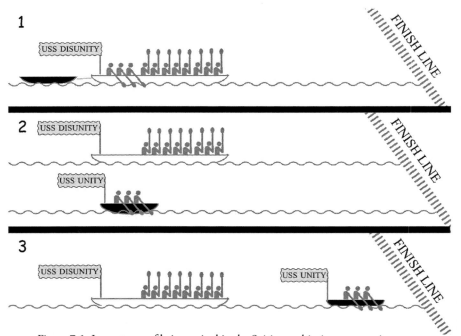

Figure 7-1. Importance of being united in the Spirit to achieving progress in prayer.

Perhaps an example modeled after an article titled "Critical Unity in Corporate Prayer For Critical Breakthroughs" will help explain what I mean.[1] Suppose there were a number of believers in a boat paddling toward a finish line as shown in Figure 7-1. Suddenly most of the believers stop paddling, and only three continue to paddle. As a result of their disunity, the boat struggles to make headway. The three believers who were paddling get in a small dinghy being towed by the big boat. By their unified efforts, they zoom toward the finish line (answered prayer). Those left in the boat are going nowhere.

Once you get into a corporate group to pray, you either contribute, or you don't contribute. You are either a help, or you are a dead weight to be carried. The more dead weight you carry, the harder it is to make progress in prayer. The strength of corporate prayer is when the entire group is on praying ground and is united in its desire to pray the will of God. When all are contributing and united in Spirit, it is easier to reach the goal of praying through to the Father.

Remember, the purpose of the gathering of the small prayer group is to do the work of the church through the ministry of prayer. It is being available for God to use us. It is finding out what God wants done on earth, and to bring it to earth in prayer. This is hard work, and all present in the group need to be open to the Holy Spirit to help.

How unfortunate it is for God's Kingdom if we come to the small group to pray and have neglected individual prayer to cleanse our lives and be filled by the Holy Spirit. As a result, we are not available for God's use! If we are unclean and have not the Holy Spirit's power, we have made the corporate prayer group a cripple as it carries out the ministry of prayer. The impact of not being united in the Spirit is illustrated in the following story.

Some years ago, my wife and I journeyed to Nashville to participate in a lay-led revival with about thirty other laymen from across the southeastern part of the United States. Our job was to share the gospel and our Christian testimony with the members of the church and with people living around the church that were open to a visit. On the way there from Atlanta, some remark by my wife caused me to sharply respond to her. An argument ensued. The issue was so trivial I cannot remember what it was about. Instead of acting Christ-like and asking for her forgiveness, I pouted. The pout continued into the prayer time before the service on the first day of arrival. For the prayer time, the prayer leader asked that we huddle up with our mates, and pray for the service. That meant I had to pray with my wife. Needless to say, we were not one in the Spirit and any prayer we made would not rise above the ceiling. Knowing we could not pray with sin in our hearts, we asked each other and God for forgiveness. Then we could come before a Holy God and do His work in prayer.

Think about this. If I had a serious burden, would I go out on the street and gather up whoever came along to pray with me? No, I would not. I would try to gather up the most Spirit-filled believers I could find to pray with me. Corporate prayer is a ministry. We need to treat it as such.

The above discussion applies to prayer groups that God has called together for the single purpose of engaging in the corporate intercessory prayer ministry of the church so they have maximum effectiveness. There are other kinds of groups who engage in corporate prayer, but corporate prayer is not their primary focus. Examples are small group Bible studies, accountability groups, and neighborhood evangelism cells. These small groups by design may have a mix of Spirit-filled believers, believers that are out-of-fellowship with God, and unbelievers present.

For instance, the small neighborhood cell group used by Dr. David Yonggi Cho, who is pastor of the world's largest church, is focused on evangelism. However, corporate prayer is a major activity of the neighborhood cell groups. Half nights of prayer are common among cell groups. God has used the corporate prayer of these cell groups in a mighty way as described in Dr. Cho's book *Successful Home Cell Groups*.[2]

Praying as One Body

Is there a difference when two or more believers pray and when one believer prays? When a single believer prays by himself, his body, soul, and spirit by definition are working in harmony because they are contained in one person. If Christ is controlling the believer, then Christ is directing the believer's prayer.

There is no difference in when one believer prays and when two or more pray corporately as one if all of the parts of the body of Christ act in harmony. The difficulty in corporate prayer is that the body parts are individual believers.

Now, all the individual believers must be filled with the Holy Spirit, controlled by the Lord Jesus, and act as one body functioning in total harmony.

In the first letter to the Corinthians, the apostle Paul beautifully characterizes the church as the body of Christ:

> For as the body is one, and hath many members, and all the members of that one body, being many, are one body: so also is Christ. For by one Spirit are we all baptized into one body, whether we be Jews or Gentiles, whether we be bond or free; and have been all made to drink into one Spirit. For the body is not one member, but many. **All parts must work in unity.** — I Corinthians 12:12-14 (KJV, emphasis added)

The Holy Spirit takes a diverse group of believers and forms them into a corporate body called the church. The church is a living organism with many interdependent parts that function as a unified corporate body with all its parts working in harmony. The church is to act as though it were a single person with one mind and body.

For a human body to function, one leg can not decide to kneel to pray while the other leg decides to go to the ice cream store. The two legs cannot have minds of their own. They have to listen to the head who tells all the body parts what to do so they can work in harmony and be productive. The body parts have a mutual interest in each other and care for one another just as each believer should have interest in and care for other believers. Each body part depends on the other. If one member suffers, they all suffer.

Similarly, the church as it is called to the ministry of prayer must be of one mind and purpose to accomplish God's work on earth today. Paul says that Jesus is the head of the body:

> And hath put all things under his feet, and gave him to be the head over all things to the church, Which is his body, the fulness of him that filleth all in all. — Ephesians 1:22-23 (KJV).

We must look to Jesus as head of the body of Christ to tell the church what to pray when the church kneels to pray. It is important to note that when the church prays, it is not what we want to pray, but what the Lord Jesus wants us to pray.

When the church has been called to pray, Jesus promised in Matthew 18:19-20 to be present with us. In fact when the church is gathered, Jesus' presence on earth is just as real as it was when He walked the earth 2000 years ago. This is why Jesus said the church can do greater things than He did.

To visualize this, think about our celebrating the Lord's Table. The loaf of bread represents Jesus' body. In our terms, it represents the body of Christ—the church. Christ at the Last Supper broke the loaf of bread and said:

> Take, eat: this is my body, which is broken for you: this do in
> remembrance of me. — I Corinthians 11:24b (KJV)

Each apostle took a piece of the loaf of bread and ate it. A symbolic "piece of Jesus" was now inside each apostle. When the apostles reassembled after Jesus' ascension to heaven, each brought their "piece of Jesus" with them. When they were in one place, all the pieces of Jesus were there, and His body was reassembled.

The point is that when men and women kneel to pray together corporately, they each bring their "piece of Jesus" with them so that Jesus' body is present. And if Jesus is among us, we can ask Him to do anything that is in God's will.

Everyone's piece of Jesus is different. The Holy Spirit gives to each believer a motivational spiritual gift or special ability that reflects a piece of Jesus:

> It is the same and only Holy Spirit who gives all these gifts and
> powers, deciding which each one of us should have.
> — I Corinthians 12:11 (LVB)

This spiritual gift (special ability) is the basic inward drive that motivates each believer in the accomplishment of God's work. The seven motivational gifts given to believers by the Holy Spirit are found in Romans 12:3-9. They are prophecy, serving, teaching, exhorting, giving, ruling, and showing mercy.

Now picture God calling a small group to pray corporately such as our seven friends where each of the friends has one of the motivational gifts listed above. They are represented by the circles in Figure 7-2.

Figure 7-2. A small prayer group comprised
of believers with differing motivational spiritual gifts.

Again all the pieces of Jesus are present when the group of seven friends
kneels to pray together corporately as one body. As promised in Matthew 18:19-
20, Jesus (represented by the Holy Spirit) is there with them as the head.

Each person engaging in corporate prayer, no matter what his motivational spiritual gift, is now available for God to use and speak through to the
small group by the Holy Spirit. The Father on a one-time basis, as He wills,
can bestow supernatural spiritual gifts to the people in the group that are called
manifestation spiritual gifts (diversities of operations):

> And there are diversities of operations, but it is the same God which
> worketh all in all. — I Corinthians 12:6 (KJV)

These manifestation gifts are "one-time" supernatural gifts from the Father to a
believer in the prayer group that relate to the burden being discussed with God.

The manifestation spiritual gifts that the Father may give the prayer group are listed in I Corinthians 12:7-11 and include such one-time supernatural gifts as a gift of wisdom, a gift of knowledge, a gift of faith, a gift of healing, and a gift of miracles.

We saw several of these manifestation gifts used in the corporate prayers found in the Bible and discussed in Chapter 5. More will be said in subsequent chapters about how these one-time manifestation spiritual gifts of the Holy Spirit relate to corporate prayer.

Paul in I Corinthians 12 to 14 addresses the use of the manifestation spiritual gifts in the conduct of the church that has gathered to worship and pray. It is clear from this scripture that an overriding consideration for the church or small group that prays together is that the believers must love each other. There is nothing that makes us love each other more than praying for each other.

Points to Remember

In this chapter, the gathering together of the believers to pray corporately was discussed. The important points were:

1. Every believer in the prayer group must prepare themselves in individual private prayer by getting on praying ground prior to coming to gathering together to pray.
2. There must be unity of the Spirit as the group gathers to pray.
3. Believers in the prayer group that are not on praying ground are a drag on the prayer time.
4. There is no difference in individual prayer and corporate prayer as long as those praying together corporately act in harmony as one.
5. Those believers called to corporate prayer as the body of Christ must operate in harmony of one heart and mind just as the human body made up of different parts must work in harmony to function properly.
6. All believers have various motivational spiritual gifts that reflect a "piece of Jesus," so that when gathered corporately Jesus is present and alive.
7. All believers gathered in corporate prayer can individually on a one-time basis, as the Father decides, receive a supernatural spiritual gift that relates to the prayer burden at hand.

Questions for Personal Reflection

Before going to the next chapter, take time to reflect on your answers to the following questions:

1. Write down one or two names of friends that you would ask to pray with you about a need. Why did you choose them?
2. If a group of friends asked you to pray with them about a burden, are you spiritually prepared to unite with them in prayer?
3. Are you willing for God to speak through you to a small prayer group by giving you a "one-time" supernatural spiritual gift that relates to the intercessory prayer burden at hand?

Chapter 8

Step 3: Taking Our Place Before God

Having completed Steps 1 and 2 of the directions for corporate prayer by getting on praying ground as individual believers and by gathering a group to pray in the unity of the Spirit, we are ready as a corporate group of believers to take our place before God the Father in prayer.

❧

Hank, Bill, and Jack have been working out at the local gym. After they finished their workout, they began to talk about Step 3 which is the topic for their next weekly meeting.

Hank: "I am having a difficult time with Step 3. I understand the need to take our place before the Heavenly Father as we pray. However, praising God as part of this process does not come naturally to me. I guess I am more intellect dominated than heart dominated."

Bill: "I'm the other way. Praise and thanksgiving come naturally to me and put me in a worshipful mood. In praise, I tell God that I understand who He is and that I love Him."

Jack: "Praise reminds me of who God is, what He has done for us, and that He is in control of our world. Hank, you might become more comfortable with praise if you begin your prayers by thanking God for all that He has done for you. Also, you might want to read aloud the Psalms to help you understand what praise is all about. By praising God, we realize the majesty of God. ”

The friends are now beginning to understand how to take their place before a Holy God so they can talk to Him.

☙

Come to the Throne Room

Our desire is to talk to our Father who is in heaven. That means that we must come to His throne room and take our place before our Heavenly Father. Paul says we are to sit in heavenly places:

> And hath raised us up together, and made us **sit together in heavenly places** in Christ Jesus. — Ephesians 2:6 (KJV, emphasis added)

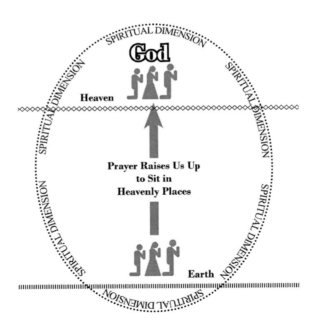

Figure 8-1. Taking our place before God by praying in the spiritual dimension.

We can pray to God in the "Spirit" as though we were actually in heaven before the throne. This is what I will call the "spiritual dimension" or "fifth dimension." Here on earth, we think in terms of four dimensions—the three spatial dimensions and time. The spiritual dimension overlays and includes the heavens and the earth and is independent of time. This concept is illustrated in Figure 8-1.

In the spiritual or fifth dimension, we can be transported independent of time and space to sit in the heavenly places with Jesus where He resides, as we see in the following verses:

> And what is the exceeding greatness of his power to us-ward who believe, according to the working of his mighty power, Which he wrought in Christ, when he raised him from the dead, and **set him at his own right hand in the heavenly places**, Far above all principality, and power, and might, and dominion, and every name that is but also in that which is to come: — Ephesians 1:19-21 (KJV, emphasis added)

John the Apostle was brought into the heavenly places via the spiritual dimension as we see in Revelations 4:1-2. While in the heavenly places, John saw the incredible glory of God:

> After this I looked, and, behold, a door was opened in heaven: and the first voice which I heard was as it were of a trumpet talking with me; which said, Come up hither, and I will shew thee things which must be hereafter. And immediately I was in the spirit: and, behold, a throne was set in heaven, and one sat on the throne. — Revelation 4:1-2 (KJV)

The Apostle Paul similarly was brought up to God's throne room in the spiritual dimension and saw astounding things in heaven.

> Fourteen years ago I was taken up to heaven for a visit. Don't ask me whether my body was there or just my spirit, for I don't know; only God can answer that. But anyway, there I was in paradise, and heard things so astounding that they are beyond a man's power to describe or put in words (and anyway I am not allowed to tell them to others). — II Corinthians 12:2 (LVB)

Prayer is independent of space and time. In fact in the spiritual dimension, we can pray to the Father for someone half way around the world, and believe that if our petition is in God's will, God can instantaneously send the answer to our petition to this person independent of space and time. The power of God is independent of space and time.

We Are to Address Our Prayers to the Father

We are now in a position to say *"Our Father..."* Matthew 6:9 (KJV). Before Jesus gave His disciples instructions on how to pray, God had never been referred to as "Father." As we come before the Father, our relationship should be the same as an earthly father and his children talking to each other. It is an intimate conversation.

As two or more believers enter into corporate prayer, we must address our prayer to "Our" Father. Our mind must be on nothing else but God the Father. In Acts 12:5, it is recorded that:

> Peter therefore was kept in prison: but prayer was made without ceasing of the church unto God for him. — Acts 12:5 (KJV)

Corporate prayer was made "unto God" for Peter. The corporate group of believers should come to the Father in prayer on the ground that we are His children.

We Are to Come to the Father through the Blood of Jesus by the Holy Spirit

The blood of Jesus has made us acceptable to the Father:

> Having therefore, brethren, boldness to enter into the holiest by the blood of Jesus... — Hebrews 10:19 (KJV)

Jesus has made us acceptable to the Father:

> To the praise of the glory of his grace, wherein he hath made us accepted in the beloved. — Ephesians 1:6 (KJV)

If we have the proper position in Jesus, God accepts us as His people.

The Holy Spirit leads us into the Father's presence. We must come united together as one corporate body by the Holy Spirit. The Holy Spirit makes God real to us. If we do not feel the presence of God, we need to ask God to fulfill His promise to send the Holy Spirit to lead us into the very presence of God and introduce us to the Father:

> Now all of us, whether Jews or Gentiles, may come to God the Father
> with the Holy Spirit's help because of what Christ has done for us.
> —Ephesians 2:18 (LVB)

The Holy Spirit will help us by prompting us to pray when we don't know how to pray, and when we don't know for what to pray:

> And in the same way—by our faith—the Holy Spirit helps us with our
> daily problems and in our praying. For we don't even know what we
> should pray for, nor how to pray as we should; but the Holy Spirit prays
> for us with such feeling that it cannot be expressed in words. And the Fa-
> ther who knows all hearts knows, of course, what the Spirit is saying as he
> pleads for us in harmony with God's own will. — Romans 8:26-27 (LVB)

We Are to Come to the Father with Boldness

We are His children. We are acceptable to God through Jesus. Just as our own earthly children come to us, we can with boldness go right up and talk to the Father. Paul explained this to us in Hebrews 4:16:

> Let us therefore come boldly unto the throne of grace, that we may obtain
> mercy, and find grace to help in time of need. — Hebrews 4:16 (KJV)

Praise Should Happen When We Approach God

Praise is the first thing that should happen as we approach God in corporate prayer. After addressing the Father, it was the first thing Jesus instructed us to do in the Lord's Prayer—_"hallowed be thy name"_ Matthew 6:9b (KJV). Also in many of the corporate prayers studied in Chapter 5, praise was the first thing done by those praying.

What is praise? As we saw in Chapter 3, praise includes the adoration and worship of God where we describe His character, wonder, mercy, ability, and love. Praise is when we recognize His greatness, achievements, and majesty. Praise is telling God we love Him. Praise is thanks to God for His blessings to us. Praise is an acknowledgement of who God is. The Bible is full of examples of praises to God:

> The Lord is my rock, and my fortress, and my deliverer; my God, my strength, in whom I will trust; my buckler, and the horn of my salvation, and my high tower. — Psalms 18:2 (KJV)

> At the Flood, the Lord showed his control of all creation.
> — Psalms 29:10 (LVB)

> In thee, O Lord, do I put my trust. — Psalm 31:1a (KJV)

> O magnify the Lord with me, and let us exalt his name together.
> — Psalms 34:3 (KJV)

> Great is the Lord, and greatly to be praised. — Psalms 48:1(KJV)

> But thou, O Lord, art a God full of compassion, and gracious, long suffering, and plenteous in mercy and truth. — Psalms 86:15 (KJV)

> O Lord God Almighty, who is like you? You are mighty, O Lord, and your faithfulness surrounds you. You rule over the surging sea; when its waves mount up, you still them. You crushed Rahab like one of the slain; with your strong arm you scattered your enemies. — Psalm 89:8-11(NIV)

> O Lord, how great are thy works! — Psalms 92:5 (KJV)

> Thou art worthy, O Lord, to receive glory and honour and power.
> — Revelation 4:11 (KJV)

God is our creator, our rock, our fortress, our deliverer, our strength, and our salvation. God is compassionate, faithful, gracious, longsuffering, merciful, and trustworthy. God is in control of all creation. God is worthy to receive glory, honor, and power. What a great God!

The Psalmist sums it up best when he tells us that everything that has breath should praise the Lord:

Let every thing that hath breath praise the Lord. Praise ye the Lord.
— Psalms 150:6 (KJV)

Corporate prayer should always begin with praise. Praise is our reminder that God is real, and God is in control! Our praise states that God is the great "I AM," and our God is everything we need! Praise brings the presence of God. When we begin to praise God, God comes to be in our midst. David writes:

But thou art holy, O thou that inhabitest the praises of Israel.
— Psalms 22:3 (KJV)

Praise is power because it expels Satan. God is in our midst when we praise Him and Satan cannot operate when God is near us. Praise ignites a fresh infusion of faith and drives doubt from the heart. Praising God should be a way of life for the church. Again David says:

"I will bless the Lord at all times: his praise shall continually be in my mouth." — Psalms 34:1 (KJV)

As we come together corporately to pray, we should have a burden to want to praise God. We must come to God desiring in our hearts to have an audience with the King of Kings. We must come to God as the wise men did looking for the baby Jesus:

Saying, Where is he that is born King of the Jews? For we have seen his star in the east, and are come to worship him. — Matthew 2:2 (KJV)

Our worship confesses that Jesus is Lord! Our worship tells Jesus that we love him!

All true praise comes from the human spirit not the human soul. The Apostle John says:

God is a Spirit: and they that worship him must worship him in spirit and in truth. — John 4:24 (KJV)

Too often we worship God with our souls—our mind, our emotions, and our will. This kind of worship is not acceptable to God. Too often we try to use the soul to engage the spirit in praise. It never works. Prayer and praise all originate in the spirit of man as prompted by the Holy Spirit. What originates in the spirit of man then spills over into the soul.

I can do many things for my wife to show her I love her. I can carry out the garbage, wash the dinner dishes, buy her flowers, or give her a present on her birthday. While these are all good things to do to show my love for her, none of these are as good as when I look at her and with heart-felt passion tell her "I love you!" That I love her will be communicated from my spirit to her spirit. Similarly, we can teach Sunday School, visit the sick, be on church committees, and attend worship services. While all of these activities are good things to do to show our love for God, none of these are as good as our spirits uniting together through praise to tell God that we personally love Him. God, like us, wants to know that we love Him for who He is. Too often, we love the religious machinery rather than loving the one who religion is all about.

In Hebrews, Paul tells us that we should continually offer praise to God:

> By him therefore let us offer the sacrifice of praise to God continually,
> that is, the fruit of our lips giving thanks to his name.
> — Hebrews 13:15 (KJV)

One of the greatest values of praise is that it moves our ego out of the way. When we praise and worship God, it moves the focus from us to God.

As we take our place before the throne, we should thank the Father for His son Jesus. We should also give thanks to God for all the blessings in our lives.

> Be careful for nothing; but in every thing by prayer and supplication
> with thanksgiving let your requests be made known unto God.
> — Philippians 4:6 (KJV)

We must also give thanks in the trials and temptations that enter our life because they shape us to look like Jesus:

> In everything give thanks: for this is the will of God in Christ Jesus
> concerning you. — I Thessalonians 5:18 (KJV)

Prayer converts our trials and tribulations into blessings and causes them to work in us for our good (Romans 8:28).

It is in worship, where we offer God our thanks and praise that we become like Him. As we worship God, we catch something of His glory and reflect it to the world. Moses spent 40 days with God, and his countenance shone like the sun. Wouldn't it be great if the church could catch some of this glory!

Points to Remember

To take our place before God as a corporate prayer group:

1. We should enter the throne room of heaven through the spiritual dimension which is independent of time and space.
2. We should address our corporate prayers to the Father.
3. We come to the Father through Jesus by the Holy Spirit.
4. We are to come before the throne with boldness.
5. We find the pathway to the Father by continuously giving Him praise.
6. We are to thank God for everything.

Questions for Personal Reflection

Before going to the next chapter, take time to reflect on your answers to the following questions:

1. How do you feel about being in the actual presence of God when you talk to the Father?
2. Think about the ability, achievements, character, majesty, and love of God. What does your heart tell you to say when you see God?

Chapter 9

Step 4: Having a Burden Given to Us by the Holy Spirit

In Steps 1 to 3, we discussed getting on praying ground individually, gathering a group of believers to pray in the unity of the Spirit, and taking our place before God by giving God praise and thanks. These steps also covered three of the four elements of prayer: pardon, praise, and thanksgiving. Steps 4 through 8 will address the fourth element of prayer—petition.

Petition is where we make intercession for ourselves and for others regarding a burden on our heart. As we intercede for ourselves and others, we are asking God to supernaturally intervene in the lives of men and women here on earth. It is where the prayer ministry work of the church is done.

Step 4 addresses how to determine what specific petitions or burdens the Holy Spirit wants the corporate body to discuss with the Father, so that the Father can answer our prayers.

❦

After the Sunday night study session with her friends on "Step 3: Taking Our Place Before God," Amanda called Sue to ask her a question:

Amanda: "Sue, when we take our place before God in corporate prayer, do we ask Him to grant all our prayer requests? Or, does the Holy Spirit tell us what burdens to bring to the Father?"

Sue: "I think we are going to cover that next week in Step 4. I've already read that chapter. Essentially, it says we are to pray about what God wants us to pray. The Father knows our needs before we pray. As we enter into corporate prayer, we are to listen to the prompting of the Holy Spirit who will tell us the burdens that need prayer. After our next session, let's talk again to make sure we both understand what it means to have a burden given to us by the Holy Spirit."

The friends are learning the importance of praying what God wants them to pray when they gather together in corporate prayer.

ఆ

The Holy Spirit Prompts Us to Pray

What prompts us to pray in the first place? It is a built-in desire in our spirits to *communicate* and have *communion* with God. God's desire to interact with us prompts us through the inspiration of the Holy Spirit to want to pray to Him. Remember God was our Creator. It is natural that He would want us to talk to Him.

Sometimes God gives us a burden for something that drives us to call upon Him. Jesus in the Garden of Gethsemane (Matthew 26:36) felt an intense desire to have fellowship and communicate with the Father. As Jesus prayed to the Father, His soul was very heavy. In Matthew 6:8, we see that God knows what we need before we ask Him:

> Do not be like them, for your Father knows what you need before you ask him. — Matthew 6:8 (NIV)

We Are to Pray What God Wants Us to Pray!

When God desires a group of two or more believers to move into intercessory prayer to petition Him for action, the Holy Spirit that indwells us will put a specific burden on our hearts. We will feel a deep sense of need to pray for

106

the burden. Relief is only obtained when we seek God in intercessory prayer.

All true prayer begins with God. God issues us the invitation to pray to Him. However, our prayer must match what is in the mind of God. We are never to pray what we want to pray, but only what the Holy Spirit wants us to pray.

Sue Curran in *The Praying Church* observes: "The power of corporate prayer is not in many people praying with each other, but in the uniting of many hearts with the Spirit of God to pray the mind and will of God."[1]

To know the mind of God, we must listen to the promptings of the Holy Spirit. This is illustrated in Figure 9-1.

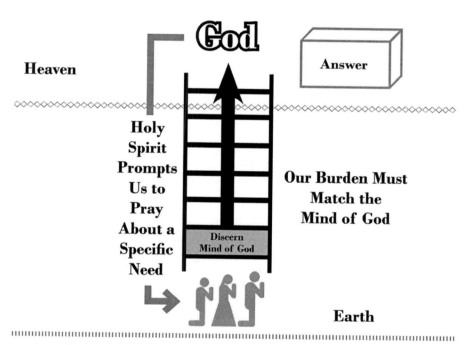

Figure 9-1. Step 4 – The corporate prayer group listens to the prompting of the Holy Spirit to discern what burden God wants us to talk to Him about.

In effect, we are partners in prayer with the Holy Spirit. Paul discusses this in Romans 8:26-27:

> And in the same way—by our faith—the Holy Spirit helps us with our daily
> problems and in our praying. For we don't even know what we should pray
> for, nor how to pray as we should; but the Holy Spirit prays for us with such
> feeling that it cannot be expressed in words. — Romans 8:26 (LVB)

The Holy Spirit helps us to know for what burden to pray and intercedes with God on our behalf. Norman Grubb writes "...the Spirit is given expressly to guide our praying, for true prayers are God's prayers prayed through us—they issue from God's mind, are taught us of His Spirit, are prayed in His faith, and are thus assured of answer."[2]

God has in mind the burdens for which He wants the corporate prayer group to pray and to pray through to an answer. God knows what we need and has the answers ready to give to us as we see in the following verse from Isaiah:

> And it shall come to pass, that before they call, I will answer; and while
> they are yet speaking, I will hear. — Isaiah 65:24 (LVB)

How might this work in a corporate prayer setting where a group of two or more believers gathers together to pray in a conversation with God? Let's look at an example.

The members of a corporate prayer group come together with burdens A, B, and C on their heart. They share their burdens with each other. The prayer group then begins to pray corporately to the Father with all the individual believers on praying ground. After a time of worship in praise and thanksgiving, the small prayer group spends a time of quiet to listen to hear what burden God is telling them to talk to Him about. Then the Holy Spirit prompts one of the believers in the small group to offer a prayer of intercession for burden C. The other believers pick up the prayer and pray only about burden C until all God wants us to pray concerning burden C is prayed. Once there is no more prayer for burden C, the Holy Spirit prompts another believer to pray for a new burden, and a similar process to the above occurs.

This process of corporately praying for one burden at a time should not surprise us when we consider how we pray as individuals in private. We pray individually about a specific burden until we have said all we want to say about it. Then, we move to a new burden. This form of prayer is called ***conversational prayer***.

To illustrate what I mean by "praying what God wants us to pray," let me share the following story. Some years ago, several men and I met together in a private room at our church to pray for our pastor (who was not there). Prior to coming to our church, our pastor served a church in Birmingham, AL. During the racial unrest in the 1960's, some African Americans came to the worship service in his church. He cordially greeted them in the name of Christ as they exited the church following the service. A picture of him shaking hands with an African American was in newspapers across the United States. As a result, many of his Birmingham church members sent him hate mail and made unkind comments to him. Our pastor was having trouble forgiving the members of his former church.

As we began to pray, the only burden on our hearts was to pray that our pastor would forgive those that had hurt him. As the men bowed their heads in prayer, there were a few minutes of quiet. Then, out of the blue the Holy Spirit prompted one of the men, who was a medical doctor, to pray for a doctor friend of his in another city. His friend was a successful doctor, but was having trouble with drug addiction. The prayer began for the doctor's well being and healing. Each of the men in the prayer group began to pray for the doctor with one prayer building on another. At the conclusion of the conversational prayer time for this burden, the men believed by faith that God would take care of this doctor and would strengthen the doctor to wage a successful battle against his addiction.

After a few minutes of quiet, no one felt the need for any more prayer, and the prayer time was concluded. Interestingly, we met to pray for one burden—our pastor—and God in effect said, "Not now. Today, I need prayer for this medical doctor. This is the burden I need you to pray about and ask me to move my will from heaven to earth."

Little did we know that at the same time we were praying for this medical doctor, he was attempting suicide by hooking a vacuum hose to his car exhaust and piping the exhaust inside his car. It was not a coincidence that the vacuum hose burned through before sufficient carbon monoxide could be introduced into the car and kill the doctor. It was corporate prayer on earth that moved God to act.

A second illustration of the Holy Spirit telling His people what they should pray is found in a story told by Jim Cymbala in his book *Fresh Wind, Fresh Fire*, about a severe test Pastor Cymbala and his wife, Carol, went through with their oldest daughter, Chrissy.[3]

At age sixteen, Chrissy started to stray and drew away from her parents and God. She eventually left home, and there were many nights when they had no idea where she was. Jim and Carol begged, pleaded, scolded, argued, and tried to control Chrissy with money. Nothing worked, and she hardened even more. Jim cried to God for help. He prayed prayers of intercession for Chrissy, but there was no change. This went on for two and a half years. During this time, Jim struggled to carry out his pastoral duties.

The Holy Spirit then told Jim that he was just to believe and obey what he had preached so often. As a result of this direction, Jim prayed with an intensity and growing faith as never before, praising God for what he believed God would do.

During one of Brooklyn Tabernacle's Tuesday night church-wide corporate prayer meetings, an usher handed Jim a note from a young woman who Pastor Cymbala knew to be a spiritually sensitive person. The note said "Pastor Cymbala, I feel impressed that we should stop the meeting and all pray for your daughter."[4] All across the sanctuary everyone joined hands to pray for Chrissy. Jim was overwhelmed with the force of the prayers from the people petitioning God on Chrissy's behalf. He knew in his heart that God had answered their prayer.

The next morning, Chrissy showed up at Jim and Carol's home. When Jim went into the kitchen to see her, Chrissy was on the floor sobbing. She asked her parents to forgive her, and then said, "On Tuesday night, Daddy—who was praying for me?" "In the middle of the night, God woke me and showed me I was heading toward this abyss. There was no bottom to it—it scared me to death. I was so frightened. I realized how hard I've been, how wrong, how rebellious."[5]

Yes, God knows the burdens that need prayer when we gather together in corporate prayer. We need to be sensitive to the Holy Spirit to let Him lead us as we pray. When God has made known to us His mind, we are ready to move to the next step where we discover God's will relative to the burden on our heart.

Points to Remember

In this chapter, we learned that:

1. As we intercede for ourselves and others, we are asking God to supernaturally intervene in the lives of men on earth.
2. God knows what we need before we pray.
3. God burdens our hearts for specific things.
4. In corporate intercessory prayer, we are to pray only the burdens which God puts on the prayer group's hearts and no more.

Questions for Personal Reflection

Before going to the next chapter, take time to reflect on your answers to the following questions:

1. What prompts you to want to pray to God?
2. Do you believe the Holy Spirit guides you in what you are to pray?

Chapter 10

Step 5: Finding God's Will Regarding a Burden

So far in Steps 1 to 4, we have gotten on praying ground individually; gathered a corporate group to pray in the unity of the Spirit; taken our place before God by giving Him praise and thanksgiving, and determined which burden God wants us to talk to Him about.

We are now at Step 5 of God's directions for corporate prayer—finding God's will regarding the specific burdens that God has put on the hearts of the prayer group.

෴

The seven friends meet at Bill's apartment for their weekly study of *When Two or More are Gathered...in Prayer*. All have studied the material in Chapter 10 and are commenting on their new discoveries:

Bill: "I always thought we couldn't know God's will for certain regarding the burdens on our heart. It wasn't until I read Step 5 that I found out that God really wants us to know His will for each burden."

Mary: "It is clear from Jesus' words that once we ask according to His will, the Father has committed to answer our petitions."

Joe: "The trick is finding God's will for a specific need."

Amanda: "To find God's will for a burden, we must continue to

	knock on the door of heaven. Plus, we must never give up until God answers, and we understand what the will of the Lord is."
Hank:	"I didn't know there were so many ways that God has given us to understand His will. How many are there?"
Sue:	"The book talks about seven ways that we can determine God's will."
Mary:	"One new discovery for me is that I didn't know friends could help me find the will of God through praying with me in corporate prayer."
Hank:	"This is another reason why corporate prayer is so powerful since you now have two or more seeking God's will together."
Jack:	"The scary thing I discovered is that God will do nothing on earth until we know His will, we align our will in harmony with His will, and we ask for His will to come from heaven to earth."

The friends have made some startling discoveries about their ability to know the will of God, and how to find the will of God for a specific burden.

೧

Understanding God's Will

If we do not know God's will concerning the burden on our hearts, we cannot do the work of the church. Paul said that we need to understand what the will of the Lord is:

> Therefore do not be vague and thoughtless and foolish, but understand-
> ing and firmly grasping what the will of the Lord is.
> — Ephesians 5:17 (AMP)

The corporate prayer group must seek to understand God's will concerning each of the burdens on our hearts. Seeking God's will regarding a burden is illustrated in Figure 10-1.

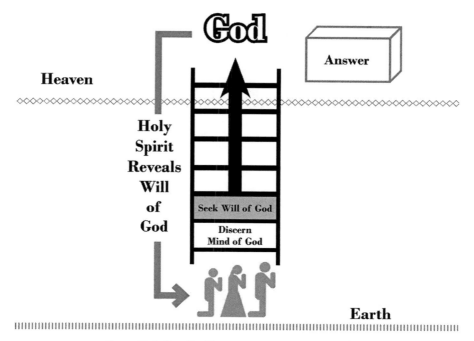

Figure 10-1. Step 5 – The corporate prayer group seeks to
understand God's will concerning the burden on their hearts.

Once we know His will, God has committed to answer our prayers:

> And this is the confidence that we have in him, that, if we ask any thing
> **according to his will**, he heareth us: And if we know that he hear us,
> whatsoever we ask, we know that we have the petitions that we desired
> of him. — I John 5:14-15 (KJV, emphasis added)

To Find God's Will, We Must Seek It with All Our Hearts

If we, as a corporate prayer group, do not know God's will in regard to
a specific burden, then we must seek God's revelation as a corporate body. We
must inquire of God as to His will with all our hearts as seen in Jeremiah:

> And ye shall seek me, and find me, when ye shall search for me with
> all your heart. — Jeremiah 29:13 (KJV)

115

Our seeking must be intense and in earnest. We must ascend to "heavenly places" with Jesus to see what God's will is in heaven. As we pray together, the will of God will emerge and be revealed to us. If we seek God's will, we have the promise that we will find it:

> And I say unto you, Ask, and it shall be given you; seek, and ye shall find; knock, and it shall be opened unto you. — Luke 11:9 (KJV)

If we do not determine His will in our first prayer, we must pray over and over until we are sure we are praying in His will. Jesus went to the Father three times (Matthew 26:39-44) in the Garden of Gethsemane to find God's will. Paul also inquired three times as to what God's will was concerning his thorn in the flesh (II Corinthians 12:7-10).

We must persist and never give up until we pray through and hear God declare His will regarding our burden. The Syrophenician woman did not give up in her petition to Jesus to heal her daughter (Mark 7:26-39). In the stories told by Jesus, the persistent widow looking for justice (Luke 18:1-7) and the determined friend looking for bread at midnight (Luke 11:1-8) did not give up.

Earth Controls Heaven in the Exercise of God's Will

The prayer ministry of the corporate prayer group is to listen and hear what God is telling us He wants to do, and then pray it down from heaven to earth. God wants to use the body of Christ to bring His will, which is found in heaven, to earth. We must be available to God through corporate prayer, find His will concerning the burden at hand, and gladly do His will when we recognize it.

God first needs a group of two or more believers to discern His will, and then He will do the work through them:

> Verily I say unto you, whatsoever ye shall bind on earth shall be bound in heaven: and whatsoever ye shall loose on earth shall be loosed in heaven.
> — Matthew 18:18 (KJV)

As earth looks into heaven and sees that which God does not want to happen, then the corporate prayer group needs to bind it. As earth looks into heaven and sees that which agrees with God's will, the prayer group needs to loose it. This is what Jesus did:

> The Son can do nothing of himself, but what he seeth the Father do.
> — John 5:19 (KJV)

Jesus saw what God wanted to do and did it the way God wanted it done.

We are to desire that His will be done on earth as it is in heaven. In the Lord's Prayer, we pray, *"Thy will be done, on earth as it is in heaven."* Matthew 6:10b (NAS). God's will is done in heaven. God desires His will to be brought to earth. We must be the channels to bring it from the spiritual dimension to earth.

As the Holy Spirit communicates His will to us, we petition God and say, "We want to do this thing." Only then will God do it. Richard C. Trench wrote "Prayer is not getting man's will done in heaven, but getting God's will done on earth. It is not overcoming God's reluctance but laying hold of God's willingness."

How to Find God's Will

We are not to pray "Lord, if it be thy will." This type of prayer is wasted breath and places the burden on God to do something. By using "if," it means we do not know His will and have no claim on God's promises, or we have doubt as to whether God can deliver on His promises.

In Mark 9:20-24, a young boy is brought to Jesus who is possessed by a demon. The disciples tried to heal him and failed. Notice Jesus' reaction of dismay when "if" is used by the father of the boy possessed by a demon:

> So they brought the boy, but when he saw Jesus the demon convulsed the child horribly, and he fell to the ground writhing and foaming at the mouth. "How long has he been this way?" Jesus asked the father. And he replied, "Since he was very small, and the demon often makes him fall into the fire or into water to kill him. Oh, have mercy on us and do something if you can." **"If I can?"** Jesus asked. "Anything is possible if you have faith." The father instantly replied, **"I do have faith;** oh, help me to have more!" —Mark 9:20-24 (LVB, emphasis added)

Jesus was saying *"If I can?"* is not consistent with believing that God will heal the boy. Challenged by Jesus' words, faith rose up in the father's heart, and he said *"I do have faith..."*

Sure, God desires to do something on earth. But God will not act until His people see His will and claim it by faith. God will do His part if we will do our part. We must get in on what God is doing. Not get God in on what we are doing. Too often, we make plans, and then pray to ask God to approve our plans. We should inquire, "God, what is your will?" Helga Bergold Gross observed, "What we usually pray to God is not that His will be done, but that He approve ours."

Before God will tell us His will, there is one requirement. Our heart must be in neutral. It must have no will of its own regarding the burden. God will not answer until we have removed self and self-interest from the matter in which we are seeking His will.

In corporate prayer, the Holy Spirit will lead us to find God's will relative to a specific burden as we pray conversationally together. Each person's prayer progressively feeds off the Spirit-led thoughts and energy of the preceding prayers until our collective hearts and minds tell us that the Holy Spirit has shown us God's will. The Bible indicates at least seven ways the Holy Spirit reveals God's will to His people regarding a specific burden.

- God speaks through His Holy Word
- God speaks through the manifestation of a spiritual gift
- God speaks through a still small voice
- God speaks through circumstances
- God speaks through other people
- God speaks through visions and dreams
- God speaks audibly

God has ordained many different ways for man to know His will. With some believers, the determination of God's will is easy and with others it is difficult. However, God has a way for every believer to know His will. Let's look more closely at the different ways to find God's will.

God Speaks Through His Holy Word

First, God's will may be revealed to us through His Holy Word. It is in God's Word that the majority of answers will be found to the question, "What is God's will regarding our burden?" The Holy Spirit will guide us into the will of God by illuminating scripture in our hearts and stimulating our minds.

If God's Word is not written on our hearts, the Holy Spirit cannot bring His will to our remembrance. The biggest reason we have trouble finding God's will is we do not know God's Word. The Apostle John addresses this in John 15:7:

> If ye abide in me, and my words abide in you, ye shall ask what ye will, and it shall be done unto you. — John 15:7 (KJV)

God's Word living in our heart is the chief way of God letting us in on what is going on in heaven:

> So then faith cometh by hearing, and hearing by the word of God.
> — Romans 10:17 (KJV)

"Word" as used in the above verse refers to specific scripture, which the Holy Spirit brings to our remembrance for use in time of need, a prerequisite being the regular storing of scripture in our minds. Once the Holy Spirit has revealed the Word (His will) and made the Word real to our hearts, then faith immediately follows.

God's will, as revealed in His Word, is communicated to our hearts through commands, principles, and promises.

Commands are straight forward and are clear descriptions of God's will. The list of specific commands in the Bible is quite lengthy. If we have disharmony in the church, the Bible clearly states what we must do to rectify the situation in Matthew 18:15-17. Similarly if we have told a lie which is a sin, the Bible clearly states what corrective action should be taken.

We are commanded to confess our sins. We are commanded to love one another. We are commanded to be filled with the Holy Spirit. We are commanded to make disciples in all nations. We are commanded to be thankful, to avoid all appearances of evil, to be patient in tribulation, to be anxious for nothing, to bring up our children in the Lord, to grow in grace, and to observe the Lord's Supper.

Principles are guides in the Bible that relate to your need. When you are reading the Word of God, the Holy Spirit will tell your spirit that this scriptural principle applies to your need. This is the will of God. Principles from God's Word give us the basis for making decisions.

Some years ago, my wife and I needed a new mattress and box springs for our bed. We had shopped around and found a set that we liked. Before we purchased the mattress and box springs, we had occasion to visit in the home of some friends in our prayer group. The wife was pregnant. In the course of the visit, I happened to glance into their bedroom. It was obvious that they needed a new mattress more than we did, and we knew they lived on a small income. My wife and I discussed what we should do. While we were talking, the words *"It is more blessed to give than to receive"* came to us.

Based on this Biblical principle, we felt the Holy Spirit leading us to give our friends the new mattress and box springs. We ordered the mattress and box springs and had them delivered anonymously. What joy and blessing it was to hear them talk about God's gift to them, wondering who had sent the new mattress and box springs.

If you want God to bless you beyond measure, use the following Biblical principle to govern your life:

> For if you give, you will get! Your gift will return to you in full and
> overflowing measure, pressed down, shaken together to make room for
> more, and running over. Whatever measure you use to give–large or
> small–will be used to measure what is given back to you."
> — Luke 6:38 (LVB)

God's Word gives clear guidance to help us decide on matters of morals, ethical behavior, and social responsibility. If faced with these issues, the Bible guides us in what our decisions should be.

Are you having problems with a boss at work? You might get guidance from the Holy Spirit by studying David's behavior when King Saul was persecuting him. Are you having financial problems? The Holy Spirit may quicken God's will to you as you read Jesus' miracles of supply. Should you accept recreational drugs? Your answer may come from a verse such as this:

> Therefore, whether you eat or drink, or whatever you do, do all to the glory of God. — I Corinthians 10:31 (KJV)

Promises are statements in God's Word that indicate "God will, if we will." They are predicated on an initial response from us.

On a Sunday night at church when I was twelve years old, my pastor asked if I would talk to him for a few minutes. He shared with me the promise made by Jesus in John 3:15-16: *"That whosoever believeth in him should not perish, but have eternal life…"* The Holy Spirit told me that this was a promise for me. This was God's will for me. As a result, I bowed by head and asked Jesus to come into my heart. I did my part by accepting Jesus as my Savior. Then God, as promised, did his part by saving my soul and giving me eternal life. Of that, I am absolutely sure.

Is your church burdened about the lack of witnessing to the lost in your community? To know what God wants you to do, see the promise in Luke 10:2:

> He told them, "The harvest truly is plentiful, but the workers are few. Ask the Lord of the harvest, therefore, to send out workers into his harvest field." — Luke 10:2 (NIV)

Based on this scripture, God has promised that if we will pray, He will send workers to help harvest souls for His kingdom. If the Holy Spirit confirms to you in your heart that this is a promise that applies to your burden, all we have to do is claim the promise. We also have to be willing for God to use us as part of the answer.

If we are in doubt about what to do in a certain situation and need guidance as to the choice to be made, we can claim the following promise:

> And if you leave God's paths and go astray, you will hear a Voice behind you say, "No, this is the way; walk here." — Isaiah 30:21 (LVB)

Based on this promise, if we pray for direction the Holy Spirit will tell us the path we should take.

If we need wisdom as to what to do regarding an issue in our life, we can claim the promise in James 1:5:

> If any of you lacks wisdom, he should ask God, who gives generously to all without finding fault, and it will be given to him. — James 1:5 (NIV)

David Wilkerson in his *The Jesus Person Pocket Promise Book* records over 800 promises from God's Word.[1] It is important to note that as we pray, the Holy Spirit will bring to our remembrance a scriptural promise that He wants us to claim.

God Speaks Through the Manifestation of a Spiritual Gift

As members of the body of Christ, we believe God uses us to be channels of His love to others as needs present themselves. It is through the believers as they pray corporately that the Holy Spirit at His discretion can manifest himself supernaturally and tell us God's will. The Holy Spirit sees a need and then allows the manifestation of a gift to flow through a believer to tell us His will. The manifestations can be thought of as spiritual gifts since the person or small group receives a gift. God can give anyone in the group a manifestation of the Holy Spirit. All can participate.

For example, as the corporate group prays regarding a specific burden, the Holy Spirit may reveal a ***word of knowledge*** (God's will) to a believer for them to share with the prayer group. This is a supernatural revelation of facts to our soul that were not learned through the intellect or physical senses.

As we saw in Chapter 5, Daniel and his friends petitioned God in corporate prayer to tell them about the King's dream and what it meant. God gave Daniel a word of knowledge to answer his prayer. This was supernatural knowledge that Daniel could not have obtained anywhere else.

There are many occasions in the Bible where God gave a word of knowledge to His people so they would have facts not learned by the natural mind. Joseph understood Pharaoh's dream; Jesus knew all about the woman at the well and had never met her; Jesus saw Nathanael under a fig tree and knew what kind of person he was before He ever met him; Ananias received a word of knowledge in a vision about Paul; and Peter used this gift to root out corruption in the early church.

A second example is when the church is burdened for a sick person. In corporate prayer, the prayer group asks God to show His will relative to the healing of the sick person. The Holy Spirit responds and reveals to one or more of the believers in prayer that He wants to give a supernatural *gift of healing* to the sick person without regard to faith, human skills, or natural means. There are many passages in the Bible where the Holy Spirit empowered Jesus, the disciples, the apostles, Paul and many others to give a gift of healing to a sick person.

A third example is a manifestation of a *gift of prophecy* where the believer supernaturally speaks the mind of God by the inspiration and revelation of the Holy Spirit and not from his own thoughts. We saw this in Chapter 5 when the nation of Judah led by King Jehoshaphat went to God in corporate prayer. God gave a man named Jahaziel a gift of prophecy. Jahaziel moved by the Holy Spirit gave God's instructions to the people of Judah. This was a supernatural gift.

Each of the nine manifestation spiritual gifts can be given by the Holy Spirit to the gathered corporate prayer group or local church at His discretion for the purpose of building up the body of Christ. It is a way God can speak to us and show us His will.

God Speaks with a Still Small Voice

The Holy Spirit who dwells in our hearts knows the will of God and reveals that will to us as we see from the following scripture:

> But as it is written, Eye hath not seen, nor ear heard, neither have entered into the heart of man, the things which God hath prepared for them that love him. But **God hath revealed them unto us by his Spirit**: for the Spirit searcheth all things, yea, the deep things of God. For what man knoweth the things of a man, save the spirit of man which is in him? even so the things of God knoweth no man, but the Spirit of God. **Now we have received, not the spirit of the world, but the spirit which is of God; that we might know the things that are freely given to us of God**. — I Corinthians 2:9-12 (KJV, emphasis added)

The will of God may be revealed to us by the Holy Spirit speaking to our spirits in a "still small voice." A still small voice generally comes to us as an impression or conviction. Please note that impressions cannot be trusted unless the believer is on praying ground and filled with the Holy Spirit. Further, no impression can go counter to the Word of God. As we continue to pray to God to test the impression, the Holy Spirit will deepen our sense of rightness about our impression even though new information to the contrary may appear. We sense that this is the will of God for us. The more Christ's life is made over in us, the more we can trust our impressions.

We can hear God speak to our spirit relative to His will through others witnessing as to what God has done for them, through sermons, through books, through videos, through Bible teachers, and through conversations with other people. Our spirit will recognize God's will when we hear it and will say "Aha! This is what God wants done."

Let me give an example where I recognized God's will through the Holy Spirit's still small voice. Some years ago, I wanted to leave my job working for NASA and go to work for private industry. I prepared an extensive resume and was considering sending it to several aerospace companies. On the spur of the moment, I decided to take a copy of the resume with me to a conference being held at the Lockheed plant in Marietta, GA.

I arrived in Marietta at night. The next morning, I knelt by my bed before going to the conference, and asked God to show me His will regarding a job at Lockheed. If He wanted me to come to Lockheed, I prayed that He would let me know. That afternoon at a break in the conference, my future boss came up to me and said "When are you going to come to work for me?" My heart flipped, and I knew without a shadow of a doubt that God had spoken to my heart and said "This is my will for you. This is the answer to your prayer." You can imagine the surprise of my future boss when I took the resume out of my briefcase and handed it to him.

Paul who was sensitive to the voice of the Holy Spirit acted when he heard Him speak to his heart:

> Now after these events Paul determined in the (Holy) spirit that he would
> travel through Macedonia and Achaia (most of Greece), and go to Jerusalem,
> saying, after I have been there, I must visit Rome also. —Acts 19:21 (AMP)

A wonderful example of using "the still small voice" to know God's will is found in *Rees Howell, Intercessor* by Norman Grubb.[2] Rees Howell, while in intercessory prayer, was told by the Holy Spirit that his invalid uncle would be healed. Rees told his uncle and his uncle, in private prayer with God, found it was true. The Lord told his uncle that the Holy Spirit was going to heal him in four and a half months at 5:00 in the morning.

By faith, Rees and his uncle told their friends that he was to be miraculously healed and the timing. Two weeks after going public, his uncle took a turn for the worse. Up until the promised day of healing, the uncle's condition continued to worsen rather than get better. Satan continued to tell the uncle up until the last minute that he would not be healed. At 5:00 in the morning four and a half months from the date of the Holy Spirit's promise, his uncle awoke fully healed.

Rees Howell heard the Holy Spirit speak to his heart with God's will, and he believed what God said by faith. God was faithful and healed his uncle.

Sometimes the impression is in the form of sanctified common sense:

> Have two goals: wisdom—that is, knowing and doing right—and common sense. Don't let them slip away... — Proverbs 3:21 (LVB)

Leslie Weatherhead in his book *The Will of God* makes the following comment regarding using common sense to know the will of God:

> Then there is the lowly signpost we call "common sense." "I prayed for advice," said a man once, "but nothing happened, and I got no answer to my prayers; so I used my common sense." But who gave him his common sense, and why was it given? If God has placed the machinery for making a judgment within the mind of man, why should he not use it, and why should man regard some uncanny way of receiving direction as more likely to be divine because it is unusual? Surely insight based on a thoughtful appreciation of the situation is more reliable than an impulse.[3]

God has given us a brain, and He expects us to use it.

God Speaks Through Circumstances

God may reveal his will through setting up our circumstances to point us to His will. There are three approaches that are discussed in the Bible. They are:

- Open door
- Putting out a fleece
- Casting lots

The **open door** approach is when God causes doors to open, or doors to close thereby pointing us toward His will. If we are living under the control of the Holy Spirit, we must believe the circumstances in our life are governed by God. Maybe the reason why a door is open for us is that God wants us to step through. He wants us to pick a course based on the best information we have. If it is the wrong course of action, God will tell us. Paul wrote about using such an approach to find the will of God in the following two scripture verses:

> But I will stay on at Ephesus until Pentecost, because a great door for effective work has opened to me, and there are many who oppose me.
> — I Corinthians 16:8-9 (NIV)

> Furthermore, when I came to Troas to preach Christ's gospel, and a door was opened unto me of the Lord... — II Corinthians 2:12 (KJV)

In both of these cases, Paul saw great opportunity to preach the gospel. In the absence of other direction from God, Paul stepped through the door. When God specifically wanted Paul to go somewhere, He told Paul His will:

> So they, being sent forth by the Holy Ghost, departed unto Seleucia; and from thence they sailed to Cyprus. — Acts 13:4 (KJV)

When God didn't want Paul to go someplace, the Holy Spirit also told him not to go:

> Now when they had gone throughout Phrygia and the region of Galatia, and were forbidden of the Holy Ghost to preach the word in Asia...
> — Acts 16:6 (KJV)

If we have prayed about a burden, searched his Word for direction, listened for His still small voice, and are still not sure what the will of God is, then we should tell God what we plan to do and ask Him to "shut the door" if it is not what He wants us to do. We must trust God's promise to work our circumstances and to direct our paths:

> Trust in the Lord with all thine heart; and lean not unto thine own understanding. In all thy ways acknowledge him, and he shall direct thy paths.
> — Proverbs 3:5-6 (KJV)

We should not trust the open door alone to show us God's will. We should continually look for confirmation by other means (Word of God, still small voice, and counsel from other believers). At best, circumstances can help us in making our decisions, but circumstances are not authoritative commands from God. In no case are we to trust circumstances if they lead us down the path to violate God's Word. Consider the following two examples of using the open door to find the will of God.

Example: A headhunter calls and offers you a job with increased responsibility, pay, and challenge. You are thrilled at the possibility of taking this job. You ask your friends to pray with you to determine God's will. Should you stay in your present job or move to the new job?

As your corporate prayer group prays, there is no clearly recognizable answer from God. You must let the headhunter know tomorrow. What should you do? Again, God expects you to use the best information you have to make a decision and then act. As we proceed, we should be very diligent to continue to ask His guidance.

Example: During Christmas vacation from college, John went by his home church in Atlanta, Georgia to see Chris, the church's youth minister. After talking about mutual college experiences for a few minutes, John told Chris, "I need you to pray with me! I have received two good job offers and have been praying to understand God's will regarding which offer God wants me to take. Although I have prayed to understand God's will, I still don't know what to do."

Chris said, "What do you want out of your new job?" John responded, "I want a challenging job where I can use my talents and education, that will be financially rewarding, and that will prepare me to start my own business here in Atlanta. I want to find a church near where I work where I can be active and continue to use my musical ability in a worship praise band. Finally, I want to live close enough that I can drive home in one day. Family is important to me."

Chris said, "Tell me about the two job offers." John said, "The first offer is a big company that is international in scope. The pay is very good and the job is exciting. I may have to live overseas. The company is located in Seattle, Washington. The second company that offered me a job is located in Charlotte, North Carolina. It is a medium size company with a good salary that will allow me to do more things with my training. Oddly enough, our college pastor told me about an exciting church in Charlotte where he was on staff that is in the process of forming a new praise band for their worship service. He said they had been praying for someone with my talent to help out. I think maybe God wants me to take the second offer, but I am not sure." Chris said, "Let's pray together."

In this story, John was serious about being open to God showing him His will. John was also willing to obey God's will when he understood it. It is clear to everyone except John that God had already opened doors for him. John needed to act on what God had already revealed to him and step through the open door while continuing to pray with others, like Chris, to ask God for confirmation.

Yes, God will open the doors for us in answer to our seeking His will, but we won't have the peace of knowing God's will for a certainty until we put our faith into action and walk through the door. Jack Hayford puts it this way:

> "The Word says: "Let the peace of God rule in your hearts" (Colossians 3:15). As you put one foot in front of another, keep saying in your heart, "Lord, if You want me to go in a different direction than the one I'm pursuing, well, I'm not in a hurry. I'm simply proceeding as best I understand." Then trust the Holy Spirit to make the way you go fruitful, or to change your direction, or reorder your way. Simply remain wide open to those possibilities in your heart. But don't fear movement simply because you don't have a specific direction for every issue or step or decision in your life."[4]

The **putting out a fleece** approach to determining God's will is really asking God to supernaturally intervene in our circumstances with a miracle or sign to tell us His will. The term "putting out a fleece" comes from the story of Gideon found in Judges 6:36-40. Gideon is asking God to arrange circumstances to confirm that He did indeed plan to use Gideon to save Israel:

> Then Gideon said to God, "If you are really going to use me to save Israel as you promised, prove it to me in this way: I'll put some wool on the threshing floor tonight, and if, in the morning, the fleece is wet and the ground is dry, I will know you are going to help me!" And it happened just that way! When he got up the next morning he pressed the fleece together and wrung out a whole bowlful of water! Then Gideon said to the Lord, "Please don't be angry with me, but let me make one more test: this time let the fleece remain dry while the ground around it is wet!" So the Lord did as he asked; that night the fleece stayed dry, but the ground was covered with dew! — Judges 6:36-40 (LVB)

A similar example where a person asks God for a miracle to confirm His will is the story of Abraham's servant who is looking for a wife for Isaac in Genesis 24:14-19. Abraham's servant prayed that God would lead him to select the wife for Isaac by arranging the circumstances to confirm God's will.

To illustrate using a sign to know the will of God, consider this situation. On a vacation cruise to Mexico, a young man and woman from different parts of the country meet who had not known each other before getting on the ship. They enjoyed being with each other for the two week cruise. As they got to know each other, they found that both were active Christians and had much in common. They parted as friends with no commitment to stay in touch. A couple of month's later at a business conference in Atlanta, they happen to see each other again. They wondered if this was a sign from God that they were destined for each other. It may have been, but more sharing, more courtship, more personal prayer, and more time is needed to confirm that it is God's will for them to be together. We must be careful asking for signs from God without confirmation from other sources that this direction is truly His will.

The third approach is the use of **casting lots** as an appeal to God for His direct intervention in our circumstances to help us decide His will regarding a burden when we cannot decide ourselves. When the lots are cast, the Lord influences where the lot should fall and thereby shows us His will. The method for discerning divine choice through "casting lots" has a long history in Israel. The animal to be used for sacrifice was determined by lot (Leviticus 16:8). The land of Canaan was divided by lot (Numbers 26:55). David divided the priests by lot (I Chronicles 24:5). Casting lots also shows up in the stories of Jonathan (I Samuel 14:41-42), Jonah (Jonah 1:7), and the selection of a successor to Judas (Acts 1:21-26).

In the case of selecting Judas' successor, the apostles had developed criteria for selecting the one to replace Judas. Two men met the criteria. The apostles could not decide which man to choose. It was natural for the apostles to use casting of lots since that is the way issues had been settled throughout the history of Israel when the parties involved could not reach a decision. It should be remembered that the apostles had not yet been empowered by the Holy Spirit. Could it have been that both Joseph and Matthias were acceptable to God, and as a result God did not make a choice between the two men?

Consider this modern day example. Suppose you wanted to buy a new house. There are two new houses that you like, and you can't make up your mind. You search the scriptures for an answer, you ask God for guidance, and you ask your corporate prayer group to pray with you about the decision. There is no answer from God. Should you flip a coin to pick? God's answer may be that either house is just fine. Again, we should make a decision, and then continually ask God to confirm the decision or redirect us.

The take away from these three approaches is that we should be very careful using circumstances to guide us to God's will. Circumstances should never guide us into doing something that is contrary to the Word of God. In the absence of definitive answers from God, we can make decisions based on the information we have, and then continually ask God to confirm as correct the direction we have taken or redirect our paths.

God Speaks Through Other People

Sometimes God gives us a burden, but we cannot seem to pray through and determine His will relative to the burden. As others pray with us, it often becomes clear what God wants us to do. In corporate prayer, God can reveal His will to others who can share God's will with us.

God Speaks Through Visions and Dreams

God speaks through visions and dreams in both the Old and New Testaments to tell us His will. In the Bible there are over 200 references to visions and dreams. A vision is defined as pictures seen by the mind. A dream is defined as a series of pictures or thoughts passing through the mind while we are asleep. Both are seen in the mind of the believer. Generally, dreams occur when we are asleep, and visions occur when we are awake. Many are symbolic and require careful interpretation.

In Joel, we read that God's people shall see visions and dreams:

> And it shall come to pass afterward, that I will pour out my spirit upon all flesh; and your sons and your daughters shall prophesy, your old men shall dream dreams, your young men shall see visions...
> — Joel 2:28 (KJV)

Peter referenced this scripture in Joel in his sermon at Pentecost (Acts 2:16) to explain what was happening with the coming of the Holy Spirit.

God may reveal His will to us through a *vision*. Paul was instructed in a vision as to what city God wanted him to go to next:

> And a vision appeared to Paul in the night; There stood a man of Macedonia, and prayed him, saying, Come over into Macedonia, and help us. — Acts 16:9 (KJV)

John also saw God's will in a vision that was recorded in the book of Revelation:

> I was in the Spirit on the Lord's day, and I heard behind me a loud voice like the sound of a trumpet, saying, "Write in a book what you see, and send it to the seven churches: to Ephesus and to Smyrna and to Pergamum and to Thyatira and to Sardis and to Philadelphia and to Laodicea."— Revelation 1:10-11 (NAS)

God may reveal His will to us through *dreams*. In Genesis 31:11, an angel came to Jacob in a dream and gave him instructions to go back to his father's land. God in a dream warned the wise men who had come to worship the baby Jesus to not return to report back to Herod (Matthew 2:12). An angel also came in a dream to Joseph telling him to flee to Egypt with the baby Jesus:

> Now when they had departed, behold, an angel of the Lord appeared
> to Joseph in a dream, saying, "Arise and take the Child and His mother,
> and flee to Egypt, and remain there until I tell you; for Herod is going
> to search for the Child to destroy Him." — Matthew 2:13 (NAS)

There are many cases in history where our church fathers have shared that they have experienced visions and dreams. For instance, Polycarp was given a vision of his martyrdom; Constantine in a dream saw a battle sign he was to carry into battle; and John Newton, a slave trader who penned "Amazing Grace," received a dream from God which totally changed his life.

If you believe you have received a vision or dream from God, then in prayer you need to confirm that it is indeed from God. Confirmation may come from scripture that speaks to your heart, from a still small voice, or from validation from other believers as you share your vision or dream with them. As mentioned before, the vision or dream cannot violate the Word of God.

God Speaks Audibly

We find several stories in the Bible where God speaks audibly to believers to tell them His will. In I Samuel 3: 3-10, God speaks to Samuel:

> ...and the lamp of God had not yet gone out, and Samuel was lying
> down in the temple of the Lord where the ark of God was, that the Lord
> called Samuel; and he said, "Here I am." ...Then the Lord came and
> stood and called as at other times, "Samuel! Samuel!" And Samuel said,
> "Speak, for Thy servant is listening." — I Samuel 3:3-4, 10 (NAS)

In the New Testament, God spoke audibly at the baptism of Jesus stating:

> "Thou art My beloved Son, in Thee I am well-pleased." — Luke 3:22 (KJV)

God also spoke audibly to Paul:

> And as he journeyed, he came near Damascus: and suddenly there shined round about him a light from heaven: And he fell to the earth, and heard a voice saying unto him, Saul, Saul, why persecutest thou me? And he said, Who art thou, Lord? And the Lord said, I am Jesus whom thou persecutest: it is hard for thee to kick against the pricks. — Acts 9:3-5 (KJV)

The times when God spoke directly to someone in the Bible with an audible voice are few in number. There are cases in church history where people claim to have heard the audible voice of God. Joan of Arc is an example.

While God can speak to man audibly in today's world, church history and the Bible indicate that this will most likely be a rare occurrence. In any event if God shares His will with one or more believers audibly, then what we hear must be tested in the same way as discussed above with dreams and visions.

Fasting

The practice of fasting that is used in the Old and New Testaments is an effective way for small corporate prayer groups to focus intensive prayer in the search for God's will regarding urgent petitions that are on their hearts. Fasting frees us from the distractions of our environment and gives the Holy Spirit the opportunity to speak to us regarding His will. In scripture, fasting is always associated with prayer. Fasting is the voluntary denial of food, water, and other basic needs for a period of time. Fasting puts our physical needs at a lower priority than the spiritual need at hand. Andrew Murray said in this regard: "Fasting helps to express, to deepen, and to confirm the resolution that we are ready to sacrifice anything—to sacrifice ourselves—to attain what we seek for the kingdom of God."

When a small corporate prayer group decides to fast together and to humbly seek God's will, it is a private matter as we see from Jesus' words:

> "And whenever you fast, do not put on a gloomy face as the hypocrites do, for they neglect their appearance in order to be seen fasting by men. Truly I say to you, they have their reward in full." — Matthew 6:16 (NAS)

133

Fasting is not for show, but for "fast" determining God's will and for bringing His power to bear on the spiritual need at hand. Some spiritual needs require more power from God than others as we see in Matthew 17:19-21:

> Then came the disciples to Jesus apart, and said, Why could not we cast him out? And Jesus said unto them, Because of your unbelief: for verily I say unto you, If ye have faith as a grain of mustard seed, ye shall say unto this mountain, Remove hence to yonder place; and it shall remove; and nothing shall be impossible unto you. Howbeit this kind goeth not out but by prayer and fasting. — Matthew 17:19-21 (KJV)

When a small corporate prayer group feels led by the Spirit of God to fast and intensely seek God's will regarding an urgent need, it brings a mighty prayer capacity to draw on God's power.

If you are not on praying ground, fasting is a waste of time as we see in Isaiah 58:

> "We have fasted before you," they say. ``Why aren't you impressed? Why don't you see our sacrifices? Why don't you hear our prayers? We have done much penance, and you don't even notice it!" I'll tell you why! Because you are living in evil pleasure even while you are fasting, and you keep right on oppressing your workers. Look, what good is fasting when you keep on fighting and quarreling? This kind of fasting will never get you anywhere with me. — Isaiah 58:3-4 (LVB)

We can be pious, attend worship services, and pray much while we fast; however, if we do not keep His commandments and continue to have sin in our heart, God will not respond and answer our prayers.

There Must Be Harmony of God's Will and Man's Will

Harmony is when man's free will and God's will are in agreement. Man has a free will. God refuses to use His will to override our wills. When man's will is not in agreement with God's will, God is restricted in what He can do. When harmony exists between our will and God's will, God will answer our prayer every time:

"Again I say to you, that if two of you agree on earth about anything
that they may ask, it shall be done for them by My Father who is in
heaven." — Matthew 18:19 (NAS)

The church must be of one mind and one spirit concerning God's will.
However, we can only ask God to do what He desires to do. Watchman Nee
remarks "...prayer is simply speaking out the will of God through the mouth
of the believer."[5]

God's will is constant, unchanging, and does not vary with time. As we
study God's Word, hear sermons, listen to Bible teachers, or seek God in prayer,
we see the need to align our will with the will of God. Bob Mumford in *Keys to
Kingdom* says our response to seeing the will of God may result in rebellion, resentment, and independence before we finally agree to align our will with God's
will.[6] These four responses are depicted in the following illustration:

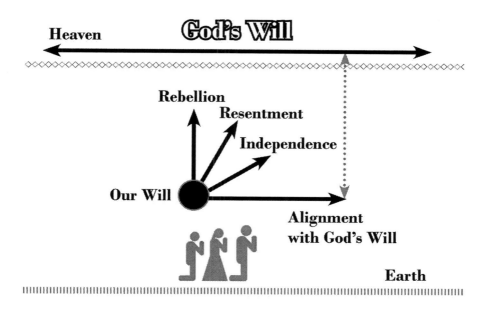

Figure 10-2. We must align our will with the will of God.

Our conversation with God, concerning doing His will once we see it, could go something like this:

Rebellion—"I understand what you want me to do, but I won't do it."
Resentment—"I will do it, but I don't want to."
Independence—"I'll do it for you Jesus, but I will do it my way."
Alignment—"I'll obey and do your will with a joyful and glad heart."

Remember earlier, it was stated that when we see His will, we must obey it every time to have answered prayer. For example, let's say you said something that hurt a friend. Then you read in Matthew 5:23-24 where it says that you shouldn't bother to pray until you have made it right with your friend.

Your first response might be "I am not going to apologize. She hurt me first. I won't do it." Now that you know God's will from reading the Bible, the Holy Spirit will continue to help you recall the need to go to your friend and apologize. You give in partially and tell God "I will apologize, but I don't want to." You still hold a grudge and really don't want to apologize. God says "that is not good enough." Again with continued conviction by the Holy Spirit, you give in and say "Ok, I will do it, but I will do it my way." Again our will and God's will are not aligned, and God says "that is not good enough." Finally, the Holy Spirit and your spirit break through your soul, and you totally give in to God's control. You say "I will go apologize and love the person as my sister." Now, there is harmony between God's will and our will.

Before God will act, our will must be aligned with God's will. Just like us, Jesus also had to align his will with the Father's will:

"My food," said Jesus "is to do the will of him who sent me and to finish his work." — John 4:34 (NIV)

Since the Father and Jesus are one and we are one with Christ, we are also to do the will of the Father.

When His Will Is Known There Must Be Agreement in the Spirit Concerning the Matter

As two or more believers come together in corporate prayer, the Holy Spirit moves the spirit of a believer to pray concerning a particular burden. Prayer then begins to pour forth from the other believers in the group in a conversational prayer with God concerning this particular burden. This continues until God says "enough" or until a believer is moved by the Holy Spirit to state that God has spoken concerning His will and claims it by faith. If this is truly the will of God, then the spirits of other believers in the prayer group should leap in agreement.

The group praying together must use the gift of discernment to test the revealed will of God as discussed in I Thessalonians 5:21 and I John 4:1:

> But examine everything carefully; hold fast to that which is good…
> — I Thessalonians 5:21 (NAS)

> Dearly loved friends, don't always believe everything you hear just because someone says it is a message from God: test it first to see if it really is. For there are many false teachers around…— I John 4:1 (LVB)

An easy test is to ask if the revelation of God's will is consistent with God's Word. To exaggerate, if someone while in corporate prayer said, "God told me to go murder Jim," the corporate prayer group would immediately know the claim of God's will was false because God's Word is clear that we should not commit murder.

Acts 13:2-3 is an example of corporate prayer where the will of God is revealed in prayer, and further prayer is made to confirm this revelation:

> One day as these men were worshiping and fasting the Holy Spirit said, "Dedicate Barnabas and Paul for a special job I have for them." So after more fasting and prayer, the men laid their hands on them--and sent them on their way. — Acts 13: 2-3 (LVB)

Points to Remember

This chapter dealt with finding God's will with respect to a specific burden. The important points were:

1. To find God's will, we must seek it with all our heart.
2. Earth controls heaven in the exercise of God's will.
   a. God will not act until the church acts.
   b. By prayer we move God's will from heaven to earth.
3. Our hearts must be in neutral concerning our burden before God.
4. God's will is revealed to us through:
   a. God's Holy Word.
   b. Manifestation of a spiritual gift by the Holy Spirit.
   c. God speaking through a still small voice.
   d. Circumstances.
   e. God speaking audibly.
   f. God speaking through visions and dreams.
   g. Other believers.
5. When harmony exists between our will and God's will, God will answer our prayer every time.
6. When God's will is stated by the church in corporate prayer, there must be an agreement by other believers present that this is truly the will of God.

Questions for Personal Reflection

Before going to the next chapter, take time to reflect on your answers to the following questions:

1. Is your life aligned with the will of God as you know it?
2. Are you willing to spend time earnestly seeking God's will for a specific burden when praying together with other believers?

Chapter 11

Step 6: Using the Authority of Jesus' Name

In Steps 1 to 5 of the directions for corporate prayer, we have gotten individually on praying ground; gathered a group to pray in the unity of the Spirit; come together corporately to praise God; determined which petition God wants us to talk to Him about; and corporately determined God's will regarding the petition.

We are now at Step 6 of the directions for corporate prayer: using the authority of Jesus' name together as the body of Christ to execute God's will concerning a specific burden and bring the answer to our prayer from heaven to earth.

&

On Saturday, Amanda sees Hank at Starbucks:

Amanda: "Hank, how are you doing? Have you found a job yet?"

Hank: "Yes, I have. Based on what we have been learning about corporate prayer and in particular 'how to know the will of God,' I have been praying for God to show me His will. I appreciate you and the rest of our friends praying with me that God would show me His will. I start Monday as a math teacher at the Middle School. I know in my heart that God has shown me

His will for my life. God has placed me in this school to work with underprivileged children. As you know, I have a heart for children. I am very excited!"

Amanda: "What do you think about tomorrow night's topic 'Step 6: Using the Authority of Jesus' Name?'"

Hank: "I find it a little uncomfortable that we can speak directly to a burden using the authority of Jesus' name and bring the answer to our prayer down from heaven to earth. I have been trying to make sense of authoritative prayer all week. I know the Bible says we can do it; nonetheless, it is going to take some getting use to."

Amanda: "The way I read it, we can only authoritatively ask God to answer our prayer when He has revealed His will on the matter. Do you agree?"

Hank: "It appears to me that using authoritative prayer is sort of like medieval days when a prince would give a knight his royal ring as a symbol so everyone would know the knight represented the authority of the prince. When the knight showed the ring to the king and made a request, the king did not see the authority of the knight but saw the authority of his son and granted the request."

Amanda: "I see. When we come to God the Father with our petitions, we *ask in the authority of His Son's name.* Jesus' name, like the ring, is entrusted to us. When we use Jesus' name as our authority, God like the king answers our petition. This is a very good analogy. Hank, you need to share this tomorrow night."

The friends are beginning to understand that God has indeed given them the power to change and control the world in which they live using the authority of Jesus' name.

℘

Step 6, where a corporate prayer group uses the authority of Jesus' name to bring God's answer to prayer from heaven to earth, is illustrated in Figure 11-1.

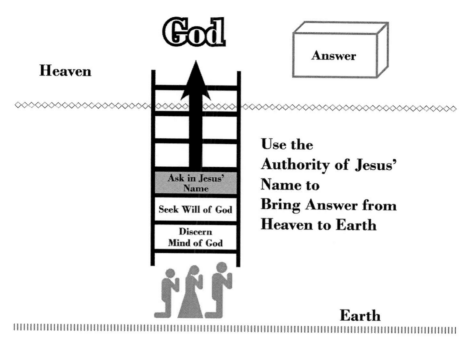

Figure 11-1. Step 6 – Using the authority of Jesus' name to bring the corporate prayer group's answer to prayer from heaven to earth.

Authoritative Prayer

"Authoritative prayer" is praying *"Thy will be done in earth, as it is in heaven."* [1] God desires us to move His will from heaven to earth. Authoritative prayer is our using the authority of Jesus' name to bring answers to prayer from heaven to earth. Authoritative prayer is not asking God to do a thing, but after finding God's will regarding a burden in prayer, it is the church (two or more) using the authority given to it by Jesus to deal directly with the all the forces of the universe.

It is important to reiterate that *we can only authoritatively ask God to do that which is in His revealed will.* As sinful humans, we do not have the power to direct God to do what we would like Him to do or in any way limit God's freedom.

Watchman Nee defines authoritative prayer as the binding and loosing prayer of Matthew 18:18:[2]

> Verily I say unto you, Whatsoever ye shall bind on earth shall be bound in heaven: and whatsoever ye shall loose on earth shall be loosed in heaven. — Matthew 18:18 (KJV)

Notice in this verse, it says: *"you shall bind"* and *"you shall loose."* That means us. The church is the one who executes authoritative prayer. The church does what any corporate business executive would do. It executes in the name of others. In our case, the church executes in "the name of the Lord Jesus."

Jesus has given us His authority to execute His will in our world. God has the power to perform anything we ask; however, He needs our authoritative prayer to make it happen. The church has all authority and power to use the name of Jesus. He gave it to us in Matthew 28:18-20:

> And Jesus came and spake unto them, saying, All power is given unto me in heaven and in earth. Go ye therefore, and teach all nations, baptizing them in the name of the Father, and of the Son, and of the Holy Ghost: Teaching them to observe all things whatsoever I have commanded you: and, lo, I am with you always, even unto the end of the world. Amen. — Matthew 28:18-20 (KJV)

Because Jesus has all power and authority, He can send us out to do the work of the church invested with all the power and authority of His office. Jesus has entrusted the church with Himself. The church is now His body. Jesus desires to use the church to execute His will on earth.

Jesus Is a Name Above All Other Names

The name "Lord Jesus" is a name above all other names. Before Jesus' resurrection, His name was simply "Jesus." After Jesus' resurrection, God exalted

142

His name above every other name, and He became "Lord Jesus." Jesus is the King of Kings and Lord of Lords. This is recorded in Philippians 2:9-11 and Ephesians 1:20-21:

> Wherefore God also hath highly exalted him, and given him **a name which is above every name**: That at the name of Jesus every knee should bow, of things in heaven, and things in earth, and things under the earth; And that every tongue should confess that Jesus Christ is Lord, to the glory of God the Father. — Philippians 2:9-11 (KJV, emphasis added)

> Which he wrought in Christ, when he raised him from the dead, and set him at his own right hand in the heavenly places, Far above all principality, and power, and might, and dominion, and every name that is named, not only in this world, but also in that which is to come... — Ephesians 1:20-21 (KJV)

At the name of Jesus, every person on earth should bow and confess that Jesus Christ is Lord. Jesus has been set at the right hand of God and has been given authority over everything in heaven and on earth in the present and in the future.

His Name Represents Authority

As we saw in Matthew 28:18, Jesus told his disciples that he had been given all authority in heaven and earth. When we pray asking in Jesus' name, we are praying in the authority of Jesus. Great things happen when we use Jesus' name. Look at what happened when Peter used the authority of Jesus' name in Acts 3:6. A lame man was healed:

> Then Peter said, Silver and gold have I none; but such as I have give I thee: **In the name of Jesus Christ of Nazareth** rise up and walk. — Acts 3:6 (KJV, emphasis added)

Peter tapped into God's power when he used the authority of Jesus' name:

> And when they had set them in the midst, they asked, By what power, or by what name, have ye done this? Then Peter, filled with the Holy

Ghost, said unto them, Ye rulers of the people, and elders of Israel, If we this day be examined of the good deed done to the impotent man, by what means he is made whole; Be it known unto you all, and to all the people of Israel, that **by the name of Jesus Christ of Nazareth**, whom ye crucified, whom God raised from the dead, even by him doth this man stand here before you whole. — *Acts 4:7-10 (KJV, emphasis added)*

The disciples used the name of Jesus to deal with the power of Satan:

And the seventy returned again with joy, saying, Lord, even the devils are subject unto us **through thy name**. — Luke 10:17 (KJV, emphasis added)

Paul also used the name of Jesus to deal with evil spirits in a young girl:

And this did she many days. But Paul, being grieved, turned and said to the spirit, I command thee **in the name of Jesus Christ** to come out of her. And he came out the same hour. — Acts 16:18 (KJV, emphasis added)

We may use the authority of Jesus name to deal with any burden that we have.

"Ask in My Name"

Over and over, Jesus said *"Ask in my name."* God has entrusted us with the use of His name. In John chapters 14, 15, and 16, Jesus instructed us numerous times to *"Ask in my name."* For example, look at John 16: 23-26a:

And in that day ye shall ask me nothing. Verily, verily, I say unto you, Whatsoever ye shall **ask the Father in my name**, he will give it you. Hitherto have ye asked nothing in my name: **ask, and ye shall receive**, that your joy may be full. These things have I spoken unto you in proverbs: but the time cometh, when I shall no more speak unto you in proverbs, but I shall shew you plainly of the Father. At that day ye shall **ask in my name**: and I say not unto you, that I will pray the Father for you...
— John 16:23-26 (KJV, emphasis added)

In the Living Bible, John 16:26 says:

"Then you will present your petitions over my signature!"
— John 16:26 (LVB)

We have a blank check signed by Jesus. We can draw on our account in heaven to answer our prayers if we are in harmony with His will. The Father will honor this check in the Bank of Heaven because it is signed by Jesus.

The Name of Jesus Is Entrusted to the Church

God does not generally intervene in our world directly. He prefers to work through the church (two or more). The work of Jesus on earth today is entrusted primarily to the church, not to individuals. The church is a group of believers entrusted with the name of the Lord Jesus on earth. Jesus is the head of the church. Whatever the church says in the name of the Lord Jesus, Jesus also says to the Father. God will answer only that which we ask in Jesus' name.

Only the church can use the name of Jesus. Unbelievers can not use the name of Jesus. In Acts 19:13-17, some wandering Jewish priests used the name of Jesus like it was a magic incantation with disastrous results.

Jesus' Name Is the Corporate Seal That Gives Us Authority

When we conclude our prayers, we say, "We ask these things in the name of Jesus." Why do we do that? Is this just a tag line we just strap on the end of the prayer without knowing what it means? We are really saying that we are offering our petitions in prayer to God in the authority that Jesus has given to the church. We are entitled to use the corporate seal,

"In the Name of Jesus"

to transact the business of the church with God.

When my wife took my last name, she was empowered to use that name anytime and anyplace. We have a joint checking account. She can write checks using my last name, and they will be honored. By analogy, Jesus has authorized us to use His name to draw down resources from heaven.

A second example of acting in someone else's name is when I approach a school zone in my car that has a crossing guard. I respect the authority of the crossing guard when she asks me to stop. I recognize the uniform, and I know it has the authority of the government behind it. Dressed up in civilian clothes, the crossing guard does not have the authority to stop cars. By analogy, when we are suited up in Jesus' uniform and use the authority of His name, God recognizes His son and grants our petition.

As a final example, consider a soldier who is given a document signed by his commanding officer that requests the quartermaster to give him a new shirt. If the soldier goes to the quartermaster by himself with no authorization, the quartermaster will not give him the shirt. But if the soldier presents his petition with the signed authority of his commanding officer, the quartermaster recognizes the commanding officer's authority and gives the soldier his petition. Again by analogy, when we come to the Father we have no standing in ourselves. It is in the authority of the Lord Jesus that we are making our request. The Father recognizes the authority of His Son and grants our petition.

The Church Owns the Keys to Unlock the Kingdom and Bring God's Will to Earth

We can move heaven to earth because Jesus has the keys to the kingdom and has given them to the church (two or more):

> I am he that liveth, and was dead; and, behold, I am alive for evermore, Amen; and have the keys of hell and of death. — Revelation 1:18 (KJV)

Jesus has given the church the keys to unlock heaven, so we can look into heaven and bring God's will to earth in authoritative prayer:

> And **I will give unto thee the keys** of the kingdom of heaven: and whatsoever thou shalt bind on earth shall be bound in heaven: and whatsoever thou shalt loose on earth shall be loosed in heaven.
> — Matthew 16:19 (KJV, emphasis added)

146

With the keys to the kingdom, the church has a special power to open heaven. We are the stewards that carry the keys and can bind and loose all the forces of the universe consistent with God's will. It is our duty and great privilege to use the keys to bring God's will to earth by speaking authoritatively that *"Thy will be done in earth, as it is in heaven."* Matthew 6:10b (KJV)

Alas, how does the church usually handle prayer concerning a burden? We say:

Lord, you do this thing.

Lord, please do this thing.

Lord, let us sing and praise you. Then maybe you will hear us and do this thing.

Lord, we beg you to do this thing.

The Lord will not answer our prayers until we use the keys to speak authoritatively that God's will be done.

Jesus used His authority given to him by the Father over and over in His ministry on earth. Jesus spoke directly to unclean spirits and cast them out of a man:

> And just then there was in their synagogue a man with an unclean spirit; and he cried out, saying, "What do we have to do with You, Jesus of Nazareth? Have You come to destroy us? I know who You are the Holy One of God!" And Jesus rebuked him, saying, **"Be quiet, and come out of him!"** And throwing him into convulsions, the unclean spirit cried out with a loud voice, and came out of him.
> — Mark 1:23-26 (NAS, emphasis added)

Jesus used His authority to heal a leper:

> And a leper came to Him, beseeching Him and falling on his knees before Him, and saying to Him, "If You are willing, You can make me clean." And moved with compassion, He stretched out His hand, and touched him, and said to him, **"I am willing; be cleansed."** And immediately the leprosy left him and he was cleansed.
> — Mark 1:40-42 (NAS, emphasis added)

147

Jesus used His authority to raise people from the dead as he did Lazarus:

> And when He had said these things, He cried out with a loud voice,
> **"Lazarus, come forth."** He who had died came forth, bound hand and
> foot with wrappings; and his face was wrapped around with a cloth.
> Jesus said to them, "Unbind him, and let him go."
> — John 11:43-44 (NAS, emphasis added)

Jesus used His authority to speak to nature to calm a storm:

> And there arose a fierce gale of wind, and the waves were breaking over
> the boat so much that the boat was already filling up. And He Himself
> was in the stern, asleep on the cushion; and they awoke Him and said
> to Him, "Teacher, do You not care that we are perishing?" And being
> aroused, He rebuked the wind and said to the sea, **"Hush, be still."**
> And the wind died down and it became perfectly calm.
> — Mark 4:37-39 (NAS, emphasis added)

Remember the story of the children of Israel crossing the Red Sea in Exodus 14? A problem arises when the children of Israel arrive at the Red Sea. The Egyptians are hot on their trail. The Israelites become afraid and begin to whine. Moses tells them the Lord will save them. I can just see Moses hiding behind a rock out of sight of the people saying, *"Lord, we are in deep trouble! You must do something!"* God says, "Moses *you* do it." He tells Moses to quit praying and to hold his rod out over the water and the sea will open up:

> Then the Lord said to Moses, "Quit praying and get the people moving!
> Forward, march! Use your rod—hold it out over the water, and the sea will
> open up a path before you, and all the people of Israel shall walk through
> on dry ground! — Exodus 14:15-16 (LVB)

Could Moses divide the Red Sea? No! But with God's authority represented by the rod, he could. It was up to Moses to take action, not God.

A final example of authoritative prayer is where Peter and John healed a lame man:

> But Peter said, "I do not possess silver and gold, but what I do have I give
> to you: **In the name of Jesus Christ the Nazarene walk!**" And seizing

> him by the right hand, he raised him up; and immediately his feet and
> his ankles were strengthened. And with a leap, he stood upright and be-
> gan to walk; and he entered the temple with them, walking and leaping
> and praising God. — Acts 3:5-8 (NAS, emphasis added)

Peter and John (two or more) saw a lame man at the temple. No doubt Peter and John felt a burden for the lame man. The Holy Spirit gave a supernatural gift of healing through Peter to the lame man. Peter spoke authoritatively and said "In the name of Jesus Christ of Nazareth rise up and walk." The lame man was instantly healed and began walking, leaping, and praising God.

Jesus directed us to speak with authorative prayer to deal directly with life's burdens:

> For verily I say unto you, That whosoever shall say unto this mountain,
> **Be thou removed, and be thou cast into the sea**; and shall not doubt
> in his heart, but shall believe that those things which he saith shall come
> to pass; he shall have whatsoever he saith. Therefore I say unto you,
> What things soever ye desire, when ye pray, believe that ye receive them,
> and ye shall have them. — Mark 11:23-34 (KJV, emphasis added)

The mountain represents a burden the church is praying about. We do not beg God to do something about this mountain. When we know God's will, we speak directly and authoritatively to the mountain and say, "In Jesus' name, be thou removed." We can do great things because it is Jesus that is moving the mountain through us.

Ordinary prayer asks God to bind and loose. Authoritative prayer is us-ing the authority invested in the church to bind and loose.

Points to Remember

In this chapter, we looked at using authoritative prayer together as the body of Christ. The important points were:

1. Authoritative prayer is where we use the authority of the Lord Jesus to deal directly with life's burdens.
2. The name "Lord Jesus" is above all other names.
3. Jesus' name represents authority.
4. Jesus' name is committed to the church.
5. Jesus' name is the seal of corporate prayer.
6. In corporate prayer, we are expected to use the authority of the name of Jesus.

Questions for Personal Reflection

Before going to the next chapter, take time to reflect on your answers to the following questions:

1. How do you feel about having the authority to use Jesus' name to move God's will from heaven to earth?
2. Are you willing to boldly use Jesus' name in public prayer to execute His will on earth?

Chapter 12

Step 7: Possessing God's Answer by Faith

In Steps 1 to 6 of the directions for corporate prayer, we have gotten individually on praying ground; gathered a corporate group to pray in the unity of the Spirit; come together corporately to praise God; determined which petition God wants us to talk to Him about; corporately determined God's will regarding the petition; and in the authority of Jesus' name asked God to move His will from heaven to earth.

We are now at Step 7 of the directions for corporate prayer—possessing God's answer to our corporate prayer through faith.

꙳

The seven friends studied "Step 7: Possessing God's Answer by Faith" all week to prepare for their Sunday night meeting at Mary's house. From talking together in Sunday School class that morning, it was clear to all of the friends that this was an important topic. Let's tune in as they discuss this step:

Mary: "Remember the old saying *seeing is believing*? From my study of this chapter, it appears the Bible turns this around when we talk about faith, and it becomes *believing is seeing.*"

Hank: "I had never realized that God has given us spiritual eyes so that we can walk by faith and not by physical sight."

Amanda: "I liked the verse in Hebrews that says *"faith is the sub-stance of things hoped for"*...If I understand it correct-ly, active faith allows us to possess God's answer and act as though the transaction with God is finished even though it is not yet a reality on earth. That is pretty deep."

Joe: "The size of my faith must be almost infinitesimal since the Bible says that if you have faith the size of a tiny mustard seed you can say to a mountain 'Move' and it will move far away. My faith is sure not big enough to move mountains."

Sue: "Looks like a really important thing for us to do is to grow the size of our faith from little faith to great faith by depending on God more and more."

Bill: "I really like the idea of the *faith-sized* prayer requests. Faith-sizing my prayer requests lets me grow my faith a little at a time and helps me deal with doubt."

Jack: "I believe that by praying together and pooling our faith, we can help sustain each other's faith and remove doubt."

Hank: "As you know, I have been struggling with praise. One thing I've found out in the last few weeks is that praise helps us recognize that God is in control of our world thereby increasing our faith and driving doubt from our hearts."

The friends have learned their lesson on possessing God's answer by faith very well. They are now prepared to present a burden to God having already de-termined His will and believe through faith that God will answer their prayer.

౿

Step 7 where the corporate prayer group possesses the answer to their prayer by faith is depicted in Figure 12-1:

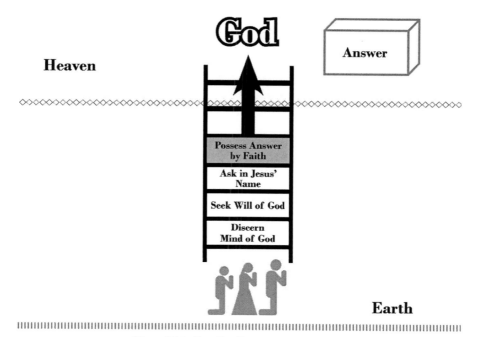

Figure 12-1. Step 7 – Corporate prayer group
possesses the answer to their prayer by faith.

Faith is Substance

Once we are clear on the will of God regarding our burden, we can claim and bring God's will to earth by faith using the authority of Jesus' name. We now live as though God's answer is a reality. It has been transacted in heaven, and it is done. Faith allows us to possess the answer. Look at Hebrews 11:1:

> Now faith is the substance of things hoped for, the evidence of things not
> seen. — Hebrews 11:1 (KJV)

What a fabulous verse! Faith is the evidence of things not seen with our physical eyes. Faith is substance. Faith is bringing the future to the present. Faith makes visible that which is not seen.

Prayer gets us to God's storehouse. Faith is the key that unlocks God's storehouse and pours down God's answer on the church. However, before God acts, there must be active faith on the part of the church. God's formula for making prayers a reality is given in Hebrews 4:1-3:

> Although God's promise still stands — his promise that all may enter his place of rest — we ought to tremble with fear because some of you may be on the verge of failing to get there after all. For this wonderful news — the message that God wants to save us — has been given to us just as it was to those who lived in the time of Moses. But it didn't do them any good because they didn't believe it. They didn't **mix** it with faith.
> — Hebrews 4:1-2 (LVB, emphasis added)

In simple terms:

$$\textit{FACT = PROMISE + FAITH}$$

If we mix God's promises with our faith, the promise is turned into a fact whether we have seen it or not in the present. Prayer is the medium that transforms God's promises mixed with our faith into reality.

Three Elements of Faith

Faith is based upon our believing the Word of God with our whole soul and not upon feelings and emotions by themselves, our human experience, or our human knowledge:

> So then faith cometh by hearing, and hearing by the Word of God.
> — Romans 10:17 (KJV)

There are three elements to faith:

- Mind—intellectual
- Emotions—emotional
- Will—volitional

By faith the mind believes in God, the emotions respond to God's love, and the will obeys the commands of God. All of the elements of faith have to work together for us to have complete faith.

Let's take your favorite football team. To have complete faith in the football team, you need all three elements of faith to come into play. The intellectual part of faith is your knowledge of the capabilities of the great players you have. Your mind tells you that the team has sufficient talent to win the national championship. This gives you intellectual faith. The emotional part of faith is your love of the team: its past performance, the passion of the team, and excitement of the game. Because you love them, it gives you emotional faith. The volitional part of faith is the decision to buy season tickets and go to each game to cheer for your team. You have put feet to your faith by an act of will. This act of will gives you the volitional part of faith.

The Holy Spirit speaks to our inner spirits which prompts all three elements of faith working together within our soul—complete faith—to move mountains. When only one or two of the elements of faith work together, we do not have complete faith.

Let's look at something every believer can identify with—their salvation experience. The Holy Spirit prompts our spirits to believe in Jesus as our Lord and Savior. We know it is the Father's will since He told us so in John 3:16:

> For God so loved the world, that he gave his only begotten Son, that
> whosoever believeth in him should not perish, but have everlasting life.
> — John 3:16 (KJV)

This is God's promise for us to claim. However, all three elements of faith have to work together.

If intellectually, my **mind** understands what the Bible says about Jesus and salvation, but my heart does not embrace the Word, I lack sufficient faith and cannot claim salvation. If my **emotions** get caught up in religious fervor wanting God to save me and wishing He would do it, but my mind does not understand the need for repentance and for asking Jesus into my heart, I lack sufficient faith and can not claim salvation. If my intellect has accepted the need for repentance and asking Jesus into my heart, my emotions want to embrace Jesus as Savior, but my will is unable to step out in faith and embrace Jesus publicly, there is insufficient faith to claim salvation.

Our spirit is prompted by the Holy Spirit to seek God. As we intellectually understand that we are sinners and that Jesus can save us from sin, emotion-ally want to accept Jesus into our hearts and repent of our sins, and are willing to step out and say so to the world, Christ will answer our prayers and save our souls to everlasting life.

Faith Requires Action

Things only happen when we put our volitional will into gear and act. In Manley Beasley's *Faith Workbook* he says, "Faith is acting as though a thing is so, when it is not, in order for it to be so."[1]

The woman with the issue of blood (Mark 5:26-29) believed by faith she would be healed if she touched Jesus' garment. She *acted* on her belief, and was healed. Jairus believed by faith that Jesus could bring his daughter back to life in spite of the laughter, doubt, and ridicule of his coworkers, family and friends (Mark 5:35-36). He *acted* on what he believed, and she was raised from the dead. The ten lepers asked Jesus to heal them (Luke 17:11-14). They were not healed as they stood there. They were healed *as they went* to show themselves to the priest.

Again Manley Beasley sums it up best in this quote "Faith is so acting on the word, and the will of God, that God has to perform a miracle to keep His Word."[2]

If we say we have faith and do not act on that faith, it is worth nothing. James writes:

> What doth it profit, my brethren, though a man say he hath faith,
> and have not works? — James 2:14a (KJV)

We Are to Walk by Faith

We are to walk by faith and not by sight. We are to use our spiritual eyes to see God's answer to prayer.

A story in the Bible about using spiritual eyes is found in II Kings 6:14-17. One night the King of Syria sent a great army to surround the city of Dothan where Elisha lived. The next morning the prophet Elisha's servant went outside and saw the great army. He reacted to only what he saw with his physical eyes.

Elisha said "Don't be afraid, our army is bigger than theirs." Elisha prayed that God would open the servant's spiritual eyes so that he could see the vast army of God. And the Lord answered Elisha's prayer and opened the servant's eyes as we see in the following verses:

> Then Elisha prayed and said, "O Lord, I pray, open his eyes that he may see." And the Lord opened the servant's eyes, and he saw; and behold, the mountain was full of horses and chariots of fire all around Elisha.
> — II Kings 6:17 (NAS)

One day Jesus asked His disciples who they thought he was, and this is what they said:

> And Simon Peter answered and said, Thou art the Christ, the Son of the living God. And Jesus answered and said unto him, Blessed art thou, Simon Barjona: for flesh and blood hath not revealed it unto thee, but my Father which is in heaven. — Matthew 16:16-17 (KJV)

Jesus told Peter that flesh and blood had not let him see this. God the Father had opened the spiritual eyes of Peter's heart.

Paul prayed for the Ephesians to have their spiritual eyes opened. It is a prayer that we can pray for each other:

> I pray that the eyes of your heart may be enlightened, so that you may know what is the hope of His calling, what are the riches of the glory of His inheritance in the saints. — Ephesians 1:18 (NAS)

We do not walk spiritually by natural sight or by our other senses. We walk spiritually by faith using our spiritual eyes:

> For we walk by faith, not by sight... — II Corinthians 5:7 (KJV)

We Must Not Doubt

To possess our answer to corporate prayer, we must ask in faith and not doubt. Jesus speaks to this in Mark 11:23-24:

"Truly I say to you, whoever says to this mountain, 'Be taken up and cast into the sea,' and does not doubt in his heart, but believes that what he says is going to happen, it shall be granted him. "Therefore I say to you, all things for which you pray and ask, believe that you have received them, and they shall be granted you." — Mark 11:23-24 (NAS)

Doubt is fatal to faith. Doubt is a weakness in the Christian's life. Doubt comes when we are not clear on the will of God. Doubt while we pray or after we have prayed will not result in a faith that brings answers to corporate prayer. Think of doubt as like a poison that enters the soul destroying our faith connection with God thereby hindering God's ability to answer our prayer. This idea is pictured in Figure 12-2.

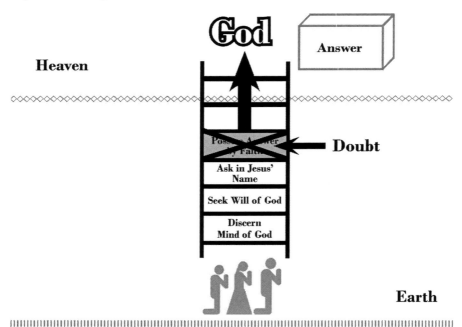

Figure 12-2. Doubt will keep the corporate
prayer group from possessing God's answer by faith.

Before God will answer our prayers, we must believe with unwavering faith that God will answer them.

Satan will try to create doubt in our minds by telling us that:

- We have committed too many terrible sins for God to answer our prayers
- We don't know how to pray and are praying incorrectly
- We don't really know the will of God

Satan wants us to vacillate between faith and doubt, making our prayers of no effect. This is addressed in James 1:6-8:

> But let him ask in faith without any doubting, for the one who doubts is like the surf of the sea driven and tossed by the wind. For let not that man expect that he will receive anything from the Lord, being a double-minded man, unstable in all his ways. — James 1:6-8 (NAS)

A wave tosses to and fro never staying in one place. We cannot expect solid answers to prayer if our minds toss back and forth between faith and doubt.

Most of us are afraid to step out in faith. We are afraid to fail. We are unwilling to get in trouble so that God can move mountains and help. What we need is mountain moving faith in the church. We, like the apostles, need to ask Jesus to teach us about mountain moving faith:

> One day the apostles said to the Lord, `"We need more faith; tell us how to get it." — Luke 17:5 (LVB)

Jesus responded by saying:

> And the Lord said, "If you had faith like a mustard seed, you would say to this mulberry tree, 'Be uprooted and be planted in the sea'; and it would obey you." — Luke 17:6 (NAS)

If we pray in faith, we can move mountains and throw trees into the sea. The Bible promises us that we will have what we ask:

> And this is the confidence that we have in him, that, if we ask any thing
> according to his will, he heareth us: And if we know that he hear us,
> whatsoever we ask, we know that we have the petitions that we
> desired of him. — I John 5:14-15 (KJV)

If God has told us His will, there is no reason to doubt. If we begin to doubt, we should immediately begin to praise God with all our hearts. Paul E. Billheimer writes "And the secret of faith without doubt is praise, triumphant praise, continuous praise, praise that is a way of life. This is the solution to the problem of a living faith and successful prayer."[3]

As we saw earlier in Chapter 8, God inhabits the praises of his people:

> But thou art holy, O thou that inhabitest the praises of Israel.
> — Psalms 22:3 (KJV)

Praise fires up faith and drives doubt from the heart. God comes to His people when we praise Him. Praise recognizes that God is in control.

There is nothing more beautiful than child-like faith that has no room for doubt. One that has a faith that simply believes that our Father can do whatever we ask of Him. E. M. Bounds relates the following story of child-like faith:

> "A child lay sick in a country cottage, and her younger sister heard the doctor say, as he left the house, "Nothing but a miracle can save her." The little girl went to her money-box, took out the few coins it contained, and in perfect simplicity of heart went to shop after shop in the village street, asking, "Please, I want to buy a miracle." From each she came away disappointed. Even the local chemist had to say, "My dear, we don't sell miracles here." But outside his door two men were talking, and had overheard the child's request. One was a great doctor from a London hospital, and he asked her to explain what she wanted. When he understood the need, he hurried with her to the cottage, examined the sick girl, and said to the mother: "It is true—only a miracle can save her, and it must be performed at once." He got his instruments, performed the operation, and the patient's life was saved."[4]

In child-like faith, the younger sister looked for a miracle and found one. We too should believe our God is able to do what we ask.

Praying Faith-Sized Requests

Rosalind Rinker in *Prayer: Conversing with God* suggests we use "faith-sized" prayer requests to increase the size of our faith and remove doubt.[5] We should make requests of the Father that are just the right "believing" size for our faith. She says "This does not limit what God can do, but it honestly recognizes the size of your faith."[6] She beautifully illustrates the power of faith-sized prayers in the following story:

> "When Karen prayed for the conversion of her boy friend, Chuck, she was unable to believe he would be saved the first week, but she was able to believe that, on the very next date, she could tell him about her own Savior. She was enabled to do this. Then she prayed that he would accept a New Testament. He did. Then, that he would be willing to read it. He was willing. And the story goes on, until two weeks after her first request, Chuck made an open acknowledgment of faith in Jesus Christ."[7]

Too often, we want to move the entire mountain all at one time. It is not that God is not willing to do it. The problem is our faith. Sometimes it is best to start moving the mountain a shovel full at a time. With successive faith-sized requests for what you believe God can do, before you know it God has moved the mountain one faith-sized prayer request at a time.

In her classic book *The Christian's Secret of a Happy Life*, Hannah Whitall Smith writes "It is a law of the spiritual life that every act of trust makes the next act less difficult, until at length, if these acts are persisted in, trusting becomes, like breathing, the natural unconscious action of the redeemed soul."[8]

What are you personally believing God to do right now that is bigger than you but is faith-sized? To live by faith we need to be actively at all times depending on God for an answer to prayer that is impossible for us to accomplish by ourselves. It is by asking God to accomplish what we cannot that we give Him the glory that is due Him. Paul addressed this in Hebrews 11:6:

> But without faith it is impossible to please him: for he that cometh to God must believe that he is, and that he is a rewarder of them that diligently seek him. — Hebrews 11:6 (KJV)

Your prayer journal should have recorded right now one or more faith-sized prayer requests that you or your corporate prayer group have by faith claimed as fact based on the Holy Spirit telling you it was the will of God. You should also have gone on record publicly that you have believed God for this answer, and you are waiting for God to perform.

John Hyde known as "Praying Hyde" had a burning in his heart for lost souls. His burden was so great that he plead with the Father "Father, give me these souls or I die!"[9]

By faith, John Hyde was led to make a definite covenant with God. This was for one soul to be saved every day. By the end of a year, 400 souls were saved. His burden for the lost intensified. He now came to God in prayer with a definite request for two souls a day. That year, 800 souls were saved. He was still not satisfied and the third year he claimed by faith four souls a day for Christ. He spent many long nights in prayer, and God delivered. The point of this story is that as John Hyde's faith grew, he could believe God for bigger and bigger things.

When I began writing this chapter, I was teaching a newly formed young adult Sunday School class about what the Bible had to say about faith. I realized that I was not practicing what I was teaching. I was not personally believing God to do something that was impossible for me to do by myself. As a result, I felt that God wanted me to undertake a faith-sized prayer request that only He could accomplish. Here is what happened.

At the time, the class had around 40 members that were all new to our church. I believed in my heart that the Holy Spirit was prompting me to ask God for 20 new class members over the next nine months—a 50% increase. I knew that by my physical efforts, I might reach 10 new members; however, it would take God to grow the class by 20 members. Since I believed it was impossible for me to do, God alone would get the glory when the prayer was answered.

I announced to the class that by faith I believed God was going to bring us 20 new class members by the end of the year. I asked the class to join me in this faith quest. We entered the fight of faith (I Timothy 6:12) to not doubt. Yes, there were whispers that asked, "What are you going to tell the class about faith when you fail to reach the 20 new members?" It was scary to step out on faith. However, I continued to believe that God would perform, and praised Him for the results I knew would come to pass but at present could not see.

Everyday, I reminded God in prayer that it was up to Him to perform. I refused to add up how many new members were joining our class because I was afraid that if we were short I would try to help God. We continued our faith quest right up to the end of the year. The class members invited their friends and visitors to our church and class. Others found their way to our class on their own. When we added up the number of new members the last Sunday in December, the total was 22! God was indeed faithful and answered our faith-sized request. You can imagine the joy in our class. What a great Christmas present it was for the class to learn that God indeed answers our prayers if we follow His directions.

You may scoff and say, "You asked for only 20 new members!" For me, this was a faith-sized request. For John Hyde, it would no doubt have been 800 members. With faith-sized prayers, we can grow our faith from "little" faith to "great" faith.

The Gift of Faith

The Bible also speaks of a "gift of faith." In corporate prayer, God may give a gift of faith to one of the believers in the prayer group for the benefit of the body of Christ:

> But the manifestation of the Spirit is given to every man to profit withal. For to one is given by the Spirit the word of wisdom; to another the word of knowledge by the same Spirit; To another faith by the same Spirit… — I Corinthians 12:7-9a (KJV)

A one time "gift of faith" is faith given to one or more believers by the Holy Spirit to know the will of God without being troubled by doubt so that they confidently believe their prayer will be answered. This is illustrated in Figure 12-3.

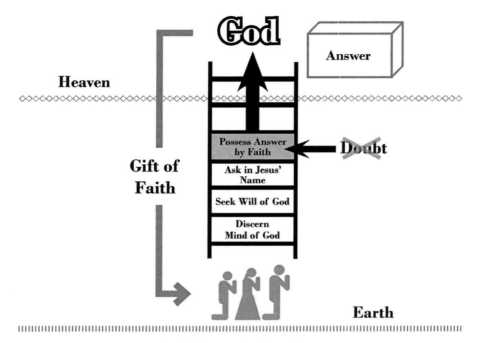

Figure 12-3. A gift of faith is given by the Holy Spirit to a corporate
prayer group to believe with absolute confidence that God has answered their prayer.

The gift of faith is given to accomplish God's purpose in the church. A gift of faith requires neither seeing nor believing on the part of the believer's soul. No question of doubt arises with a gift of faith as it can with ordinary faith.

I first experienced a gift of faith when Becky and Terry (two members of our corporate prayer group) asked a few of us to pray with them concerning two burdens. Terry was an intercity Baptist missionary, and Becky was a registered nurse. They had been unable to have children, and Becky had recently had an x-ray that showed a potentially cancerous spot on the bone in one of her legs that might require amputation. They asked us to pray for them in the manner of James 5:14.

As we prayed for Becky and Terry, the Holy Spirit gave several of us absolute confidence that Becky would be healed, and that they would have children. In the next x-ray taken by her doctor, the spot on her leg was gone. They had twins less than a year later. Becky and Terry gave God all the glory for His answer to prayer. Both have been greatly used by God in their intercity ministry.

There is another wonderful example of a gift of faith being given by the Holy Spirit in R. A. Torrey's book *The Power of Prayer*. Mr. Torrey says:

> "For example, while I was pastor of the Moody Church in Chicago, the little daughter of a man and woman who were members of our church was taken ill. She first had the measles, and the measles were followed by meningitis. She sank very low, and the doctor said to her mother, "I can do no more for your child. She cannot live." The mother immediately hurried down to my house to get me to come up to their house and pray for her child. But I was out of town holding meetings in Pittsburgh. So she sent for the assistant pastor, Rev. W. S. Jacoby, and he went up to the house with one of my colleagues, and prayed for the child."
>
> "That night when I got home from Pittsburgh he came around to my house to tell me about it, and he said, "Mr. Torrey, if I ever had an answer to my prayers in my life, it was today when I was praying for the Duff child." He was confident that God had heard his prayer and that the child would be healed. And the child was healed right away. This was Saturday."
>
> "The next morning the doctor called again at the home and there was such a remarkable change in the child that he said to Mrs. Duff, "What have you done for your child?" She told him just what she had done. Then he said, "Well, I will give her some more medicine.""
>
> "No, she said, "you will not. You said you could do no more for her, that she must die and we went to God in prayer and God has healed her. You are not going to take the honor to your self by giving her some more medicine." Indeed, the girl was not only improved that morning, she was completely well."[10]

The important point in these two examples is that the gift of faith brings into your heart *absolutely unshakeable confidence* that God has answered the corporate prayer. You do not have to go through the fight of faith where doubt assails you.

Points to Remember

In this chapter, we have possessed God's answer to our prayer by faith. The important points are:

1. Faith is substance, the evidence of things not seen.
2. Faith unlocks God's storehouse.
3. If we mix God's promises with our faith, it is a fact whether we have seen it or not with our physical eyes in the present.
4. We are to walk in faith and not by physical sight. We are to use our spiritual eyes to see God's answer to prayer.
5. There are three elements to faith: intellectual, emotional, and volitional. All of the elements of faith have to work together for us to have complete faith.
6. To possess our answer to prayer, we must not doubt.
7. Praise is the secret to drive doubt from our heart.
8. Faith-sized prayer requests allow us to grow our faith and help remove doubt.
9. In corporate prayer, God may give a gift of faith to one or more believers for the benefit of the body of Christ.

Questions for Personal Reflection

Before going to the next chapter, take time to reflect on your answers to the following questions:

1. Are you walking by faith and actively depending on God every day for answers to prayer that are impossible for you to accomplish by yourself?
2. Do you like the idea of praying faith-sized prayer requests to increase the size of your faith and remove doubt?

Chapter 13

Step 8: Persisting in Prayer and Praising the Lord

In Steps 1 to 7, we have: taken our place before God by getting individually on praying ground; come together corporately to praise God and determined corporately which petition God wants to hear and act on; corporately determined God's will regarding the petition; in the authority of Jesus' name asked God to move His will from heaven to earth; and by faith possessed God's answer to our prayer.

We are now at the final step of God's directions for corporate prayer—to persist in prayer believing God has answered our prayer and to praise God for the answer whether we can see it physically or not.

❧

The seven friends gather at Hank's condo on Sunday night to discuss "Step 8: Persisting in Prayer and Praising the Lord." This is the last step they will study before starting a corporate prayer group. Let's listen as they begin their meeting:

> Amanda: "Now, I understand more about why faith is so important after studying this chapter. We must keep our faith strong while we persist in prayer until the answer comes."

Bill: "It is important that we not give up before the answer is a reality on earth."

Joe: "Seems like it would be so easy for God to just go ahead and answer our prayer if our will is in harmony with His will."

Jack: "It appears that God answers our prayers in heaven as soon as we pray. However, sometimes He allows a delay in the answer coming to earth to teach us how to overcome Satan and to refine our soul by further changing us into the image of His Son."

Sue: "That is why we must persist, persist, persist and never give up on God making His answer a reality on earth. We must be patient."

Hank: "Recognizing we already have what we ask even if it has not appeared on earth, it is right that we offer praise and thanks to God.

Jack: "Based on what we have learned, we should offer praise and thanks to God when we begin our prayers, and when we end our prayers."

Mary: "I really look forward to starting our new prayer group next Sunday night."

The friends now understand they need to persist in prayer to God until the answer comes to earth. And, believing that God has answered their prayer, they need to offer Him continuous praise and thanksgiving.

☙

Step 8 addresses the need for the corporate prayer group to persist in prayer until the answer comes to earth. This step is illustrated in Figure 13-1.

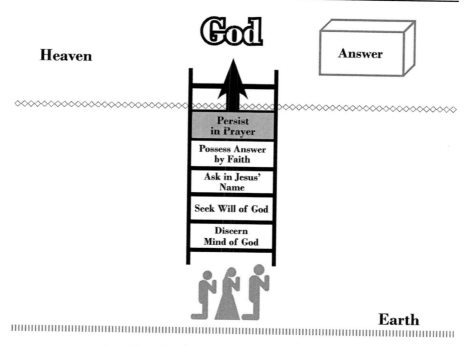

Figure 13-1. Step 8 – Corporate prayer group must persist
in prayer and praise believing God has answered their prayer.

Persist In Prayer Until the Answer Comes

Jesus told his disciples that there was a need for constant prayer that persists in faith until the answer comes. To emphasize the need to persist in faith until God answers our prayer, Jesus told the following story to His disciples:

> One day Jesus told his disciples a story to illustrate their need for constant prayer and to show them that they must keep praying until the answer comes. Now He was telling them a parable to show that at all times they ought to pray and not to lose heart, saying, "There was in a certain city a judge who did not fear God, and did not respect man. "And there was a widow in that city, and she kept coming to him, saying, `Give me legal protection from my opponent.' "And for a while he was unwilling; but afterward he said to himself, `Even though I do not fear God nor respect man, yet because this widow bothers me, I will give her legal protection, lest by continually coming she wear me out.'" And the Lord said, "Hear what the unrighteous judge said; now shall not God bring about justice for His elect, who cry to Him day and night, and will He delay long over them?"
> — Luke 18:2-7 (NAS)

169

Earlier in Luke 11:5-8, Jesus used the parable of the persistent friend who needed bread to make the same point. If we persist in prayer and have faith, God will deliver.

The church obeyed Jesus' directions to keep praying until the answer comes and prayed without ceasing for Peter's release from jail:

> Peter therefore was kept in prison: but prayer was made without ceasing of the church unto God for him. — Acts 12:5 (KJV)

Paul echoed Jesus' directions to persist in prayer as he spoke to the Thessalonians by commanding that we are to:

> Pray without ceasing. — I Thessalonians 5:17 (KJV)

In Ephesians 6:18, Paul again tells us to pray all the time:

> Pray all the time. Ask God for anything in line with the Holy Spirit's wishes. Plead with him, reminding him of your needs, and keep praying earnestly for all Christians everywhere. — Ephesians 6:18 (LVB)

It is clear from the preceding scripture that we are to pray without ceasing once we know God's will. We are to persist in prayer believing in faith until the answer comes to earth. Jesus said that after seeking and finding God's will, we are to knock until the doors of heaven are open to us:

> Ask, and it shall be given you; seek, and ye shall find; knock, and it shall be opened unto you... — Matthew 7:7 (KJV)

We are to persist in our knocking until the impossible becomes the possible.

Our prayer must be intense and earnest. Every part of our being must be focused as we pray to God. Jesus prayed earnestly in the Garden of Gethsemane. In Luke 22:43-44, it says that Jesus was praying so earnestly that sweat like great drops of blood fell to the ground:

> Now an angel from heaven appeared to Him, strengthening Him. And being in agony He was praying very fervently; and His sweat became like drops of blood, falling down upon the ground. — Luke 22:43-44 (NAS)

Few men and women have ever experienced the intense and earnest intercessory prayer of Jesus in the Garden of Gethsemane. God has called some men to be prayer intercessors like Rees Howell, David Brainerd and John Hyde. The Holy Spirit moved them to pray in great intensity and with great earnest. In response to their prayers, God greatly changed our world.

David Brainerd was a missionary to the North American Indians in Northern Pennsylvania. He was wracked with illness, but continued in intercessory prayer for the Indians. He spent many nights in prayer. The intensity of his prayer was such that he would be wringing wet with sweat. God answered his prayer by sending a mighty revival among the Indians. His persistence in prayer is seen from his journal;

> "...near the middle of the afternoon God enabled me to wrestle ardently in intercession for absent friends; but just at night the Lord visited me marvelously in prayer. I think my soul never was in such agony before. I felt no restraint, for the treasures of divine grace were opened to me. I wrestled for absent friends, for the ingathering of souls, for multitudes of poor souls, and for many that I thought were children of God, in many distant places."[1]

The intensity of John Hyde's prayers is seen in the following observation:

> "The place where John Hyde met God was holy ground. The scenes of his life are too sacred for common eyes. I shrink from placing them before the public. But near the prayer closet of John Hyde we are permitted to hear the sighing and the groaning, and to see the tears coursing down his dear face, to see his frame weakened by foodless days and sleepless nights, shaken with sobs as he pleads, "O God, give me souls or I die!"[2]

These men would wrestle God and not let up until they had prayed through to the will of God, claimed it as reality, and then persisted in faith until the answer came to earth. We have God's promise in Jeremiah that we will find God if we look in earnest:

> And ye shall seek me, and find me, when ye shall search for me with
> all your heart. — Jeremiah 29:13 (KJV)

If we don't get an answer the first time we pray, we should pray again and again.

The great prayer intercessor George Muller says we fail in prayer because we do not continue in prayer until the blessing is obtained. He writes;

> "It is not enough to begin to pray, nor to pray aright; nor is it enough to continue *for a time* to pray; but we must patiently, believingly continue in prayer, until we obtain an answer: and further, we have not only to *continue* in prayer unto the end, but we have also to *believe* that God does hear us and will answer our prayers. Most frequently we fail *in not continuing* in prayer until the blessing is obtained, and in not expecting the blessing."[3]

Often we give up when the goal is in sight and would be obtained if we just persisted a little longer. We are to never give up. Never give up. Never give up until the answer comes!

The blessings from persisting in prayer until the answer comes are demonstrated in a story told by Pastor Bill Hybels:

> "Some years ago we had a baptism Sunday where many people publicly affirmed their decision to follow Christ. I thought my heart would explode for joy. Afterward, in the stairwell, I bumped into a woman who was crying. I couldn't understand how anyone could weep after such a celebration, so I stopped and asked her if she was all right.
>
> 'No,' she said, 'I'm struggling. My mother was baptized today.'
>
> This is a problem I thought.
>
> 'I prayed for her every day for twenty years,' the woman said, and then she started crying again.
>
> 'You're going to have to help me understand this,' I said.
>
> 'I'm crying,' the woman replied, 'because I came so close—so close—to giving up on her. I mean after five years I said, 'Who needs this? God isn't listening.' After ten years I said, 'Why am I wasting my breath?' After fifteen years I said, 'This is absurd.' After nineteen years I said, 'I'm just a fool. But I guess I just kept praying, even though my faith was weak. I kept praying, and she gave her life to Christ, and she was baptized today.'
>
> The woman paused and looked me in the eye. 'I will never doubt the power of prayer again,' she said."[4]

Why Must We Persist Until the Answer Comes?

Jesus has told us we must persist in faith until the answer comes. The question naturally arises as to why our prayers aren't answered immediately. Listen to the words of Isaiah:

> I will answer them before they even call to me. While they are still talk-
> ing to me about their needs, I will go ahead and answer their prayers!
> — Isaiah 65:24 (LVB)

Also, Jesus says in Mark 11:24 that if we pray in faith according to the will of God, the answer to our prayer is immediately sent by God to us from heaven:

> Listen to me! You can pray for anything, and if you believe, you have it;
> it's yours! — Mark 11:24 (LVB)

If God answers our prayers immediately, then why is the answer delayed in getting to us, and why must we persist in prayer? We will attempt to answer both of these questions.

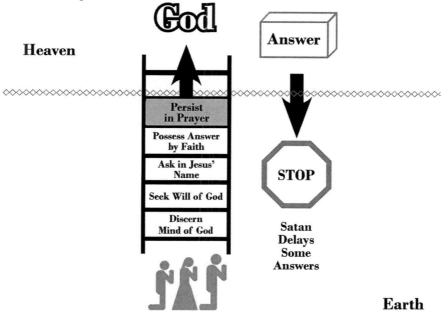

Figure 13-2. God sometimes allows Satan to delay answers to
prayer to grow our faith and further change us into the image of His Son.

Even though God has immediately answered our prayers of faith in heaven, God has permitted Satan and his evil forces to delay the answer to some of our prayers being received on earth from heaven. This is illustrated in Figure 13-2 on the previous page.

There are at least two reasons as to why God permits Satan to delay our answers. The first is to teach us how to overcome Satan and his evil forces while we are here on earth and thereby bring us to greater spiritual maturity. The second reason is to refine our soul and further change us into the image of His Son.

To Learn to Overcome Satan

The first reason that God permits Satan to delay our answers to prayer is to help us learn how to overcome Satan and his evil forces here on earth by being persistent in prayer.

Satan is a defeated enemy. God could have put Satan and his evil forces completely away after Calvary. However, He chose to use Satan to give the Church "on-the-job" training in overcoming the forces hostile to God. This training is to prepare us to be co-rulers with Christ in heaven.[5]

As a result, God allows Satan and his evil forces to attempt to prevent the answer to our prayers from getting through to us. Satan's goal is to defeat our faith. God's goal is for us to grow our faith. We find that this was the experience of the prophet Daniel:

> And I heard his voice —"O Daniel, greatly beloved of God," he said,
> "stand up and listen carefully to what I have to say to you, for God has
> sent me to you." So I stood up, still trembling with fear. Then he said,
> "Don't be frightened, Daniel, for your request has been heard in heaven
> and was answered the very first day you began to fast before the Lord and
> pray for understanding; that very day I was sent here to meet you. But
> for twenty-one days the mighty Evil Spirit who overrules the kingdom
> of Persia blocked my way. Then Michael, one of the top officers of the
> heavenly army, came to help me, so that I was able to break through
> these spirit rulers of Persia." — Daniel 10:12-13 (LVB)

A messenger angel from God came to Daniel in a vision. He told Daniel that God had answered his prayer the very first day that Daniel had prayed.

The messenger angel had been dispatched from heaven to bring the answer to Daniel. However the messenger angel was detained on the way to deliver God's answer to Daniel for three weeks by one of Satan's evil spirits. It was only due to the intervention of the archangel Michael that the messenger angel was able to deliver God's answer to Daniel.

In this passage of scripture there are some very important facts for us to learn. First, a human being was required to ask God in prayer through intercession and have sufficient faith to move the answer from heaven to earth. Second, God answered Daniel's prayer the very first day he prayed. Third, a messenger angel was dispatched from heaven to bring the answer to Daniel. Fourth, one of Satan's evil spirits opposed the messenger angel and delayed the answer getting to Daniel. Fifth, God needed Daniel to persist in prayer and demonstrate his faith while the forces of God and Satan fought. Sixth, God intervened as a result of Daniel's persistent prayer and sent the archangel Michael to clear the way for the answer to be delivered. Seventh, Satan opposed the purpose of God, but in the end he failed.

J. Oswald Sanders observes about Daniel in *Prayer Power Unlimited* that "It was not that his prayers had not been heard, but that they had triggered a conflict in the heavenly realm."[6] Prayer is spiritual warfare. Paul acknowledges this in Ephesians 6:12:

> For we wrestle not against flesh and blood, but against principalities,
> against powers, against the rulers of the darkness of this world, against
> spiritual wickedness in high places. — Ephesians 6:12 (KJV)

Satan is currently the prince of this world. He and his unseen minions rule the earth and the space above the earth as seen in the following two scripture passages:

> Satan, who is the god of this evil world, has made him blind, unable
> to see the glorious light of the Gospel that is shining upon him, or to
> understand the amazing message we preach about the glory of
> Christ, who is God. — II Corinthians 4:4 (LVB)

You went along with the crowd and were just like all the others, full of
sin, obeying Satan, the mighty prince of the power of the air, who is at
work right now in the hearts of those who are against the Lord.
— Ephesians 2:2 (LVB)

We should recognize that unseen evil forces rule the world in which we
live. Satan never allows an answer to prayer to reach earth from heaven if he can
stop it. He will oppose and contest the answer to prayer in order to defeat our
faith. If Satan can get us to give up and not persist in prayer and to doubt, he
can suppress the answer to prayer that is rightfully ours.

Unfortunately, the answer to many prayers that have already been granted in heaven may never show up on earth because the one praying becomes
tired and discouraged and gives up the fight of faith. We must never give up.
We must keep on praying until the answer comes.

So why should we persist in prayer? If we persist in our prayer of faith
and do not doubt, Satan cannot keep God's answer to our prayer from getting
through to us. It is through this fight of faith that God brings us into greater
spiritual maturity. While we persist in our fight of faith, we need to recognize
that we can use the whole armor of God:

Therefore, take up the full armor of God that you may be able to resist
in the evil day, and having done everything, to stand firm.
— Ephesians 6:13 (NAS)

Also available to us in the fight of faith to overcome Satan are all of
the heavenly angels. When Daniel persisted in prayer, never doubting that he
would have his prayer answered, God sent the archangel Michael to clear the
way to deliver the answer. Jack Taylor in his book *Victory Over the Devil* presents
an interesting quote on this subject written by the Puritan minister, Increase
Mather, in 1696 that he had translated from Old English: "Angels both good
and bad have a greater influence on this world than men are generally aware of.
We ought to admire the grace of God toward us sinful creatures in that He hath
appointed Holy Angels to guard us against the mischiefs of wicked spirits who
are intending our hurt both to our bodies and our souls."[7]

We need to be aware that ministering angels abound in heaven. The Apostle John in the book of Revelation states there are millions of angels that surround the throne of God in heaven:

> Then in my vision I heard the singing of millions of angels surrounding the throne and the Living Beings and the Elders... — Revelation 5:11 (LVB)

God uses messenger angels to bring us our answers to prayer. God uses angels to minister and care for us:

> And did God ever say to an angel, as he does to his Son, "Sit here beside me in honor until I crush all your enemies beneath your feet"? No, for the angels are only spirit-messengers sent out to help and care for those who are to receive his salvation. — Hebrews 1:13-14 (LVB)

There are angels waiting to serve us in our time of need since the angels in heaven are under the authority of Christ:

> And now Christ is in heaven, sitting in the place of honor next to God the Father, with all the angels and powers of heaven bowing before him and obeying him. — I Peter 3:22 (LVB)

The important point I want to make here is that as we pray, the forces of good and evil are at work in spiritual warfare. We must, as Jesus told us, persist in prayer, holding fast to our faith until our answer comes. Prayer is the battleground where all our victories are won. We must persist. We must overcome the enemy.

To Further Change Us into The Image of His Son

The second reason God allows Satan to delay our prayers is to refine our soul and further change us into the image of His Son thereby bringing us to greater spiritual maturity.

Even though we have confessed all the sins of which we are aware, God may desire to shape us up in some area of our life that has as yet not been touched by the light of the Holy Spirit. It may be an area where we are totally unaware that we are not pleasing God.

God allows Satan to delay His answer to our prayer until we, in our persistence to receive an answer to our prayer, recognize the area of our life that needs changing. God is looking for a life of brokenness. There may be hidden sins of which we are not aware that He wants us to recognize, repent, and confess. There may be areas of our life that we have not let the Holy Spirit control, and God now wants to control them.

O. Hallesby in *Prayer* sums up why we must persist in prayer when God is trying to change some area of our life so that we look more like Jesus in these words:

> "If wrestling in prayer becomes a hard and bitter struggle, and you feel that your soul is out of touch and tune with God, and your prayers only empty words, then pray trustingly for the Spirit of prayer. He will point out the sin which is acting as a hindrance to your prayers and will help you to acknowledge it. And then He will make Christ so precious to you that you will voluntarily give up that sin which is threatening to sever your connection with God."[8]

Once we acknowledge and confess our sin or surrender the area of our life that God wants to control, answers to our prayers will flow.

There is a wonderful story told by F. J. Huegel in his book *Successful Praying* about the aviator and businessman Eddie Rickenbacker that illustrates why God's answer to prayer is sometime delayed when he has us in His school of prayer:

> "The story of Eddie Rickenbacker and his companions on their rubber rafts for some twenty-two days out on the Pacific Ocean at the mercy of sun and cold and wind and waves, beautifully illustrates the matter of prayer according to the will of God. It will be remembered that one of the men had a Testament which the group asked him to read to them when they saw the comfort he derived from its perusal. The Word awakened faith and the men began to call on the Lord in their desperate need. The answers came thick and fast. Rain to quench their all-consuming thirst, a bird from the sky to feed their famished bodies, in fact everything they asked for was given. All except one thing: that they might be seen and rescued. This was denied them. They could not understand. Why was it that their Heavenly Father gave them everything they asked for save this the chief desire of their hearts?

Finally one of the men suggested that it must be that it was not God's will that they be sighted. They were in a good school—the school of prayer. They had never before taken into account God's Word or called upon His Name in prayer. Surely, when His purposes were fulfilled and they had had more training in the school of prayer, He would see to it that they would be sighted. And so it was. On the twenty-second day a plane that passed overhead sighted them, and they were rescued. *"If we ask anything according to his will, he heareth us."* [9]

In this story, God used the delay in answer to their prayer for rescue to further mature their spiritual faith. Sometimes the period between when we first pray and when God answers our prayer draws us closer to God than the actual answer to prayer itself.

Praise the Lord!

Corporate prayer begins and ends with praise. Believing in faith that God has answered our prayer, we have the victory, and we should praise God for the answer even though with our physical eyes we have not yet seen it on earth. This is illustrated in Figure 13-3.

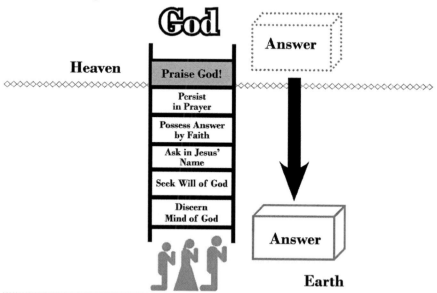

Figure 13-3. We should end our corporate prayers
with praise for God and thank Him for the answered prayer.

As we saw in Chapter 5, Daniel praised God after receiving an answer to his prayer. David praised God *for* answering his prayers:

> When I called, you answered me; you made me bold and stouthearted.
> — Psalms 138:3 (NIV)

Moses praised God for answering the prayer of the children of Israel for deliverance from Pharaoh:

> Then sang Moses and the children of Israel this song unto the Lord, and spake, saying, I will sing unto the Lord, for he hath triumphed gloriously: the horse and his rider hath he thrown into the sea. The Lord is my strength and song, and he is become my salvation: he is my God, and I will prepare him an habitation; my father's God, and I will exalt him. The Lord is a man of war: the Lord is his name.
> — Exodus 15:1-3 (KJV)

Let us along with David shout unto the Lord with a voice of triumph for this is the pattern of the saints in the Bible:

> O Clap your hands, all ye people; shout unto God with the voice of triumph. — Psalms 47:1 (KJV)

Let us praise God together for answering our prayers using Psalms 150:

> Praise ye the Lord. Praise God in his sanctuary: praise him in the firmament of his power. Praise him for his mighty acts: praise him according to his excellent greatness. Praise him with the sound of the trumpet: praise him with the psaltery and harp. Praise him with the timbrel and dance: praise him with stringed instruments and organs. Praise him upon the loud cymbals: praise him upon the high sounding cymbals. Let every thing that hath breath praise the Lord. Praise ye the Lord.
> — Psalm 50 (KJV)

Yes, let everything that hath breath praise the Lord!

Points to Remember

This chapter dealt with the need for constant prayer that persists in faith until the answer comes and our praise for His answer. The important points are:

1. We are to persist in prayer until God's answer is a reality on earth.
2. Our prayer must be intense and earnest.
3. God sometimes allows Satan to delay an answer to prayer in order to deepen our spiritual faith.
4. Just as we begin our corporate prayers with praise, so also are we to end our prayers in praise.

Questions for Personal Reflection

Before going to the next chapter, take time to reflect on the answers to the following questions:

1. Were you aware that Satan's goal is to delay God's answer to your prayer and defeat your faith?
2. If you know the will of God and have claimed the answer by faith, are you willing to persist in prayer until the answer is a reality on earth?

Chapter 14

God's Answers to Our Corporate Prayers

We have completed the discussion of all eight steps of God's directions for corporate prayer. With these directions in mind, we are now ready to gather together in prayer with the confident expectation that God is going to answer our prayers.

❧

The seven friends meet at Hemingway's on Wednesday night after church for Trivia Pursuit. As they play the game, the friends talk about what they have learned from the study of God's directions for how to pray together corporately:

Joe: "It looks to me like the purpose of our starting a corporate prayer group is to ask God to use His supernatural power to do those things we can't do ourselves."

Sue: "I agree. If we can do them in our own power, we don't need to call on God to use His resources."

Mary: "My problem is recognizing God's answers to our prayers. Have any of you received an answer to prayer?"

Bill: "From our study, I have come to understand that I receive a number of answers to prayer daily—God forgives me of my sins, fills me with His Spirit, and protects me. In addition, He tells me what petitions I need to bring to Him in prayer."

Mary:	"What I meant to ask was, have any of you had answers to big prayer requests? Like, our asking God to heal someone who is really sick."
Amanda:	"My Dad has a friend that the doctors gave no hope of recovery. His church, friends, and family all prayed for him to be healed. His illness miraculously went away much to the doctor's amazement."
Bill:	"On the other hand, I had a five-year old cousin who was diagnosed with leukemia. I remember her as sweet and energetic. My aunt and uncle were strong Christians. Their church, friends, and family prayed continuously for her to go into remission. She was not healed and is now in heaven with Jesus. I don't know why God said 'No' to her healing. I am sure when we get to heaven we will understand."
Jack:	"I, like most of you, have prayed for God to cure some one that is sick. After our study of *When Two or More are Gathered...in Prayer*, I now realize that I have been skipping an important step in the process to receive an answer from God. I have been going straight from having a burden for the sick person to asking God to heal them. This totally skipped the step of finding God's will for the situation. I had been praying for healing without knowing what God wanted for the sick person, because I had not asked Him."
Amanda:	"If we don't know His will, it is hard to have the faith needed to possess the answer to our prayer."
Hank:	"My problem is that I want God to tell me 'Yes, it is my will for the sick person to be healed.' I don't want to hear Him say 'No, it is not my will for them to be healed' or 'Continue to pray and seek my will.'"
Jack:	"We must be open to how God wants to answer our petition and not demand that it be a certain way. The outcome of our prayer is not always what we want."

Sue: "Even when I know that God's will is 'Yes' relative to a prayer request, I want Him to bring the answer from heaven to earth right now! Unfortunately, I am not blessed with patience and have a hard time waiting on God's timing. It has been difficult to learn that I must patiently wait, and let the answer come in God's time."

The friends have discovered the wonderful news that God is in the business of changing our world through providing His children answers to their prayers.

෴

God has the answer to our prayers before we make our petitions known to him. We should not be amazed when God answers our prayers. We should expect God to answer every prayer that we pray when we follow God's directions. The answers are stored in heaven with our names on them just waiting for us to possess them as illustrated in Figure 14-1.

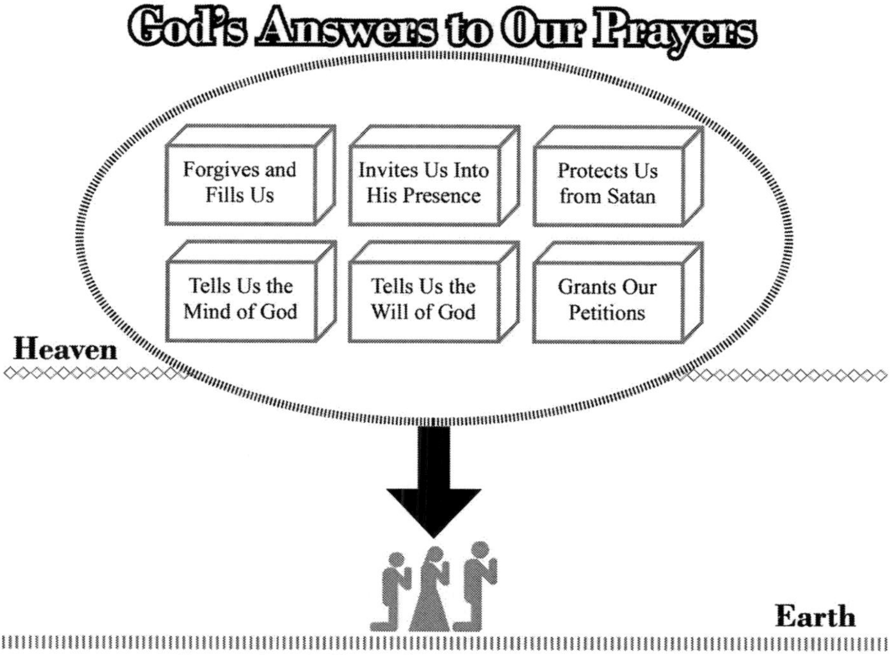

God's Answers to Our Prayers

Forgives and Fills Us

Invites Us Into His Presence

Protects Us from Satan

Tells Us the Mind of God

Tells Us the Will of God

Grants Our Petitions

Heaven

Earth

Figure 14-1. God's specific answers to our prayer requests.

Specific Answers to Prayer

As the corporate prayer group gathers for intercessory prayer, we need to recognize that during our time of prayer, God blesses us with many answers to prayer *before* He answers our prayers of petition. The specific answers to prayer we receive are depicted in Figure 14-1.

In chapter 6, we discussed the importance of coming before God with clean hands and a clean heart. In our private prayer time, before gathering to pray corporately, our first prayer is to ask the Father to forgive us of our sins, ask Jesus to be Lord of our lives, and ask the Father to fill and empower us with His Holy Spirit. The ***first answer*** to prayer we receive, as we prepare to gather in corporate prayer, is God's forgiveness and the filling of the Holy Spirit. We are now on praying ground. We can now be part of the united body of Christ and do the work of the church.

As the corporate prayer group gathers, prayer is made that asks God to bring us into His presence so that we can talk to Him. We saw in Chapter 8 that God inhabits the praise of His people. The ***second answer*** to prayer we receive is God joining us in fellowship and conversation. We are now gathered with Him in the throne room of heaven.

Before the corporate prayer group begins to pray for a specific petition, prayer is made to God for protection from Satan. The ***third answer*** to corporate prayer that we receive is God's protection from Satan and His evil forces while we pray. We are now under God's protection.

We are to pray what God wants us to pray. The Holy Spirit will prompt our spirits to tell us the specific burdens that God has in mind for us to talk to Him about. The ***fourth answer*** to prayer we receive is God telling us the specific burdens for which we are to pray.

As the corporate prayer group starts to pray for a specific petition, it begins by seeking the will of God regarding the petition. The ***fifth answer*** to prayer we receive is God's response to our seeking His will. God wisely and lovingly determines if our prayer request is consistent with His will which is in heaven. Based on whether our will is in harmony with God's will, the Father responds accordingly. God's answer to our seeking His will regarding our petition generally falls into three categories:

- Yes, this is my will!
- No, this is not my will!
- Continue to seek my will!

The outcome of our corporate prayer for a specific petition may not always be what we want or expect. We must be open to how God wants to answer our prayer and not demand that He answer it in a certain way.

The response from the Father could be *"Yes, this is my will. The petition you are asking for is in perfect alignment with my will."* There are many examples in the Bible where God heard his people and answered their prayer. We saw this in Moses and the people of Israel in Egypt. We saw this in the early church's prayer for deliverance of Peter from jail. We saw this in response to authoritative prayer for healing and miracles by Jesus, the apostles, and disciples. We saw this in answer to Cornelius' prayer that resulted in God sending Peter to preach to him.

The response from the Father could be *"No, this petition you are asking for is not my will!"* How would we know if God's answer is no? Your spirit or someone else's spirit in the corporate prayer group may hear the Holy Spirit say "no." Another believer in the gathering may counsel the group that what is being prayed for is not God's will since what is being asked for is contrary to God's Word. You may have a strong impression from the Holy Spirit that what is being requested is not God's will.

Why would God tell us that our petition was not His will? It could be because we have asked for a petition that if granted would not be good for us or for others. It could be because the petition is not consistent with God's purpose. It could be that what is being requested of God violates the free will of the person who is the object of the prayer. This God will not do.

It could be that God does not grant our petition because it is within our own ability to meet the need. If we have the means to meet a need, God expects us to use our means to meet the need, not ask Him to meet the need. This is addressed in James 2:14-16:

> Dear brothers, what's the use of saying that you have faith and are
> Christians if you aren't proving it by helping others? Will that kind of

faith save anyone? If you have a friend who is in need of food and cloth-
ing, and you say to him, "Well, good-bye and God bless you; stay warm
and eat hearty," and then don't give him clothes or food, what good
does that do? — James 2:14-16 (LVB)

An example of God saying "no" to a petition is David's plea to God for
the life of his son that was conceived in adultery (II Samuel 12:13-20). God did
not grant David's petition since it was not consistent with His purpose. When
the baby died, David accepted the will of God, cleansed himself, and worshipped
the Lord.

If God does not grant the group's prayer request because it is not His will,
He will give sufficient grace to cope with the burden. As we saw earlier, Paul requested God to heal him, and God said "no." Instead, God gave him abundant
grace (I Corinthians 12:7-9). God said *"My grace is sufficient for thee."* God will
not leave us without strength and comfort if the answer is no.

The response from the Father as we seek His will could be *"Continue to seek
my will."* If the corporate prayer group cannot find God's will regarding their petition, they should reexamine their individual lives to see if there is some obstruc-
tion between them and God. It may be that God has already spoken and that the
prayer group is unwilling to listen. It may also be that the corporate prayer group
has corporate sins that need to be identified and confessed. After self and group
examination, the group should watch and wait on God to see if their petition
should be changed. If there is a change in the situation regarding the petition,
they should change their prayer and seek new guidance as to God's will.

While we wait on God to tell us His will, we are to pray without ceasing as
we saw in the last chapter. When we pray, if we don't get the answer the first time,
we are to be persistent and pray again, again, and again.

God also may have in mind to give you something better than for what
you are asking. This is captured in the following poem:

He was a Christian, and he prayed,
He asked for strength that he might do greater things,
but he was given infirmity to do better things.
He asked for riches that he might be happy;
he was given poverty that he might be wise.

He asked for power that he might have the praise of men;
he was given weakness that he might feel the need of God.
He asked for all things that he might enjoy life;
he was given life that he might enjoy all things.
He had received nothing that he asked for;
But all that he hoped for.
His prayer is answered, he is most blessed.[1]

We have been told over and over by Jesus that if we would just ask we would receive. But our corporate prayer group has prayed and nothing has changed. In fact, things have taken a turn for the worse. It seems even though we have followed God's directions for corporate prayer, our prayers to determine His will have gone unheeded by the Father. Even King David had a problem sometimes feeling that he was not getting answers to his prayers as we see in the following verses from Psalms:

Hear me when I call, O God of my righteousness: thou hast enlarged me when I was in distress; have mercy upon me, and hear my prayer. — Psalms 4:1 (KJV)

Day and night I keep on weeping, crying for your help, but there is no reply... — Psalms 22:2 (LVB)

O Jehovah, answer my prayers, for your loving kindness is wonderful; your mercy is so plentiful, so tender and so kind. Don't hide from me, for I am in deep trouble. Quick! Come and save me. — Psalms 69:16-17 (LVB)

Yet, God did answer David's prayers:

When I pray, you answer me, and encourage me by giving me the strength I need. — Psalms 138:3 (LVB)

The corporate prayer group has now prayed through and determined the will of God regarding the petition. It has also authoritatively prayed in Jesus name that God's will be moved from heaven to earth. Finally, it has persisted in faith. The *sixth answer* to prayer that we receive is our prayer becomes a reality on earth.

Timing of God's Answers

The question that is left is God's timing as to when the answer to our petition is moved from the spiritual dimension to the physical dimension. The timing of when the answer to our petition gets to earth generally falls into two categories. The first is that the answer comes immediately in time from heaven to earth. The second is that the answer comes in God's time, and we must patiently wait for the answer.

Throughout the Bible and the history of the church, we see God answering prayer immediately. As a result of prayer, the blind see, the lame walk, diseases are healed, miracles are performed, and circumstances are changed.

However, in many of our corporate prayers, the answer does not come to earth immediately. We must be patient and wait for it to come. We have already discussed in Chapter 13, the role of Satan in delaying our prayers getting from heaven to earth and the need to persist in prayer until the answer comes. We may wait a long time to see the evidence of answered prayer, but we can be certain that God does hear us and responds on His timetable.

Look at the story of Moses and the children of Israel that were in bondage in Egypt. They were in bondage for hundreds of years.

> Several years later the king of Egypt died. The Israelis were groaning beneath their burdens, in deep trouble because of their slavery, and weeping bitterly before the Lord. He heard their cries from heaven, and remembered his promise to Abraham, Isaac, and Jacob [to bring their descendants back into the land of Canaan]. Looking down upon them, he knew that the time had come for their rescue. — Exodus 2:23-25 (LVB)

God heard their cry and answered their prayer:

> Then the Lord told him, "I have seen the deep sorrows of my people in Egypt, and have heard their pleas for freedom from their harsh taskmasters. I have come to deliver them from the Egyptians and to take them out of Egypt into a good land, a large land, a land `flowing with milk and honey'…" — Exodus 3:7-8a (LVB)

The people of Israel waited a long time for God's response, and in the end God did not let them down.

The Lord is good to those that are patient and wait upon him for an answer to their prayers:

> The Lord is good unto them that wait for him, to the soul that
> seeketh him. — Lamentations 3:25 (KJV)

Sometimes God determines it is in our best interest to be patient. Men like King David knew he had to be patient. He wrote:

> Rest in the Lord, and wait patiently for him... — Psalms 37:7a (KJV)

It may be that we are not able at the present time to receive what we ask even though God wants to give it to us. We have not matured sufficiently to handle the answer. So time needs to pass while we gain maturity. To illustrate consider the following story.

Your five year old son asks for a cookie just before supper time. It is not that you don't want to give him a cookie. Your son is told to wait until after supper, and he can have the cookie. The time is not appropriate since the cookie will spoil his supper. As your son grows to maturity, he will understand why he had to wait for the cookie.

Jesus talked about this relative to spiritual things when speaking to his disciples in John 16:12. He said there were many things He wanted to tell them, but they were not mature enough to understand:

> "Oh, there is so much more I want to tell you, but you can't understand
> it now." — John 16:12 (LVB)

Tying God to a timetable to answer our prayers is not consistent with our hearts being in neutral and open to His leading. In Psalms 69:13, the Psalmist asks God to answer his prayer on God's timetable:

> But as for me, my prayer is to You, O Lord, in the acceptable time; O
> God, in the multitude of Your mercy, Hear me in the truth of
> Your salvation. — Psalms 69:13 (KJV)

Our problem is that we want answers to our prayers on our timetable rather than God's timetable. We may indeed wait a long time to see the physical evidence of answered prayer, but God does hear us, answer us, and respond to us in His time.

Herbert Lockyer sums it up this way:

> He answered prayer—not in the way I sought,
> Nor in the way that I had thought He ought;
> But in His own good way, and I could see
> He answered in the fashion best for me.[2]

Points to Remember

In this chapter, we looked at God's answers to corporate prayer. The important points are:

1. As we enter into corporate prayer for a specific petition, we need to recognize that God gives us many answers to prayer during this journey. He:
    a. Forgives us and fills us with the Holy Spirit.
    b. Brings us into His presence.
    c. Provides us protection from Satan.
    d. Tells us the burdens for which prayer is needed.
    e. Shows us His will regarding our petition.
    f. Grants our petition.
2. God's response to our seeking His will regarding our petition generally falls into three categories:
    a. Yes, this is my will!
    b. No, this is not my will!
    c. Continue to seek my will!
3. God's answer to our prayer can arrive on earth from heaven either immediately or be delayed in time. If there is a delay, we must patiently wait for the answer.

Questions for Personal Reflection

Before going to the next chapter, take time to reflect on your answers to the following questions:

1. When coming before the Lord in corporate prayer, are you surprised at the number of answers to prayer you receive during the journey?
2. Are you willing to wait patiently on God's timing to answer your prayer on earth?

Part III

How to Use God's Directions to Pray Together

Chapter 15

Historical Use of Corporate Prayer
Over the Last Several Centuries

In Part I, we looked at what the Bible had to say about corporate prayer. In Part II, we discussed God's directions for corporate prayer and looked at the answers to prayer we receive from God during our prayer journey. In Part III, we will put all of this together to see how we can practically put God's directions for corporate prayer to use in our daily lives.

In this chapter, we will examine the historical use of corporate prayer to see how God's directions for corporate prayer have been used by the church in a powerful way over the last several centuries. The purpose of this examination is to see if there are practical things about how the directions for corporate prayer have been used in the past that we can learn for our use today.

Corporate Prayer Ministry by Small Group

We have already shown the power and effectiveness of small groups in corporate prayer from scripture in previous chapters. Since the beginning of the church, the prayer ministry of the church has been carried on by small groups. The small prayer group has historically been the foundation of the local church's prayer ministry. Over and over throughout history, it has been small prayer groups in intercessory prayer that have brought revival to their churches and cities.

Small groups known as prayer societies emerged in Europe and England in the seventeenth century. The goal of the prayer societies was to have the organization of the church resemble the early Christian church, which met in small groups in their homes. In Robert Bakke's excellent book *The Power of Extraordinary Prayer*, he indicates prayer societies spread rapidly through Scotland and by the end of the seventeenth century every social class was a part of them.[1] The societies in the early 1700's became fully integrated into the Scottish church and were carefully regulated and organized.

In Cambuslang, Scotland in the early 1740's, men and women were organized into small prayer societies by William M'Culloch the parish pastor. As a result of the intercessory prayer from these societies and gifted preaching from George Whitefield, a great spiritual awakening came to the city of Cambuslang.

Count Nicholas Von Zinzendorf was a man of noble birth with considerable wealth. In 1727, Count Zinzendorf, allowed a group of Protestant refugees, who had been forced to leave their homes because of Roman Catholic persecution, to build a village on his estate. But the refugees, who were from every theological persuasion, could not live in peace. They fussed and argued among themselves. After five years of this, Count Zinzendorf assembled the entire group together so they could apologize to one another, have communion, and pray corporately together. As they confessed their sins to one another and corporately prayed together over several weeks, the Holy Spirit fell on them with amazing power and grace.

So great was this outpouring of the Spirit that the prayer meeting continued for 100 years without stopping night or day. Twenty four men and twenty four women decided that intercessory prayer should continue unabated in their community. They divided themselves into small prayer societies to allow them to pray around the clock. Out of these prayer societies came the Moravian movement.

What was the result of the intercessory prayer from this group of Moravian refugees? Over the next 200 years, more than 3000 evangelists were sent out from this small village.[2] Bakke points out that it was the prayer societies founded in the early eighteenth century by the Moravians at Aldersgate Street and Fetters Lane that brought John and Charles Wesley to salvation and deeply influenced William Carey and George Whitefield.[3]

Prayer societies were organized in the American colonies at the end of the seventeenth century. They grew in popularity throughout the colonies. Men like Cotton Mather believed that lay Christians needed to be mobilized. He felt prayer societies were the best way to achieve this mobilization. He encouraged the organization of prayer societies made up of neighborhoods, men's groups, women's groups, and young people's groups.

Many say it was in answer to the corporate prayers of John Wesley and a small group of people that the church and nation of England were saved from revolution and social unrest in the early part of the eighteenth century. God gathered a group of believers and prompted them to intercede for the church and their nation. As a result, there was a revival that in a few years changed the whole character of the English nation.

In 1857, a little known New York City missionary and a group of people who shared the missionary's burden for revival in New York began to pray together. As a result of this small corporate group praying for revival, churches were attended by the thousands, prayer meetings held 24/7, and thousands were saved.

In the book *Praying Hyde*, we read of the revival in India in the late nineteenth century that started with 30 days and nights of corporate prayer by John N. Hyde and R. McChenye Paterson. George Turner joined them after nine days, and these three men prayed and praised God for a mighty outpouring of His power. It is said that their three hearts beat as one in agreement. Finally they prayed through and believed that God would send a mighty outpouring of His Spirit. They shouted "It shall be done."[4] What was the result? Thousands were saved.

In the book *The Shantung Revival*, C. L. Culpepper writes that in 1927 China was in a state of internal war. Southern Baptist missionaries as well as missionaries for other faiths were asked to come to the port city of Chefoo for possible evacuation.[5] The missionaries came together for Bible study and corporate prayer.

One of the missionaries, Ola Culpepper, was experiencing pain and deteriorating vision due to a long-term eye problem. The Baptist missionaries urged Ola to come to one of their homes to have a corporate prayer of healing according to the promise of James 5:14-16. They prayed for several hours and were in a complete spirit of communion. They felt heaven come down and glory fill their souls. The pain left Ola's eyes and never returned.

This was the prelude to the Shantung Revival. God began to use this small corporate prayer group in a mighty way in China to see souls saved and churches reborn. They saw the power of the Holy Spirit at work.

One of the most successful uses today of prayer in small groups is by Dr. David Yonggi Cho in his church in South Korea. His church is structured centering on the regular gathering of small home cell groups. In his book *Successful Home Cell Groups*, he describes how home cell groups operate in detail.[6] His church is currently the world's largest congregation, with a membership of over 800,000. In the home cell groups, half nights of corporate prayer are common.

In Ralph W. Neighbor Jr.'s book, *Where Do We Go From Here*, he describes the use and structure of home cell groups in use throughout the world.[7] He indicates that as much as one third to one half of the time spent in their weekly meetings is devoted to corporate prayer.[8] In their corporate prayer time, the home cell groups are open to the manifestation of the gifts of the Spirit for the common good. Cell groups expect God to answer their prayers.

Home cell groups form a sense of community often not present in traditional churches. Each member of a cell group knows he or she is loved. That home cell groups are successful in reaching the lost for Christ cannot be denied. Today, the world's two largest Presbyterian churches and the world's largest Methodist church are cell group congregations in Seoul.[9]

Small corporate prayer groups flourish throughout the world in many forms. A quick Google will see over a million hits for the word "prayer group."

Most prayer groups have a group leader that convenes and conducts the prayer group through the time of prayer. Experience has shown that to maximize the sense of group community, the small corporate prayer group should be around 15 people. When the group size reaches around 30 people, the group should organically divide into two groups.

There are small corporate prayer groups of all kinds: married and single adult groups, all male adult groups, all women adult groups, all single groups, all young people groups, neighborhood groups, workplace groups, and other special interest groups. Prayer groups meet in churches, in restaurants, in offices, and in homes.

Small corporate prayer groups today sometimes meet together for many years. They can also come together for a particular activity over a finite time. For instance in a church revival, they may meet beforehand, they may pray together during the revival, they may gather after the revival to praise and thank God for the changes wrought in the church and the harvest of souls and then disband. A special interest prayer group may be made up of believers who meet every Sunday morning to pray for one burden—the filling and empowerment of the pastor as he speaks the Word of God.

Some churches use "huddles" or "prayer circles" as small corporate prayer groups during their dedicated prayer time. The prayer leader breaks the congregation into small prayer groups (2 to 6 people) and directs the groups to pray for one or two specific burdens.

Corporate prayer groups today follow a variety of outlines. The format generally includes:

- A short devotional
- Singing of praises to God
- Sharing of answers to prayer
- Sharing of prayer requests
- Prayers of praise and thanksgiving
- Prayers of petition (intercession)
- Concluding with prayers of praise and thanksgiving
- Social time

Corporate Prayer Ministry by Local Church

In chapter 5, we have already shown from scripture the power and effectiveness of corporate intercessory prayer by the local church. While small prayer groups are the foundation of intercessory prayer by the church, there are times when the prayer capacity of the entire local church is needed in intercessory prayer for a burden to pray through to determine the will of God and bring it to earth.

An example in the mid-eighteenth century of the marvelous impact of corporate prayer by the local church was the implementation of united synchronized prayer called the "Concert of Prayer." William M'Colloch the pastor of Cambuslang, Scotland, mentioned earlier organized his ninety families into prayer societies, but went one step further. He coordinated the prayer efforts of the societies so they could all focus on the same prayer burdens.[10] The agreement among the prayer societies to pray for a specific burden was called a "concert." The word "concert" was used since M'Colloch saw the implementation of Matthew 18:19 as a kind of concert based on the word "agree."

M'Colloch corresponded with the great American preacher Jonathan Edwards, who expanded the idea of a "Concert of Prayer." He urged the 18th century New England churches to see corporate prayer as a kind of symphony where all prayed in concerted agreement. Each person that prays is a different instrument to be used of God, but all playing in harmony.

Jonathan Edwards' vision was to coordinate the prayer agendas of all prayer societies, and focus the intercessory prayer on specific burdens that would have broad acceptance among all denominations and across the social spectrum. This would combine the prayer capacity of the church world wide into a mighty force that would bring God's will to earth.

The basic premise of a concert of prayer was to pray for two specific burdens: the outpouring of God's Holy Spirit on the church (renewal and revival) and the advancement of the Kingdom of God around the world (missions and world evangelism).

In each church, small prayer societies would meet weekly in concerts of prayer to pray for revival and world evangelism. Once a quarter, the separate prayer societies would gather together in one place and coordinate all prayer societies into a single movement of concerted prayer.[11] This was real prayer capacity!

Robert Bakke observes that "The new plan (The Concert of Prayer) was launched by Scottish Presbyterians and embraced by Congregationalists such as Jonathan Edwards, David Brainerd, and Timothy Dwight; Anglicans John Wesley and George Whitefield; Baptists such as Andrew Fuller, Isaac Backus, and William Carey; and countless others."[12] Bakke goes on to say that "The concert of prayer was also the foundation of the Second Great Awakening, called "America's Pentecost" or the revival of 1800, the most powerful religious episode in United States history."

In 1840, a group of people in Boston at Park Street Church began a concert of prayer for the outpouring of the Holy Spirit. They met daily for prayer and monthly for citywide concerts of prayer. After two years the church reported many being saved. Sadly, as the attendance at prayer meetings fell off or stopped in the fourth year, there was a drastic reduction in those being added to the church.

In 1851 several laymen that had been part of the Park Street meeting began a daily prayer time at the Old South Church in Boston. The prayer meeting invited Christians from all denominations to pray. They had a single focus for their prayer: "to pray for the revival of religion, and the outpouring of the Spirit on the inhabitants of the city."[13] They prayed together every day before going to work. By 1857, the men at Old South Church had prayed for six years. Their faith continued to grow stronger each week as they persisted in prayer for their city. God's blessings began to pour down on them with the church filled to running over and the audience filled with tears.

Encouraged by the moving of God at the Old South Church, Jeremiah Lanphier started a meeting near the financial district in New York. They met daily at the lunch hour. It started small but in just a few months the meeting had grown to an estimated 10,000 people. It has been estimated that one million people came to Christ during the first year of the prayer meeting.

The "Concert of Prayer" concept is still being used effectively around the world today by many churches and religious groups to combine the power of small prayer groups to pray corporately on a regular basis for revival of our land and for lost souls in our world. David Bryant, in his book *Concerts of Prayer*, gives details on the format for conducting a concert of prayer.[14] The format for a concert of prayer is similar to the format given earlier in this chapter for a corporate prayer group.

The city-wide revivals of Billy Graham which involved many local churches of many denominations have been successful for many years in bringing revival to communities and seeing many souls saved. All of Graham's crusades were undergirded with the power of millions of prayer warriors who, praying corporately, interceded with God for lost souls.

In 1999, a group of young people in England got the crazy idea to pray non-stop for a month. God worked in a wonderful way, and they could not stop praying. As a result, the 24-7 prayer movement was begun. It now involves more than 1,500 churches and groups in the United States and 4,500 worldwide with people participating from many denominations and age groups. Participating groups commit to keep prayer going for 24 hours a day for a week or more in a dedicated prayer room. Then, they pass the "prayer baton" in a never ending flow from location to location. Hundreds of non-stop prayer groups link up on the web (www.24-7prayer.com) to form a continuous chain of prayer. They are a virtual church praying corporately in many different locations.

Today, the "old time" church-wide prayer meeting still flourishes in some local churches.[15, 16, 17] These corporate prayer meetings are usually focused on a series of burdens. The people can be directed to pray in "huddles" of two to six for a specific burden, or the entire local church can be brought to corporate prayer by the prayer leader for a specific burden.

Cell churches also assemble regional congregations of small home cell groups together for regular celebrations that include praise, worship, training, testimonies, public baptism, Bible Study, and half nights of prayer.[18]

In summary, corporate intercessory prayer by the local church can come in many forms which include traditional church prayer meetings, multiple small prayer groups meeting together, concerts of prayer, a virtual community of prayer rooms connected by the web, and regional congregations of home cell groups.

Corporate Prayer by the Nation

From Chapter 5, we saw from scripture that nations have felt the need to come as one united body to pray corporately to God, usually focused around a time of crisis in the nation.

In America, our nation was born in crisis. Throughout its history, America's leaders have called the nation to a time of corporate prayer. Before we became a nation, John Hancock led the Provincial Congress in calling for a Day of Fasting and Prayer on April 15, 1775. The Governor of Connecticut called upon the colony to observe April 19, 1775 as a "Day of Public Fasting and Prayer...that God through repentance would graciously pour out his Holy Spirit on us, to bring us to a thorough repentance and effectual reformation..."[19] God's providential hand is evident since it was on April 19, 1775 that the shot heard round the world was fired at Lexington and Concord.

When England put the colonies under martial law in July 1775, the Continental Congress called for a Day of Fasting and Prayer. Throughout the war the Continental Congress continued to call the people to prayer to see our nation through this crisis. The Congress also called for days of thanksgiving to celebrate the victories in war and other significant events in the life of the new nation. For instance, on November 1, 1777 Congress issued a proclamation calling for a day of prayer and fasting after the victory at Saratoga where citizens were urged to ask "...Jesus Christ mercifully to forgive and blot out (our sins)" and "to prosper the means of religion for the promotion and enlargement of that Kingdom which consisteth in righteousness, peace, and joy in the Holy Ghost."[20]

Following the issuance of the Emancipation Proclamation, which declared all slaves free, President Abraham Lincoln called for a National Day of Humiliation, Fasting, and Prayer on April 30, 1863. A few of his words were:

> "...It is the duty of nations as well as of men to own their dependence upon the overruling power of God; to confess their sins and transgressions in humble sorrow, yet with assured hope that genuine repentance will lead to mercy and pardon; and to recognize the sublime truth, announced in the Holy scriptures and proven by all history, that those nations only are blessed whose God is the Lord..." and "It behooves us, then, to humble ourselves before the offended Power, and confess our national sins, and to pray for clemency and forgiveness."[21]

America has been unusually blessed by God! The writer of Psalms says it best:

Blessed is the nation whose God is the Lord. — Psalms 33:12 (KJV)

From the birth of our nation until today, the Congress of the United States has declared over 200 National Days of Prayer and Fasting. The tradition continues today. On April 17, 1952, President Truman signed a bill proclaiming the National Day of Prayer into law. Twenty years later in 1972, a National Prayer Committee was formed whose purpose was to coordinate the events of the National Day of Prayer. In 1988, President Ronald Reagan signed into law a bill decreeing that the National Day of Prayer is to be held annually on the first Thursday in May.

As America faces serious issues around the world, the National Day of Prayer is a time for American citizens to join with their national leaders to celebrate their freedom to corporately gather to worship and pray. Millions on the first Thursday of May attend services held in public venues to pray for the nation, governmental leaders, media, churches, families, and schools.

Corporate Intercessory Prayer Model

From our study of the historical use of corporate prayer, the following corporate intercessory prayer model evolves:

Type of Prayer	Number of People	Frequency of Meeting	Number of Burdens
Individual	1	Daily	Multiple
Small Prayer Groups	2 to 30	Weekly	Modest Number
Local Church	Multiple Small Groups	Weekly to Monthly	Small Number
Community	Multiple Churches	Quarterly	2 or 3

Points to Remember

In this chapter, we looked at the historical use of corporate prayer in the last several centuries to see if we could learn lessons to help us today apply God's directions to corporate prayer. From looking at a historical perspective, we learned:

1. Small corporate intercessory prayer groups have had a profound impact on the history of the church.

2. In practically all the great revivals and great awakenings that have occurred down through history, the common threads have been the earnest intercessory prayer of a small corporate prayer group of Spirit-filled people who had a burden for revival in their church and city.

3. Small corporate intercessory prayer groups do the work of the local church and are generally made up of only believers.

4. Small corporate prayer groups can continue for a long period of time or be for a specific event or need over a finite time.

5. Small corporate prayer groups can be made up of all types of people gathered together of different ages, interests, education and social status.

6. Small corporate prayer groups generally meet weekly.

7. Small corporate prayer groups develop a community that cares, trusts, and loves each other. To maximize the sense of community, the size of the small corporate prayer group should range from 2 to 15 people.

8. Throughout Christian history, small corporate prayer groups have experienced the manifestation of the gifts of the Spirit for the common good.

9. Most intercessory small prayer groups follow an agenda of devotional, praise, sharing of burdens, intercessory prayer, and close with praise.

10. Many great city-wide revivals throughout the last several centuries have started when local churches began to pray corporately for specific burdens. When the churches quit praying, God's blessings quit coming.

11. Corporate intercessory prayer by the local church can come in many forms which include traditional church prayer meetings, multiple small prayer groups meeting together, concerts of prayer, a virtual community of prayer rooms connected by the web, and regional congregations of home cell groups.

12. Historically, when nations have major national issues, a national day of prayer was called by the nation's leaders because the nation was in crisis.

Questions for Personal Reflection

Before going to the next chapter, take time to reflect on your answers to the following questions:

1. How has the historical use of corporate prayer pointed the way for you to practically use corporate prayer today?

2. Do you think corporate prayer by you, your church, and your city can bring about revival in our land?

Chapter 16

Practical Use of Directions for Corporate Prayer Today

We began Part III by examining the historical heritage of the church in the last several centuries to see how the directions for corporate prayer have been applied in the past. The purpose of this examination was to determine if there were practical things about how the directions for corporate prayer were used in the past that we can use today. In this chapter, we will combine what we have learned from scripture and from our historical heritage to look at how to practically apply the directions for corporate prayer in our lives today.

While corporate prayer for our nation is important, a call for national corporate prayer is not within the control of the vast majority of the readers of this book. Therefore, the practical use of directions for corporate prayer will focus on the intercessory corporate prayer ministry of small prayer groups and the local church.

Uniting believers into a corporate body of Christ can best be achieved with a small group of people loving, sharing, and praying together. The small group praying corporately is the foundation on which to build a praying church. The prayer ministry of the church is most effectively accomplished by small prayer groups (two or more) since it can involve every believer in prayer. The more small prayer groups within a local church, the more prayer capacity the church has.

It is in small prayer groups that people learn to love each other and trust each other. Charles Finney said "Nothing tends more to cement the hearts of Christians than praying together. Never do they love one another so well as when they witness the outpouring of each other's hearts in prayer"

Corporate prayer ministry at the local church level is generally given to praise, thanksgiving, and general prayers of intercession. Specific prayers of intercession by the whole membership of the local church to find the will of God are powerful due to the increased prayer capacity of so many people praying.

Once small prayer groups begin to operate within the local church, the church can periodically gather the small prayer groups corporately in one place to pray about specific burdens that affect the church, the community, and the nation.

Conversational prayer, as described by Rosalind Rinker in *Prayer: Conversing with God*, is an excellent way of implementing the directions for corporate small group prayer in everyday life.[1] A *conversational prayer* is defined as a conversation between two or more people and God about a number of specific burdens.

Everyday Conversation

To help understand the use of conversational prayer as we pray corporately, let's first examine how we normally talk to each other by listening to the conversation of the seven friends we met earlier in the book at a typical social gathering.

&

The seven friends met for dinner at a local restaurant after work. After ordering their meal, they begin to talk about the recent events in their lives. They usually spend 1½ to 2 hours together before heading home. Let's look at part of their conversation:

Sue:	"I just saw the movie *The Passion of Christ* by Mel Gibson. Have you seen it?"
Jack:	"Yes I saw it. It was very realistic. There was blood everywhere."
Mary:	"I don't know if I want to see the movie if it is so bloody."

210

Hank: "Can you believe the suffering Jesus went through for us?"

Bill: "I must tell you that I closed my eyes during the time he was being whipped and nailed to the cross. I can't imagine what that was like."

Amanda: "You know, he did that for us!"

Mary: "How did the other people in the movie react?"

Amanda: "Many, like me, cried."

Jack: "I left there with a new understanding of John 3:16. God loved us so much that He gave his only Son to undergo that suffering and death that we might be saved. This movie was heavy!"

Sue: "Speaking of suffering, you remember my telling you about Pamela, my next door neighbor. Pamela moved in a couple of months ago. She is my age and has cancer. Her husband left her, and she has been raising two sons by herself."

Hank: "Is she a Christian?"

Sue: "I don't know."

Joe: "What can we do to help her?"

Amanda: "I went to school with her. I will go by and talk to her and see what her situation is."

Sue: "Amanda, let me know when you are going, and I will go with you."

Bill: "That reminds me. We have church visitation tomorrow night. Can any of you come?"

&

You have conversations like this everyday. It could be a conversation about your job, children, homework, or anything. This is the way we talk to each other. Notice, only one subject at a time is discussed. The first subject was the movie, the second subject was the neighbor that has cancer, and the third subject was church visitation. All the friends gave their opinion on the first subject before moving to the second subject. Then all discussed the second subject before moving to the third subject.

The friends' conversation was in short sentences. No one monopolized the conversation with a long-winded speech. Every one of the friends had something to say. No one was afraid to speak or was left out of the conversation. As the conversation proceeded and more information was given, the conversation got more extensive in nature.

Typical Small Group Prayer

How boring it would be if Sue who mentioned the movie had brought a list of all the things she wanted to talk to her friends about, and then proceeded to take the next 15 minutes to tell them about the movie, her job, trouble with neighbors, and so on. Next, Jack would tell about all the happenings in his life over the last week. This would proceed until all seven, one at a time, had gone over their entire lists. One person talking and everyone else listening is not a conversation.

Unfortunately, typical corporate small group prayer meetings are a lot like the boring conversation above. We have been taught to make a list of the burdens we want to discuss with the Lord. Then, as the small group prays, one person after another prays for all the things that have been shared as burdens by going down the list of burdens one at a time: latest church crisis, Harry's loss of job, Connie sick with cancer, or two friends that are in conflict. This list gets prayed over and over.

W.C. Lantz in his essay "Conversational Prayer Meetings" describes this kind of prayer (which is typical of many churches today) as like a line of children standing at the department store with their Christmas lists to see Santa Claus.[2] Everyone in line reads their entire list to Santa in a series of individual communications. The corporate small group prayer where a list of burdens gets prayed over and over is not a conversation with God. This kind of prayer is boring, boring, boring.

Another problem in the typical small group is that we want to decide the burdens for which we want to pray instead of letting God decide. Our soul governs our prayer rather than our spirit, as prompted by the Holy Spirit. Prayer, not in the Spirit of God, will quickly deflate a corporate prayer time.

The format of the small group prayer meeting discussed above is how we typically prayed in the small rural Baptist church where I grew up. My family took me to church on Wednesday night for "prayer meeting." Everyone prayed the same list of burdens over and over. Every Wednesday night you could count on the same people to pray. Many people at the prayer meeting would not pray out of fear of praying in public. No wonder that today Wednesday night prayer meeting in our churches is almost extinct. Only when we begin to truly have a conversation with God will we recapture the organic prayer meetings of the early church.

Small Group Conversational Prayer

Conversation with God in prayer by a small corporate group of two or more people should be no different than everyday conversation with each other. As a result, our conversation with God should be as though we were present with Him, as indeed we really are. Our prayer should cover only one burden at a time. Each prayer should be short and build on the previous prayers. Everyone present should have a chance to talk to God.

Using what we have learned about the directions for corporate prayer, considering the historical use of corporate prayer, and recognizing how we should carry on a conversation with God, let's look at the seven friends again as they have a conversation with God.

During a special revival in their church that focused on living a Spirit-filled life, each of the seven friends asked Jesus to cleanse his/her heart and to take control of their lives. Also as part of their church's emphasis on small prayer groups, the seven friends formed a small corporate prayer group that gathered at 7:00 PM each Sunday night for two hours at one of their homes. Together, they studied a new book, *When Two or More are Gathered...in Prayer*, that outlined God's directions on how to pray when two or more are gathered together in His name. This gave them a common understanding about how to pray together corporately.

All of the friends understood the need to be on praying ground before coming to the small prayer group. As a result, each of the friends had already spent time alone with the Lord to "get on praying ground."

The friends greatly enjoyed each other's company. Since they had been meeting for some time, they had come to trust and deeply care for each other. This trust overcame their fear of praying out loud in front of each other. The friends asked Jack to be the convener of the prayer group.

⁓

On a recent Sunday evening, when all had arrived at Amanda's house, Jack initiated the corporate prayer time with a period of worship by asking Mary to lead the group in some songs of praise. Following the singing, Jack asked each one to share what was the most important thing that had happened to them since the last meeting. Then Jack asked the group to share things for which they wanted to thank and praise God. Hank shared a verse of scripture that had really spoken to him in the past week. Next, Jack asked the friends to share the burdens that were on their hearts. Let's sit in again on part of their conversation:

Mary: "Several in our Sunday School class, who have children, have mentioned that there is a need for children's workers in Sunday School. I would like us to pray for more workers in Sunday School."

Hank: "Could we pray for our President? I sense he is in real need of prayer."

Sue: "I would like us to pray for my next door neighbor, Pamela, who has cancer. She is separated from her husband and has two small boys."

Joe: "We are having so many visitors in our church. I would like us to pray that we can get them all involved in Sunday School."

Amanda: "I am traveling next week, please pray that I will return home safely."

Jack: "If there are no more burdens to share, let's go to the Lord in prayer."

Jack: "Father, we want to come into your throne room as your children and talk to you. We ask to be in your presence. As we begin our conversation, we ask that you would protect us as we pray. We pray that you will bind any evil forces that will hinder us focusing on this prayer time and loose your holy angels to assist us as needed."

All: "Lord, we agree."

After a moment of quiet time,

Joe: "Lord, we thank you for your goodness and grace to us. Most of all we thank you for your son Jesus who died for us."

Mary: "Father, we praise you for your goodness, your everlasting mercy, and your faithfulness. We praise you for your creation. You are our rock and our place of refuge from the storm. You are all that we ever need in this world!

Bill: "Father, I would like to pray the words of David in Psalms 150 (KJV) as my offering of praise. "Praise ye the Lord, Praise God...Let everything that hath breath praise the Lord. Praise ye the Lord."

Jack: "Lord, I want to specifically praise you for new life. Thank you for sending my brother and his wife a new son that is healthy and beautiful.

After a moment of quiet time,

Sue: "Father, I have a neighbor, Pamela, who has cancer and has been on my heart for several weeks. Show me your will concerning her healing. Also, show me what I can do to help her."

Amanda: "I went to school with Pamela. I don't think she has ever gone to church. Lord, use us to lead her to Christ. Show us how to approach her with the gospel."

Hank: "Your Word says that you do not want any to perish. We know it is your will that she be saved."

Bill: "Lord, in faith, we ask that over the next week you prepare Pamela's heart and provide the opportunity for Amanda and Sue to visit with Pamela and to show their love for her."

Sue: "Father, I do believe you are saying to me that this week I need to love and help Pamela with whatever needs she has. We will trust you to provide the opportunity in your time for us to share Jesus with her."

Jack: "Our sense, Father is that this is your will. We all agree and thank you for this lost sheep for which you have given us the privilege to minister to in your name."

After a moment of quiet time,

Bill: "Father I agree with Mary about the need for more workers in our children's Sunday School. We recognize that the children are our responsibility to educate in your Word"

Joe: "In Luke 10:2, your Word says that if we need workers, we should ask you for workers, and you will send them. The Holy Spirit is speaking to my heart that this is a promise for us. We know this is your will. Father, we claim this promise by faith."

Hank: "Father, I believe you are calling me to work with children in Sunday school. I know I have the motivational gift of teaching. I have felt that I needed to be teaching children for some time and have been struggling for a month as to what to do. Confirm to me that this is what you want me to do."

Joe: "Lord, we join Hank in his prayer asking for guidance as to your will in what Hank should do."

Jack: "I recall a verse (Mark 10:14) that says something like "Let the little children come unto me for theirs is the Kingdom of Heaven." Our children are indeed in our charge to educate in the Word. Hank, it is my sense from the Holy Spirit that the Lord is calling you to this ministry."

Amanda: "Father, we agree with Jack and praise you for answering Hank's prayer."

Hank: "Lord, my spirit confirms what Jack and Amanda have said. I am excited about this opportunity to use my gift in your service. I pray that you fill me with your strength, wisdom, and power as I begin to minister to the children."

Jack: "Father, we pray for an anointing of the Holy Spirit to empower Hank to do this ministry."

After a moment of quiet time,

Bill: "Father, my heart is heavy for our pastor. He is under such a heavy work load."

Mary: "Yes, I too am concerned. Because of the demands on his time, it takes away from his time to study and pray."

Jack: "Lord this is a real problem. We love our pastor. He gives and gives and gives. Help us to love him even more and give back to him."

Hank: "In your Word, you have told us to pray for each other that we might be strengthened."

Amanda: "Father I pray for our pastor, the prayer Paul prayed in

217

Colossians 1:9-11 (KJV): *For this cause we also, since the day we heard it, do not cease to pray for you, and to desire that ye might be filled with the knowledge of his will in all wisdom and spiritual understanding; That ye might walk worthy of the Lord unto all pleasing, being fruitful in every good work, and increasing in the knowledge of God; Strengthened with all might, according to his glorious power, unto all patience and longsuffering with joyfulness;"*

Sue: "Lord, I agree with Hank and Amanda's prayer that our pastor be strengthened and always full of the joy of the Lord."

After a few minutes of silence,

Jack: "Father thank you for sharing your presence with us tonight. We thank you for the answered prayers and the directions you gave us. We all join together to praise you and give you honor and glory. We ask all of these things in the name of your son Jesus Christ. Amen"

Following this time of corporate prayer, the friends continued to enjoy each other's fellowship. They also continued to chat about the prayer time. Since Amanda was the host this Sunday night, she had oatmeal cookies and coffee for everyone to enjoy. It was obvious that there was great love among the friends.

∽

Observations on Small Group's Conversational Prayer

The seven friends in the small prayer group spent time to understand God's directions on how to pray corporately. This allowed them to be confident

218

in their prayer time that God would answer their prayers. They met in a comfortable place—Amanda's home. The same group met weekly at a definite time for an agreed to period of time. They agreed on a convener to lead the prayer group. He opened the conversation with an icebreaker to get everyone in the group talking. He asked them to share the most important thing that had happened to them since the last meeting.

The corporate prayer by the small group was indeed a conversation with God. They addressed the Father as though they were physically together in the same place. The convener prayed on behalf of the group to request God's protection for the prayer time. There was a time of praise and thanksgiving to God that expanded the friend's faith.

As the small group gathered, the friends shared their joys and answers to prayer, as well as, burdens. This sharing deepened their faith and increased the love of the entire group. The small group prayed the burdens that God wanted addressed in this prayer time. They prayed for definite things.

The prayers were short, and everybody participated. Each prayer built upon the other prayers by adding insights or knowledge that God had put on each speaker's heart. As the Holy Spirit directed, the prayer continued conversationally until the seven friends agreed that they had prayed all that God wanted regarding each burden.

The group was able to determine God's will relative to the burdens and spoke with authority to ask God to move his will to earth. The seven friends agreed in the Spirit as to what was being asked of God.

Not all was finished work. For example, knowing what God wanted to do about the healing of Sue's neighbor, Pamela, was not finished. The focus in this conversational prayer started on Pamela's physical needs and ended up focusing on her salvation. The prayer group could have claimed Pamela's salvation based on God's promises. Instead, they faith-sized their request by asking the Father to prepare Pamela's heart and arrange an opportunity for Amanda and Sue to meet Pamela during the next week to begin to love and help her. In subsequent prayer meetings, the Holy Spirit may prompt further movement toward Pamela's healing and salvation.

Notice, there were five burdens raised by the friends. Prayer was not made for three of the burdens. Also, prayer was made for one entirely new burden (the pastor) that had not previously been mentioned by the group. In effect, God was saying "I have the three burdens that you didn't talk about under control. Prayer is not needed on these burdens today. However, I do need to have prayer for your pastor today."

Following the time of corporate prayer, the seven friends signified their agreement to what had been prayed by saying "Amen." Amen means "so be it." By saying "Amen," every member of the small group agreed, in the Spirit, that this prayer was their prayer too.

Additional Practical Thoughts on Conversational Prayer

In addition to the above guidelines and the observations in the previous section, I would like to add some practical thoughts.

New members of the prayer group require instruction in how to pray corporately. Otherwise, they will not understand conversational prayer and may either pray long and windy prayers or not participate in the prayer time at all.

The ideal location of a corporate prayer meeting by a small group is in the home of one of the members of the prayer group. Homes are environments conducive to small group prayer and social interaction. A room at the church would also work fine. The room temperature needs to be comfortable. Wherever you meet, every attempt should be made to limit interruptions from cell phones, children, and people coming and going.

There should be comfortable places to sit or kneel if desired. Ideally, all should be in an arrangement facing each other. This is how we would normally carry on a conversation with other people. Young people often find sitting on the floor facing each other to be a good arrangement.

A specific time, date, and duration of the small group prayer meeting should be agreed upon. Meeting in a small prayer group requires commitment. We should plan our schedule to attend every meeting possible.

There should be an opportunity at the beginning of the meeting for a time of worship through sharing praises to God, answered prayers, testimonies, a Word of scripture, and burdens. This should be done in a very short time so as not to take away from the prayer time. The prayer group must be careful not to take more time discussing prayer requests than praying about them.

The prayer time should include primarily the prayer elements of praise, thanksgiving, and petition as the Holy Spirit leads. Since each person in the prayer group has spent time alone with God in confession, the element of pardon is not usually part of the prayer time. On occasion if a sin is public and a member of the prayer group needs to confess the sin to the entire group, then the element of pardon is appropriate. What is shared and prayed in the small prayer group must stay there! This builds trust in the group.

Only one burden at a time should be addressed by the prayer group in conversational prayer. The Holy Spirit decides which burdens are to be discussed with the Father. This is an organic process, not an organized one. It is alive and not structured by man. God must be free at any point during our corporate prayer to move the conversation from one burden to another. We need to trust God to lead us as we pray. Henry T. Blackaby and Claude V. King observe: "When God wants to work in a group, He can and will give the guidance needed for that time. Your job is to recognize His voice or His activity and then do everything you sense He wants you to do."[3]

Believers should feel free to pray about a specific burden as often as they want. Prayer for each specific burden should be offered until all that the Holy Spirit wants prayed is said. Each individual prayer should be fairly short. Just as in an ordinary conversation. Short prayers also put believers that have not prayed out loud before in a more comfortable position to participate in the group prayer. After prayer for a specific burden is finished, the group should be silent until the Holy Spirit prompts prayer for another burden.

A time of social fellowship at the end of the prayer group allows time for the members of the prayer group to further share their lives and deepen their love for each other.

There are additional helpful guidelines for leading a corporate prayer gathering and for keeping a prayer group flowing smoothly that are discussed in the following books: *The Power of Praying Together,* by Stormie Omartian, *The Prayer Saturated Church*, by Cheryl Sacks, and *Together In Prayer: Coming To God In Community* by Andrew Wheeler.[4,5,6]

Guests to a small intercessory prayer group are welcome, but only if they are on praying ground. A small corporate "intercessory" prayer group is not a place for bringing new people for social enjoyment or to interest them in salvation if they are lost. Their motivation for gathering is not the same as the small intercessory prayer group. Small prayer groups are to do the work of the church in prayer!

Members of the prayer group are expected to visit non-Christian friends, relatives, and neighbors, develop loving relationships with them, and then lead them to Jesus outside of the small intercessory prayer group. However, unbelievers are indeed welcome if a small group is convened primarily for Bible study, worship, or fellowship.

It has been the practice of some churches to have small prayer groups that meet weekly in corporate prayer. Once a month, all the small prayer groups in the local church gather together to share what God has done in their group as it relates to the church, community or nation. Then there follows a time of corporate prayer where the local church prays prayers of agreement. By ourselves, our faith may weaken, but with a small group that is in agreement regarding God's will, it is harder to doubt.

There is incredible power available to the church if the entire church is in agreement regarding God's will and corporately believes that God has answered their prayer. It is the difference in using a hammer and an atomic bomb.

Maintain God's Protection

Satan will do everything he can to keep the small prayer group from praying. As a practical matter, we need to ask for and maintain God's protection over the group as we pray to counter the hindrances Satan will throw in our path. We need to be alert to the disruptive things Satan will try to do.

Satan will try to keep the corporate prayer group from having time to pray. Numerous difficulties will arise to hinder our prayer. Satan is willing to let us be active in the church as long as we do not pray. He will keep us busy doing good deeds, visiting the sick, having fellowship with other believers, and listening to sermons. All of these are good things, unless we do them while neglecting to pray.

Satan will try to divide the prayer group to keep it from praying. Jealousy and suspicion will arise among the believers, preventing harmony in the body of Christ.

Satan will disturb our prayers as we begin to pray. Our thoughts will begin to scatter. The daily pressures in our life will intrude. We become aware of noises created by children, telephone, outside disturbances and movement by other believers. We become uncomfortable due to temperature, get sleepy, become tired, or feel ill.

Satan will suggest to us that we are not good enough for God to answer our prayers. We are too guilty of sin. We are so bad there is no way God can forgive us. We are unworthy.

Satan also tells us we do not know how to pray. We are too immature as Christians to expect answered prayer. We do not really know God's will. We have so little faith that we will at some point begin to doubt and lose our answer to prayer.

Satan will tell us that we will look foolish if we pray in public and people will laugh at us. We should fear public prayer and avoid it at all costs. You cannot trust other people with your burdens.

Satan will try to get us to pray in the flesh. Clutter our prayers with empty words. Pray overly long prayers for a long list of things only at the surface level without praying any one burden through to find God's will.

Satan will suggest that your prayer group is super-spiritual and has a special relation with God because you are filled with the Holy Spirit and open to the gifts of the Spirit. He will use pride to cause division in the group and will use it to hinder your prayers.

We must be vigilant to make sure we do not let Satan use any of his reasons to disrupt the time God's people spend in corporate prayer.

Points to Remember

In this chapter, we studied conversational prayer as a way to implement the directions for corporate prayer. The important points were:

1. Conversational prayer is a conversation between two or more people and God about a number of specific burdens.
2. We are to converse with God just like we converse with friends.
3. We pray about one burden at a time to God.
4. The Holy Spirit tells us what burdens to talk about to the Father.
5. We need to be practical about how we conduct a small prayer group.
6. We need to ask for and maintain God's protection over the group as we pray to counter the hindrances Satan will throw in our path.

Questions for Personal Reflection

Before going to the next chapter, take time to reflect on your answers to the following questions:

1. Would you be comfortable praying with a group of people using conversational prayer?
2. Are you interested in being part of a small corporate prayer group?

Chapter 17

How Do I Get Started Praying
with Other People?

Now that you understand God's directions for how to pray together to
bring God's power from heaven to earth and have studied how to practically
apply God's directions for corporate prayer in today's world, one question re-
mains. "How do I get started praying together with other people?" Let's look
at how to start praying together using five scenarios: praying with a prayer
partner, praying with your husband or wife, praying with your family, praying
with a small group of Christians, and praying together as a church.

In each of the scenarios, the participants need to meet together for several sessions to discuss and fully understand God's directions for corporate
prayer and how to practically apply the directions. If needed, invite one of
your ministers or an experienced prayer warrior to meet with you to help you
learn about how to pray together. Next, the participants should covenant together to pray on a regular basis. The final step in getting started is to gather
together and begin to pray.

The simplest way to start your journey in corporate prayer is to ask
a friend to become your prayer partner. Remember, God can use corporate
prayer groups as small as two people. After studying God's directions for praying together with your friend, then commit to pray together using conversational prayer on a frequent basis. With two people this can be in person, by
telephone, or by using the internet. Having a close friend that can pray with
you 24/7 is indeed a pearl of great price. The writer of Ecclesiastes expressed
it well:

> Two can accomplish more than twice as much as one, for the results can
> be much better. If one falls, the other pulls him up; but if a man falls
> when he is alone, he's in trouble. — Ecclesiastes 4; 9-10 (LVB)

If you are a husband or wife, ask your mate to join you in daily prayer. A husband and wife praying together, as one, is a powerful force in our world. Many Christian husbands and wives do not pray together except at meal time. What a blessing they are missing. You will recall that in I Peter 3:7 it states that a husband and wife are partners in receiving God's blessings and answers to prayer.

Husbands and wives, as part of their daily devotions, can conversationally pray for everything that impacts their family's world. To get started, the husband and wife need to commit to setting aside time to pray together each day.

If you pray with your wife or husband daily, good things will happen to your marriage. For example, Cheryl Sacks makes this observation based on a 1993 Gallup poll: "The divorce rate among couples who go to church together regularly is 1 out of 2—the same as among unbelievers. But the divorce rate among couples who pray together daily is 1 out of 1,153."[1] This is an incredible testimony to the love that grows between a husband and wife when they pray together.

Teaching your children how to pray is your responsibility. At a very early age, many children learn to pray out loud in front of adults at meal time and bed time. This freedom to pray in front of other people should be encouraged. In addition, parents should teach their children God's directions for how to pray and receive answers to their prayers as they become mature enough to receive the Word. To get started, as a family praying together, introduce the concept of conversational prayer in daily devotions with your family. This way, as they grow spiritually, conversational prayer with others will be a natural occurrence. There is a saying that is so true: "The family that prays together stays together."

If you would like to start praying with a small group of Christians, ask your church staff or Christian friends if they know about an existing small group that you could join. If you cannot find an existing small corporate prayer group, then you need to find "two or more" people that have the same desire to pray together as you do. In private individual prayer, ask God to send you some fellow Christians with which you can pray on a regular basis. It could be someone that is already close to you—friends, family, people at work, neighbors, or members of your Sunday School class. Don't be afraid to speak to someone you believe God is leading you to ask. They may turn you down, but that doesn't mean God didn't want you to ask them. Talk to your pastor about individuals who might join with you in a small prayer group. When two or more participants have indicated their interest, ask them to read this book. Then meet for several sessions to discuss and fully understand its contents. Next, ask those that would like to begin praying together as a small prayer group to covenant to pray together on a regular basis. Finally, gather together with your new prayer group and begin to pray using the practical guidelines in Chapter 16 to help you.

If you would like to implement a time of corporate prayer into an existing small cell group, affinity group, or accountability group of which you may already be a part, then approach the group leader about including corporate prayer as part of your meetings. It is recognized that some of the members of these groups may be unbelievers or are believers not on praying ground. Over time, the members of the group should be educated on God's directions for praying together to the maximum extent possible. The concept of praying together conversationally should be introduced early. The group leadership should set aside a regular portion of their meeting for corporate prayer, and then the group should begin to pray together using the guidelines in Chapter 16 to assist them.

To start a time of church-wide corporate prayer is the responsibility of your church leadership. It is their task to transform your church from a church that just prays into a church that is a house of prayer. If you have a burden for church-wide prayer, meet with your pastor and staff to discuss your burden. Work together with your pastor and staff to create a corporate prayer strategic plan that suits your worship style. Cheryl Sacks' book *A Prayer Saturated Church*, outlines an excellent structured approach that can be used to develop a corporate prayer strategic plan for your church.[2] Next, the church leaders need to prepare the hearts of the church members by teaching them what God's Word has to say about how to pray individually and corporately. Then, the church leadership needs to lead the church in a regular time of corporate prayer that might include prayer meetings with the entire church in attendance, multiple small prayer groups meeting together, church-wide concerts of prayer, a virtual community of prayer rooms connected by the web, or bringing together regional congregations of home cell groups.

There are many ways for you and your church to experience and implement corporate prayer. John Franklin's book *A House of Prayer* is an excellent resource that summarizes the wide variety of ways churches today are praying together corporately.[3]

The only way to really learn to pray corporately is to put your will in motion and start praying together with other Christians. We cannot learn without practice. If we will only begin to gather in corporate prayer, God will show us how to bring His will from heaven to earth!

Points to Remember

In this chapter, we looked at how we get started praying with others. The important points were:

1. We can start praying corporately with other people by praying with a prayer partner, with our husband or wife, with our family, with a small group, and with our church.
2. The only way to learn how to pray corporately is to put your will in motion and start praying together with other Christians.

Questions for Personal Reflection

Before going to the next chapter, take time to reflect on your answers to the following questions:

1. Are you willing to start using corporate prayer in your home?
2. Are you willing to start meeting with other believers in a small prayer group for the purpose of corporate prayer?

Chapter 18

Final Word

In the preceding chapters, I have described my journey to understand the importance of God's people engaging in corporate prayer; what the Bible says about corporate prayer; and how to put God's directions for corporate prayer into practice. In this chapter, our study concludes with a final word on corporate prayer as we journey into the future. The journey to learn about God's directions on how to pray corporately is never over. There is still much for all of us to learn:

- God is looking for a people to pray together so that the church is known as a house of prayer.
- God is looking for a people who will commit to gather together as two or more to do the work of the church through corporate prayer.
- God is looking for a people that will humble themselves in corporate prayer and seek His face.
- God is looking for a people who will love Him and desire to spend time with Him in fellowship and conversation.
- God is looking for a people who will obey His commandments.
- God is looking for a people who will come to Him in corporate prayer with clean hands and clean hearts.
- God is looking for a people who will offer praise and thanksgiving to Him with their lips.
- God is looking for a people that will share the burdens of others by bringing them to the throne through intercessory corporate prayer.

- God is looking for a people that will seek His will regarding their burdens.
- God is looking for a people that will obey His will every time they see it.
- God is looking for a people that will use the authority of His Son to bring His will from heaven to earth through corporate prayer.
- God is looking for a people that will pray with much faith and persist in prayer until the answer comes.
- God is looking for a people that will give Him glory and honor by acting on behalf of His Son here on earth through corporate prayer.

My hope is that you will be part of the people for which God is looking. Upon you depends the coming of the Kingdom of God to earth!

Questions for Personal Reflection

We have completed our study of corporate prayer. Take time to reflect on your answers to the following questions:

1. **List the most important insights that you have learned from this study of corporate prayer?**
2. **What changes will you make in your prayer life as a result of what you have learned?**

Notes

Chapter 1—Introduction

1.   Omartian, Stormie with Hayford, Jack. *The Power of Praying Together.*
     Eugene, OR: Harvest House Publishers, 2003. Page 148.
2.   Price, Nelson. *Prayer: Closet Power.* Kennesaw, GA: Nelson Price
     Ministries, Inc., 2007. Page 52.

Chapter 2—Why Should We Pray Together Corporately?

1.   Torrey, R.A. *The Power of Prayer.* Grand Rapids: Zondervan, 1971. Page
     40.
2.   Spurgeon, C. H. "The Story of God's Mighty Acts." Sermon delivered at
     the Music Hall, Royal Surrey Gardens, July 17, 1859.
3.   Bounds, E. M. *The Complete Works of E. M. Bounds on Prayer.* Grand
     Rapids: Baker Books, 1990. Page 76

Chapter 3—What Did Jesus Teach About Prayer?

1.   Barclay, William. *The Daily Bible Study Series* (NT). Philadelphia: The
     Westminister Press, 1975.
2.   Grubb, Norman. *C. T. Studd.* Fort Washington: Christian Literature
     Crusade, 1972. Page 173.

Chapter 4—Prayer in the Early Church and Today's Church

1.   Henderson, Daniel with Saylar, Margaret. *Fresh Encounters.* Colorado
     Springs: NavPress, 2004. Page 47.
2.   Billheimer, Paul E. *Destined for the Throne.* Fort Washington: Christian
     Literature Crusade, 1975. Page 18.
3.   Bounds, E. M. *Power Through Prayer.* New Kensington: Whitaker House,
     1982. Page 11.

Chapter 5—Corporate Prayers in the Bible

1.   Lockyer, Herbert. *How Can I Make Prayer More Effective.* Grand Rapids:
     Zondervan, 1953. Page 51.
2.   Bounds, E. M. *Power Through Prayer.* New Kensington: Whitaker House,
     1982. Page 129.

3. Wiersbe, Warren W. *The Wiersbe Bible Commentary*. David C. Cook, 2007. Page 362.

4. For the purposes of this book, "Praying through" is defined as praying about an issue until God gives you peace in your spirit that you have fought the fight of faith and God has answered your prayer.

Chapter 6—Step 1: Getting on Praying Ground

1. Grubb, Norman. *C.T. Studd*. Fort Washington: Christian Literature Crusade, 1972. Pages 47-48.

2. Sanders, J. Oswald. *Prayer Power Unlimited*. Minneapolis: World Wide Publications, 1977. Pages 147-148.

3. The idea for the Sin Sheet in Appendix I came from a tract "Not I, But Christ" published by Tract Evangelistic Crusade. P.O. Box 998, Apache Junction, AZ 85220.

4. Blackaby, Henry T. and King, Claude V. *Fresh Encounter: Experiencing God Through Prayer, Humility and A Heartfelt Desire to Know Him*. Nashville: Broadman and Holman Publishers, 1996. Pages 107-108.

5. *The United Methodist Hymnal*. Nashville: The United Methodist Publishing House, 1989. Page 8.

6. Sheldon, Charles M. *In His Steps*. Old Tappan, N.J.: Pyramid Publications, 1963.

7. Ibid. Page 10.

8. Ibid. Page 11.

9. Ibid. Page 11.

10. Ibid. Page 12.

11. Ibid. Page 16.

Chapter 7—Step 2: Gathering to Pray In the Unity of the Spirit

1. "Critical Unity in Corporate Prayer For Critical Breakthroughs." Eagle Vision Ministry, http://www.eaglevision.com (accessed March 1, 2007).

2. Cho, David Yonggi. *Successful Home Cell Groups*. Gainesville: Bridge-Logos Publishers, 1981.

Chapter 9—Step 4: Having a Burden Given to Us by the Holy Spirit

1. Curran, Sue. *The Praying Church*. Lake Mary, FL: Creation House Press, 2001. Page 40.

2. Grubbs, Norman. *Touching the Invisible*. Fort Washington: Christian Literature Crusade, 1976. Page 10.

3. Cymbala, Jim with Merrill, Dean. *Fresh Wind, Fresh Fire*. Grand Rapids: Zondervan, 1997. Pages 59-66.

4. Ibid. Page 63.

5. Ibid. Page 65.

Chapter 10—Step 5: Finding God's Will Regarding a Burden

1. Wilkerson, David. *The Jesus Person Pocket Promise Book*. Glendale: Regal Books, 1972.

2. Grubb, Norman. *Rees Howells, Intercessor*. Fort Washington: Christian Literature Crusade, 1973. Pages 129-132.

3. Weatherhead, Leslie D. *The Will of God*. Nashville: Abingdon Press, 1944. Page 43.

4. Hayford, Jack. *Pursuing the Will of God*. Sisters, Oregon: Multnomah Publishers, 1997. Page 167.

5. Nee, Watchman. *Let Us Pray. New York*: Christian Fellowship Publishers, 1977. Page 3.

6. Mumford, Bob. *The King And You*. Old Tappan: Fleming H. Revell Company, 1974. Pages 29-30.

Chapter 11—Step 6: Using Authority of Jesus' Name

1. A comprehensive discussion of authoritative prayer is found in Watchman Nee's book *The Prayer Ministry of the Church*. New York: Christian Fellowship Publishers, Inc., 1973. Page 90.

2. Nee, Watchman. *The Prayer Ministry of the Church*. New York: Christian Fellowship Publishers, Inc., 1973. Page 90.

Chapter 12—Step 7: Possessing God's Answer by Faith

1. Beasley, Manley. *Faith Workbook*. Evangelist Manley Beasley, 2318 Fourth Street, Port Neches, Texas 77651. Page 5.

2. Ibid. Page 43.

3. Billheimer, Paul E. *Destined for the Throne*. Fort Washington: Christian Literature Crusade, 1975. Page 18.

4. Bounds, E. M. *The Complete Works of E. M. Bounds on Prayer*. Grand Rapids: Baker Books, 1990. Pages 357-358.

5. Rinker, Rosalind. *Prayer: Conversing With God*. Grand Rapids: Zondervan, 1959.

6. Ibid. Page 79.

7. Ibid. Page 81.

8. Smith, Hannah Whitall. *The Christian's Secret of a Happy Life*. Fleming H. Revell Co., 1952. Page 76.

9. McGaw, Francis. *Praying Hyde*. Minneapolis: Bethany Fellowship, 1970. Page 43.

10. Torrey, R.A. *The Power of Prayer*. Grand Rapids: Zondervan, 1971. Pages 118-119.

Chapter 13—Step 8: Persisting in Prayer and Praising the Lord

1. Edwards, Jonathan. *The Life and Diary of David Brainerd*. Lafayette: sovereign Grace Publishers, 2001. Page 13.

2. McGaw, Francis. *Praying Hyde*. Minneapolis: Bethany Fellowship, 1970. Page 16.

3. Miller, Basil. *George Muller Man of Faith & Miracles*. Minneapolis: Bethany Fellowship, 1941. Page 123.

4. Hybels, Bill. *Too Busy Not to Pray*. Downer's Grove: InterVarsity Press, 1998. Pages 120-121.

5. A detail discussion of God using Satan to train the church to rule with Jesus is found in Paul E. Billheimer's book *Destined for the Throne*. Fort Washington: Christian Literature Crusade, 1975.

6. Sanders, J. Oswald. *Prayer Power Unlimited*. Minneapolis: World Wide Publications, 1977. Page 84.

7. Taylor, Jack R. *Victory Over the Devil*. Nashville: Broadman Press, 1973. Page 77.

8. Hallesby, O. *Prayer*. Minneapolis:Augsburg Publishing House, 1931. Page 170.

9. Huegel, F. J. *Successful Praying*. Minneapolis: Bethany Fellowship, 1959. Pages 38-39.

Chapter 14—God's Answers to Our Corporate Prayers

1. Prayer: "A Major Study Outline," http://www.bible.ca/ntx-prayer.htm, page 9 (accessed March 1, 2007).

2. A Lockyer, Herbert. *How I Can Make Prayer More Effective*. Grand Rapids: Zondervan, 1953. Page 115.

Chapter 15—Historical Use of Corporate Prayer over the Last Several Centuries

1. Bakke, Robert. *The Power of Extraordinary Prayer*. Crossway Books, Wheaton, 2000.

2. 24-7 Prayer. http://www.24-7prayer.com/cm/resources/60 (accessed February 8, 2007).

3. Bakke, Robert. *The Power of Extraordinary Prayer*. Crossway Books, Wheaton, 2000. Pages 37-38.

4. McGaw, Francis. *Praying Hyde*. Minneapolis: Bethany Fellowship, 1970. Page 24.

5. Culpepper, C. L. *The Shantung Revival*. Dallas, Crescendo Book Publications, 1971.
6. Cho, Dr. David Yonggi. *Successful Home Cell Groups*. Gainsville: Bridge-Logos Publishers, 1981.
7. Neighbour, Ralph W. Jr. *Where Do We Go From Here*. Houston: Touch Publications, 1990.
8. Ibid. Page 38.
9. Ibid. Page 41.
10. Bakke, Robert. *The Power of Extraordinary Prayer*. Crossway Books, Wheaton, 2000. Page 47.
11. Ibid. Page 53.
12. Bakke, Robert. Prayer: *God's Catalyst for Revival*. http://www.navpress.com/EPubs/DisplayArticle/2/2.1.2.html (accessed June 8, 2007).
13. Bakke, Robert. *The Invisible Hand*. http://www.navpress.com/EPubs/DisplayArticle/2/2.22.2.html (accessed June 8, 2007).
14. Bryant, David. *How Christians Can Join Together in Concerts of Prayer for Spiritual Awakening and World Evangelization*. Ventura: Regal Books, 1984.
15. Cymbala, Jim with Merrill, Dean. *Fresh Wind, Fresh Fire*. Grand Rapids: Zondervan, 1997.
16. Henderson, Daniel with Saylar, Margaret. *Fresh Encounters*. Colorado Springs: NavPress, 2004.
17. Curran, Sue. *The Praying Church*. Lake Mary, FL: Creation House Press, 2001.
18. Neighbour, Ralph W. Jr. *Where Do We Go From Here*. Houston: Touch Publications, 1990. Pages 224-227.
19. Beliles, Mark A. and McDowell, Stephen K. *America's Providential History*. Charlottesville: Providence Foundation, 1989. Page 141.
20. Ibid. Page 176.
21. Ibid. Pages 236-237.

Chapter 16—Practical Use of Directions for Corporate Prayer Today

1. Rinker, Rosalind. *Prayer: Conversing With God*. Grand Rapids: Zondervan, 1959.
2. Lantz, W. C. *Conversational Prayer Meetings*.
3. Blackaby, Henry T. and King, Claude V. *Fresh Encounter: Experiencing God Through Prayer, Humility and A Heartfelt Desire to Know Him*. Nashville: Broadman & Holman Publishers, 1996. Page 185.

4. Omartian, Stormie with Hayford, Jack. *The Power of Praying Together*. Eugene, OR: Harvest House Publishers, 2003.

5. Sacks, Cheryl. *The Prayer Saturated Church*. Colorado Springs: NavPress, 2007.

6. Wheeler, Andrew. *Together In Prayer: Coming To God In Community*. Downers Grove, IL: InterVarsity Press, 2009.

Chapter 17—How Do I Get Started Praying With Other People?

1. Sacks, Cheryl. *The Prayer Saturated Church*. Colorado Springs: NavPress, 2007. Page 150.

2. Ibid.

3. Franklin, John. *A House of Prayer*. Nashville: LifeWay Press, 1999.

Appendix I

Sin Sheet

Set aside sufficient quiet time and go down the "Sin Sheet" sin by sin prayerfully asking the Holy Spirit if you have committed this sin. If you feel convicted of this sin, agree with God that you have committed the sin and put a check in the space provided with a soft lead pencil.

Ask God to convict you of other sins that may not be on this sheet. Listen for a while quietly in communion with God to see if there are sins the Holy Spirit wants you to add to this list. Specifically, there may be sins of omission that you need to list. For instance, things God told you to do, and you failed to do them.

Now in prayer repent to God and ask His forgiveness for each individual sin you have checked on the sin sheet. As you repent of the sin, take an eraser and remove your check mark from the sin sheet. God will forgive you for each individual sin for which you repent and ask His forgiveness (I John 1:9).

Some of your sins are against other people. These can only be erased from the sin sheet after you have made apology or restitution to those you have hurt. If the sin against other people is public, then the apology must be as public as the sin.

1. **Sin of Pride (exalted feeling). Are you prideful:**
   a. Because of your success?   ( )
   b. Because of your position?   ( )
   c. Because of your possessions and wealth?   ( )
   d. Because of your natural gifts and abilities?   ( )
   e. Because of your intellect?   ( )
   f. Because of your physical appearance?   ( )
   g. Because of your good training?   ( )
   h. Because of your spiritual gift?   ( )
   i. Because you think you are better than others?   ( )

2. **Sin of Loving Human Praise. Do you have:**
   a. A secret fondness to be noticed?   ( )
   b. A love of power and supremacy?   ( )

241

    c. A desire to get all the credit and praise? ( )
    d. A habit of drawing attention to yourself in conversation? ( )
    e. A swelling of self after a good job of speaking or praying? ( )

3. **Sins of the Tongue. Do you:**
    a. Quarrel with others? ( )
    b. Gossip about others? ( )
    c. Boast about self? ( )
    d. Have an arguing, talkative spirit? ( )
    e. Have a tendency to use harsh, sarcastic expressions? ( )
    f. Have a disposition to criticize and pick flaws? ( )
    g. Use unclean conversation (cursing)? ( )
    h. Tell dirty stories? ( )
    i. Use God's name in vain? ( )
    j. Have a desire to throw sharp heated barbs at another? ( )

4. **Sins of the Heart. Do you:**
    a. Anger quickly and lose your temper? ( )
    b. Become impatient with the fault of others? ( )
    c. Have a touchy sensitive spirit? ( )
    d. Have a disposition to resent and retaliate when others
       disapprove or contradict? ( )
    e. Have hatred of others? ( )
    f. Practice prejudice or discriminate against others? ( )
    g. Become jealous of others? ( )
    h. Lash out and hurt those you love? ( )
    i. Envy prosperity or success of others? ( )
    j. Constantly try to get the best for yourself ( )
    k. Have a stubborn, unteachable spirit? ( )
    l. Have a driving commanding spirit? ( )
    m. Have a feeling you are always right and others are
       wrong? ( )
    n. Exhibit selfishness? ( )
    o. Enjoy formality and deadness? ( )
    p. Remain spiritually dry and indifferent? ( )
    q. Have no concern for lost souls? ( )

5. **Sins of Avarice and Greed. Do you have:**
    a. A love of ease and pleasure? ( )

    b. A love of money and material goods? ( )
    c. A love of the things of the world? ( )

6. **Sins of Inactivity. Are you:**
    a. Shrinking from God's call to service? ( )
    b. Not doing your duty because of wealth, vocation, or other circumstances? ( )
    c. Neglecting to help the poor and sick? ( )
    d. Inactive in church because you are too busy? ( )
    e. Complacent about the things of God? ( )
    f. Afraid of what God will want you to do? ( )
    g. Spending too much time in front of the TV? ( )
    h. Neglecting worship? ( )
    i. Neglecting to pray? ( )
    j. Neglecting to study the Bible? ( )
    k. Neglecting to take care of your physical body? ( )
    l. Lazy? ( )

7. **Sins of Dishonesty. Are you:**
    a. Guilty of lying to someone? ( )
    b. Deceitful? ( )
    c. Evading or covering the truth? ( )
    d. Leaving a better impression of yourself than is strictly true? ( )
    e. Straining the truth? ( )
    f. Covering up sins of the past? ( )
    g. Exaggerating the truth? ( )
    h. Hypocritical? ( )
    i. Covetous? ( )

8. **Sins of Unbelief. Do you:**
    a. Become discouraged in times of pressure, opposition, and circumstance? ( )
    b. Lack confidence in God? ( )
    c. Lack faith and trust in God? ( )
    d. Fail to claim and act on God's promises? ( )
    e. Worry/complain in the midst of pain, poverty, and illness? ( )

9. **Sin of Stealing. Have you:**
   a. Stolen from others? ( )
   b. Stolen from God (tithes and offerings)? ( )
   c. Defaulted on a debt you borrowed and did not repay? ( )

10. **Sin of Murder** ( )

11. **Sin of Lust. Have you:**
    a. Committed adultery? ( )
    b. Committed fornication? ( )
    c. Practiced homosexuality? ( )
    d. Had impure thoughts? ( )
    e. Lusted after the flesh? ( )
    f. Become a slave to harmful habits? ( )
    g. Participated in substance abuse? ( )

12. **Sins of Gluttony. Have you participated in:**
    a. Overeating? ( )
    b. Drunkenness? ( )
    c. Wild parties? ( )
    d. Materialism? ( )

13. **Sin Against Father and Mother. Have you:**
    a. Failed to honor and respect them? ( )
    b. Failed to give them love? ( )
    c. Failed to obey your parents? ( )
    d. Failed to care for your parents? ( )

14. **Sin Against Husband or Wife. Have you:**
    a. As a husband failed to honor and love your wife? ( )
    b. As a wife failed to honor and love your husband? ( )
    c. Deprived your husband or wife of their marriage rights? ( )
    d. Divorced your mate? ( )
    e. As a parent failed to love and care for your children? ( )

15. **Sins Against Others. Have you:**
    a. Failed to love one another? ( )
    b. Failed to love your enemies? ( )

  c. Failed to ask forgiveness and make restitution to
    those you have hurt? ( )
  d. Failed to forgive those that have hurt you? ( )
  e. Tried to get others to join you in sin? ( )
  f. Betrayed a confidence? ( )

16. Sins Against God. Have you:
  a. Rejected Christ as Savior and Lord? ( )
  b. Failed to repent of your sins? ( )
  c. Failed to love God with all your heart? ( )
  d. Not continued to be filled with the Holy Spirit? ( )
  e. Been unwilling to surrender control of your life to God? ( )
  f. Been unwilling to die to self? ( )
  g. Dabbled in Idolatry and spiritism? ( )
  h. Not obeyed God's will when you know what it is? ( )

17. List Other Known Sins
  a. ( )
  b. ( )
  c. ( )
  d. ( )

18. Ask God to Reveal Secret Sins (Psalms 19:12-13)
  a. ( )
  b. ( )
  c. ( )

Appendix II

Surrender Sheet

For those things the Holy Spirit prompts you to surrender to God for Him to control, use a soft lead pencil and put a check in the space provided. Add others to the list as the Holy Spirit directs.

In prayer, surrender each one you have checked to God's control and erase the check mark.

After surrendering control of everything you possess, ask God to control your life and fill you with His Holy Spirit.

1. Your wife or husband ( )
2. Your children ( )
3. Your job or career ( )
4. Your business ( )
5. Your plans ( )
6. Your family ( )
7. Your home ( )
8. Your money ( )
9. Your security ( )
10. Your health ( )
11. Your friends ( )
12. Your possessions ( )
13. Your position in the community ( )
14. Your ministry ( )
15. Your schedule ( )
16. Your ego ( )
17. Your natural talents ( )
18. Your intellect ( )
19. Your emotions ( )
20. Your will ( )
21. Your whole life ( )
22. ( )
23. ( )

Appendix III

Study Guide

This study guide is designed to provide the reader an opportunity to gain a deeper understanding of corporate prayer and help the reader put in practice God's directions for how two or more are to pray together with power to receive answers to their prayers. Open your heart to the voice of the Holy Spirit and let Him lead you as you begin your journey of practicing corporate prayer.

Chapter 1—Introduction

1. What is the difference between individual prayer and corporate prayer?
2. Jesus said that those believing in Him would continue His work on earth and do even greater works than He had done. What kind of works do you think Jesus was talking about?
3. Do you think the delegation of spiritual authority to the early church carries over to today? Explain.
4. Why do you think Christians participate to such a very limited extent in public corporate prayer with other people?
5. Describe the most exciting prayer meeting of which you have ever been a part. Why was it exciting?
6. What are some ways in which you participate in corporate prayer with other Christians during a typical week?
7. Why is it important for the church to regularly gather together and pray corporately?
8. Why does God require more than one person to pray for some burdens to receive an answer to prayer?
9. Recall a time when you prayed with someone else about a burden. What was the result?

Chapter 2—Why Should We Pray Together?

1. What reasons does the Bible give for why we should engage in corporate prayer?
2. What is the difference between having a conversation with the Father and having fellowship with the Father?

3. Why does the Father want to talk to us and have fellowship with us?

4. Which is more important: us talking to God or us listening to God? Why?

5. What draws us to the Father so that we want to pray?

6. How is the Father glorified when we pray together corporately?

7. What kind of things will God do for His children on earth if they ask Him in corporate prayer?

8. What difference has prayer made in your life?

9. Why is God looking for men and women who will spend much time together in corporate prayer?

10. How much time are you willing to spend with other believers in corporate prayer?

11. Would you call your church a "house of prayer?" If you answered no, what needs to change for it to be a house of prayer?

12. The Bible commands us to "pray without ceasing." What does this mean?

Chapter 3—What Did Jesus Teach About Prayer?

1. Why do you think a disciple approached Jesus and asked Him to teach the disciples to pray?

2. Jesus taught that prayer contains four basic elements. What are they? Which elements do you use the most in prayer? Why?

3. Which of the basic elements of prayer are found in the Lord's Prayer?

4. What is the difference in praise and thanksgiving?

5. What are three specific petitions in the Lord's Prayer that Jesus says we should pray about every day?

6. List the times you can remember when Jesus prayed to the Father. What was the purpose of each prayer?

7. Think of your most recent prayer to God. What basic elements did it contain?

Chapter 4—Prayer in the Early Church and Today's Church

1. As recorded in the book of Acts, how important was prayer in the early church?

2. In Acts 6, questions arose in the early church regarding the allocation of the apostle's time devoted to administration versus prayer and ministry of the Word. What activities did the apostles feel were most

248

important? How do your ministers allocate their time?

3. In the last three centuries there have been times of great revivals where the church resembled the early church. Why do you think the revivals died?

4. Compare your church to the early church. What would make your church more like the early church?

5. Do you think the early church believed in the power of prayer more than Christians today? Explain?

6. Why do you think "prayer meeting" as a dedicated time for believers to pray together in public has disappeared from many of our churches in favor of other activities?

7. Why does today's church neglect to regularly gather together and pray?

8. Are there worthy church activities you substitute for meeting together in corporate prayer?

9. Why are we afraid of praying aloud in front of other believers? Under what conditions would you be comfortable praying in public?

10. When we do pray, we often ask amiss by not following God's directions for answered prayer. In what ways do we ask amiss?

Chapter 5—Corporate Prayers in the Bible

1. In Matthew 18:19 when it says *"if two of you agree on earth,"* what are we required to agree on?

2. What does it mean when the Bible says a group of believers was united in one accord?

3. The Apostle Paul in his letters to the churches asked them to pray for him. Why did he ask them to do this? For what specific things did he ask them to pray?

4. In the examples given in this chapter of corporate prayer by the early church, how many burdens were they praying about in each prayer? What were the burdens?

5. In the examples of corporate prayer in small groups given in this chapter, list the burdens for which they were praying.

6. In the corporate prayers found in the Bible, what things do you find in common?

Chapter 6—Step 1: Getting on Praying Ground

1. What are three reasons why believers are not on praying ground and cannot come into God's presence?

2. To be on praying ground, we must keep God's commandments. Other than the Ten Commandments, what commandments do you recall that God wants you to keep?
3. How does God view even the smallest of sins regarding your being on praying ground?
4. Are you willing to spend time alone with God and ask Him to show you any sin that is in your heart? Are you willing to confess the sin, ask for forgiveness, and make restitution to those you have hurt?
5. Describe an occasion when you tried to use your own power to undertake a ministry for the Lord without relying on His power and strength. How did it turn out?
6. How important is it for each believer to be filled and empowered by the Holy Spirit before they approach God in prayer?
7. What must you do to let the Holy Spirit control every aspect of your life?
8. What is the role of the Holy Spirit in getting you on praying ground?
9. What sins do you think your church and nation should corporately confess to God, ask forgiveness, and make restitution?
10. Why is it important for a church to be on praying ground?
11. Name several corporate sins that are common in churches today.
12. What must a church or nation do when it recognizes it has committed a corporate sin?

Chapter 7—Step 2: Gathering to Pray in the Unity of the Spirit

1. As a group of believers gather to pray corporately, is it required that they all have the same beliefs and spiritual maturity? Why or why not?
2. What does "being united in the Spirit mean?"
3. What is the difference in being united in the Spirit and united in the faith?
4. Why is it important for each believer to be in right relationship with the Father before they participate in a group gathered to pray together?
5. What is the impact to your small group's ability to pray corporately if some believers are not on praying ground or unbelievers are present?
6. In what ways is the human body like the church?
7. What is the difference in the way we pray when one individual

believer prays and when two or more believers pray corporately as one body?

8. How do you feel about having a special "piece of Jesus" in you?

9. When you gather with other believers in a small group to pray, how do you know that Jesus is alive and right there with you?

10. What kind of one-time spiritual gifts might the Father give to a small prayer group in corporate prayer?

Chapter 8—Step 3: Taking Our Place before God

1. Why is prayer independent of space and time?

2. Since we are sinful people, how has Jesus made us acceptable to come to the Father in prayer?

3. As we approach the throne of God in heaven in prayer, what is the role of the Holy Spirit?

4. Why is praise important when we pray to the Father?

5. Why is it so hard for us to praise the Father in our prayers?

6. How is our ego impacted when we praise God?

Chapter 9—Step 4: Having a Burden Given to Us by the Holy Spirit

1. Do you think that God supernaturally intervenes in the lives of men and women in response to corporate prayer for a specific burden? Why or why not?

2. Should we pray for what we want to pray or what God wants us to pray? Explain your answer?

3. Have you ever felt the Holy Spirit leading you to pray about a specific burden? Describe how you knew you were to pray about this burden.

Chapter 10—Step 5: Finding God's Will Regarding the Burden

1. When we pray, why is it important to know God's will regarding the specific burdens on our heart?

2. What did Jesus mean by the words *"Thy will be done, on earth as it is in heaven"* as found in the Lord's Prayer?

3. Why spend time searching for God's will regarding a burden when we could just pray "Lord, if it be thy will fix this burden?"

4. If you ask God to show you His will regarding a burden, do you need to be willing to be part of the answer? Why or why not?

5. List the ways the Bible indicates we can find His will regarding a burden. Which of the ways have you experienced?

6. What part does the Bible play in determining the will of God?
7. Write down the things the still small voice of God has spoken to you about in the last several weeks.
8. Why is it important for our will to be in harmony with God's will for Him to answer our prayer?
9. Why is it important for all the believers praying together in corporate prayer to agree that what is stated as the will of God is truly the will of God?
10. How can we be sure that what our spirit tells us is the will of God is really from God and not from Satan?

Chapter 11—Step 6: Using the Authority of Jesus Name
1. If God has given us His power and authority through Jesus, why does the church not use it more often?
2. Jesus said over and over "Ask in my name." Why is it important to ask in Jesus' name?
3. Do you feel your church or small prayer group uses Jesus' authority to unlock heaven and bring God's will to earth? If not, how can this situation be changed?
4. Why does the church often hesitate to speak authoritatively in Jesus name and prefer to say "Lord, you do this thing?"

Chapter 12—Step 7: Possessing God's Answer by Faith
1. What is the relationship between faith and prayer?
2. Why is being clear on the will of God so important to having faith?
3. Think back to the time when you accepted Jesus as Savior. Can you identify the three elements of faith in your experience?
4. Must all three elements be operative for you to have complete faith? Why or why not?
5. What are spiritual eyes?
6. Why is doubt poison to faith?
7. What is the impact of praise on faith?
8. What is meant by a faith-sized prayer request?
9. Are you more comfortable praying a faith-sized request or a mountain-size request? Explain?
10. What answers to prayer are you (or your prayer group) publicly claiming today by faith that are bigger than you but are faith-sized?
11. What is a one-time gift of faith?
12. What mountains do you want to move by prayer today?

Chapter 13—Step 8: Persisting in Prayer and Praising the Lord

1. Why does God want us to persist in faith until the answer comes?
2. In what ways are Satan's evil forces and God's angels involved with answers to our prayers?
3. How does God use our conversations with Him to refine our soul and further change us into the image of His son?
4. Corporate prayers in the Bible begin with praise. Why do they also conclude with praise?
5. In what ways does your church or small prayer group conclude with praise after a time of prayer?

Chapter 14—God's Answers to Our Corporate Prayers

1. As we pray together corporately, God provides many answers to our prayers. What kind of answers should we expect to receive from God?
2. What kind of things will Satan do to keep you from praying?
3. God's response to our seeking His will generally falls into what three categories?
4. For what reasons might God give "no" as an answer to our prayers?
5. When we don't get a response from the Father as to His will regarding a burden, why would God tell us to continue to seek His will in prayer?
6. What is the role of fasting in corporate prayer?
7. What does the Bible say about when (in time) the answer to our prayer will come?

Chapter 15—Historical Use of Corporate Prayer in the Last Several Centuries

1. What are the common threads found in all great revivals that have occurred down through history?
2. Why do you think there is such a close link between corporate prayer and revival?
3. Historically, how important have small corporate intercessory prayer groups been to the work of the local church?
4. In what forms does the local church practice corporate intercessory prayer in today's world?
5. Why is it important for a nation to pray corporately to the Father?

Chapter 16—Practical Use of Directions for Corporate Prayer Today

1. How would you define "conversational prayer?"
2. How does the concept of talking to God in conversational prayer strike you?
3. List as many characteristics of conversational prayer as you can.
4. Generally, what type of format do corporate prayer groups follow as they pray?
5. How does conversational prayer make us more comfortable praying aloud in front of other people?

Chapter 17—How Do I Get Started Praying with Other People?

1. List the all the ways you can become involved in praying together with other people.
2. What are the first two actions you need to take today to start praying together with other people?
3. If you are married, what does the message of I Peter 3:7 say to you?
4. How can you introduce the concept of conversational prayer into the daily devotions with your family?
5. What actions do you need to take to become part of a small corporate prayer group?
6. What is required to transform your church from a church that prays into a church that is a house of prayer? What can you do to help make this happen?

About The Author

James "Micky" Blackwell grew up on a farm in rural North Alabama, and attended a small Baptist Church, where he was active from his earliest memory. He was fortunate to receive a very thorough grounding in the Bible from outstanding Sunday School teachers.

Over the next four decades since graduating from college, Micky has taught numerous college and adult Sunday School classes and has held most lay positions in the church. He has participated in lay revivals around the country, enjoys leading spiritual retreats, and speaks to many faith-related organizations.

Micky attended college at the University of Alabama and received a degree in Aerospace Engineering in 1962. He continued with postgraduate work in Aerospace Engineering at the University of Virginia, where he received his masters degree in 1966. This was followed with doctoral work at Georgia Tech, advanced management work at Harvard, and an honorary Doctor of Laws from Mercer University in 1994.

In his senior year of college, Micky married his childhood sweetheart, Billie, also an active Christian. They have two daughters, Kaye and Kelley, who married fine Christian men and have given them one granddaughter, Cecilia, and three grandsons, Garrett, Ethan, and Matthew.

Micky began his engineering career in 1962 with NASA, and was fortunate to learn his trade under one of the true aeronautical geniuses of the time—the wing shapes of modern aircraft and the winglets on commercial aircraft are products of his work.

In 1969, Micky came to Lockheed and moved rapidly through its managerial ranks. In 1987, he became Vice President and General Manager of the F-22 stealth fighter program, where his team won the largest contract ever awarded by the Department of Defense up until that time. In 1993, he was promoted to President of the Lockheed plant in Marietta, Georgia, and two years later, would become President and COO of Lockheed Martin Aeronautical Systems Sector, with oversight of all Lockheed Martin aeronautical companies and products worldwide. Among the aircraft developed or produced under his leadership were the F-22 fighter, the F-35 (JSF) fighter, the F-16 fighter, the F-117 fighter, the C-130 transport, the C-5 transport, the C-27J transport, the U-2 reconnaissance aircraft, the X-33 space plane, and the JASSM cruise missile. He managed 36,000 employees with yearly sales exceeding $6 billion and initiated the largest implementation of Enterprise Resource Planning in the aerospace industry. Among other accomplishments to his credit are one of the industry's largest implementations of "Lean Thinking" to reduce cost and cycle time and the invention and implementation of the Integrated Product Team (IPT) management concept, which is currently being used worldwide.

Micky was named a 150th Anniversary Distinguished Engineering Fellow by the University of Alabama's College of Engineering in 1988, and was inducted into the Alabama Engineering Hall of Fame in 1995. In 1999, he was selected as the winner of the prestigious Reed Aeronautics Award, the highest award an individual can receive for achievements in the field of aeronautical science and engineering.

He retired from Lockheed Martin in 2000. Since that time, he has chaired Georgia's Military Affairs Committee and worked with the Mayor of Marietta, Georgia, chairing the Marietta Redevelopment Task Force. Currently active in the development of the Marietta Aviation Museum and Discovery Center and the restoration of the Strand Theater, he serves on both boards. Previously he has served on the Mercer University Board and the University of Alabama Engineering Advisory Board. He was named Cobb County, Georgia's Citizen of the Year in 2002, one of *Georgia Trend Magazine's* "Top 100 Most Influential Georgians" in 2002, 2003, and 2004, and one of *James Magazine's* "Most Influential Georgians" in 2005 and 2006 for his work with the city and state. He was a founding member of the Kennesaw State University Board on Character, Leadership, and Ethics.

Until recently, Micky has served as Board Chairman of ScanTech Sciences, LLC—a company which specializes in products for homeland security. A consultant to aerospace clients in the U.S. and abroad, Micky also leads strategic planning retreats for charitable nonprofits in service to the community.

Micky actively supports the Marietta First United Methodist Church where he teaches a Sunday School class of young adults. He is an active participant and board member of "Lead Like Jesus," an organization dedicated to teaching business leaders how to do what its name suggests, and enjoys golf, reading, traveling, writing, and community service.

To Purchase Additional Copies of

When Two Or More Are Gathered...In Prayer

Please visit
www.unitedwriterspress.com

Volume discounts are available for those wishing
to purchase ten or more copies.

All proceeds from the sale of this book will go to the benefit
of church and religious educational organizations.

To contact the Author, write to:

James Blackwell
311 Hardage Drive
Marietta, GA 30064

Or e-mail him:

mickybla@bellsouth.net

In the small country church where he grew up, James "Micky" Blackwell remembers Wednesday night "prayer meetings" as the time when people in his community gathered to pray for each other, their nation, and the world. But somewhere along the way, in many churches, a regular time set aside for God's people to unite in intercessory prayer has gotten lost.

In *When Two or More are Gathered...in Prayer*, Blackwell takes us back to our roots, reminding us that our Creator gave us explicit directions for how to communicate with Him, and then brings us forward through the centuries, showing how "corporate prayer"—praying *together*—has brought change in the past...and how it can still change a troubled world today.

Jesus said, "...if **two of you** agree on earth about anything that they may ask, it shall be done for them...For where **two or three have gathered** together in My name, there I am in their midst."
— Matthew 18:19-20 (NAS, emphasis added)

James "Micky" Blackwell retired as Executive Vice President of the Lockheed Martin Corporation with responsibility for their aircraft business. numerous awards for his professional work and community service. Micky has held many lay positions in the church and has taught young adults for over 40 years. He has participated in lay revivals, led spiritual retreats and spoken to many faith-related organizations around the country—and actively worships at the First United Methodist Church of Marietta, Georgia. Micky and wife Billie have been married for 48 years. They have two children and four grandchildren.

ISBN 978-1934216583

$18.95 US
United Writers Press, Inc.

51895
9 781934 216583